CHRIS CLARK is a r
He is the author of sev
serial killers Christophe
Sinclair and Robert Black. He participat
documentary on Sutcliffe following his death in 2020.

TIM HICKS is a retired chartered accountant with experience in audit, fraud investigation and data processing. Tim is now a member of the National Union of Journalists and the Crime Writers' Association, writing on crime and intelligence subjects. His research has been published in *The Times, Sunday Express, Daily Mirror, The Sun, Private Eye, North Yorks Enquirer, The Yorkshire Post, Birmingham Post* and *The Journalist*.

INSIDE THE MIND OF THE

YORKSHIRE RIPPER

THE FINAL INVESTIGATION

CHRIS CLARK AND TIM HICKS

First published in the UK in 2023 by
Ad Lib Publishers Ltd
15 Church Road
London SW13 9HE
www.adlibpublishers.com

Text © 2023 Chris Clark and Tim Hicks

Paperback ISBN 9781802472042
eBook ISBN 9781802472134

A CIP catalogue record for this book is available
from the British Library.

Every reasonable effort has been made to trace copyright-holders of material reproduced in this book, but if any have been inadvertently overlooked the publishers would be glad to hear from them.

Printed in the UK
10 9 8 7 6 5 4 3 2 1

Dedicated to Sutcliffe's victims, their families and friends – both those who received justice and some degree of closure, but also those who didn't, particularly those victims who did not come forward or whose bodies were not discovered.

Contents

Forewords

Detective Superintendent Bob Bridgestock

As a career detective in West Yorkshire Police between 1974 and 2004, retiring at the rank of Detective Superintendent, I was involved in many different kinds of criminal investigations.

Whilst any crime has an enormous impact on the lives of those involved, the emergency services and the community, none was more harrowing than the five years when Peter Sutcliffe, dubbed the 'Yorkshire Ripper', terrorised Britain, claiming to be on a mission from God to kill sex workers – whilst evading capture time and time again.

During these five years, no woman felt safe, no matter how many officers patrolled the streets of Yorkshire.

As the stories spread of how the victims were butchered, men – both young and old – took it upon themselves to escort females to and fro, night and day.

We all dreaded that early morning call: 'We've another body.' Or, waking up to the headline that 'the Ripper' had struck again.

As time went by, the public confidence in the police's ability to catch Sutcliffe waned, and the investigation became one of the largest and most expensive manhunts in British history.

As a young detective, with only four years' service, I found myself involved in the murder investigation of Sutcliffe's eighth victim, Helen Rytka, purely by chance. Sutcliffe had had a lucky escape, as my partner and I spent the previous seven nights on observations, on Great Northern Street in Huddersfield. The matter was totally unrelated to the Ripper enquiry, except for where Helen's body was found, behind a pile of wood, by employees on 31 January 1978.

Speaking to Helen's twin sister, Rita, it became clear that although they were both alerted to the 'Ripper', they had felt safe knowing that one was looking out for the other.

Just over a year later, I was also one of the first detectives on the scene of the murder of nineteen-year-old Josephine Whitaker, on Skircoat Moor, Halifax, when her body was discovered in heavy, persistent rain, driven across the open parkland by strong winds. Back then, forensic science was not very advanced; we did not even have readily available equipment to protect a crime scene from the elements.

The Byford Report led to many improvements in investigative procedures that were adopted across all forces. In my last three years alone, I took charge of twenty-six murder enquiries. Fortunately, I had the HOLMES system at my disposal throughout the rest of my career, which was a huge improvement.

Chris Clark

I joined the police force to make a difference. On Thursday 10 March 1966, I boarded the train at King's Lynn for the fifty-mile journey to Norwich. There, in the city's Shirehall Magistrates Court, I was sworn in as an officer of the Norfolk Constabulary.

When the ceremony was over, I was Constable 409, Clark C: 'A citizen locally appointed but having authority under the Crown for the protection of life and property, the maintenance of order, the prevention and detection of crime and the prosecution of offenders against the Peace.' I then collected my warrant card, uniform and the tools of my new trade: one set of handcuffs, a whistle and a truncheon. After a thirteen-week training course in Oxfordshire I was ready to pound the beat as a probationary constable. I was sent to an urban district on the fringes of Norwich, which at that time had its own separate police force.

By the mid-1960s, crime was growing and changing fast. The world we had known was changing. By the time I'd finished, the police force itself had changed. Like other forces up and down the country, the old city, county and borough constabularies were merged into the larger forces we know today. This was, I think, the beginning of the end for much that had been traditional: the bobby on the beat was losing out to the patrol car.

The hierarchy was changing too: the senior officers we had worked under were solid World War Two veterans who had grafted their way to the top and had both real experience and the ability to deal with their officers in a fatherly way that got the best out of them. Gradually, they were squeezed out by high-flyers who came into the job with higher educational qualifications – no bad thing, of course – but more worryingly, with old-school ties and memberships of secretive masonic lodges.

It was during this time that divisional intelligence collators were introduced. I was instrumental in setting up the office for the King's Lynn district in 1968. This set the tone for my future twenty-year-old role as Deputy Intelligence Officer for West Norfolk, dispersed with the role of researcher/indexer in Major Incident Rooms both on the paper card index MIRIAM (Major Incident Room Indexing and Monitoring) system, to the advent of HOLMES (Home Office Large Major Enquiry System). This culminated in me becoming a Local Intelligence

Officer from 1987 until 1991, during which time I watched the Yorkshire Ripper investigation unfold.

There has still not been a complete account of the Yorkshire Ripper or of the full number of his victims. Hence my decision to work with Tim on this account of Peter Sutcliffe's Crimes.

Tim Hicks

Tim Hicks is a chartered accountant with experience in audit and investigation, data processing and fraud investigation.

Tim is a member of the National Union of Journalists and the Crime Writers' Association, writing on crime and intelligence subjects. He has sourced articles in *The Times*, *Sunday Express*, *Daily Mirror*, *The Sun*, *Private Eye*, *North Yorks Enquirer* (NYE), *The Yorkshire Post*, *Birmingham Post* and *The Journalist*. He has also been interviewed on the BBC *Today* programme, GMTV, ITV, Channel 4 and BBC Television, and is a published historian.

In 1984 he received a judge's commendation for assisting Northumbria Police to arrest members of a major paedophile ring.

In 1994 he submitted evidence to the Nolan Committee on Standards in Public Life concerning arrangements for 'whistleblowing', following his exposure of a fraud and security scandal within the Ministry of Defence.

In 2007 he submitted evidence to the Treasury Select Committee of the House of Commons on the collapse of the Halifax Bank of Scotland Group.

In 2013 he worked with the BBC to expose the Peter Jaconelli and Jimmy Savile paedophile ring in Scarborough. Following this, he submitted evidence to 'Operation Yewtree' (the Metropolitan Police Service (MPS) investigation into Savile), 'Operation Hibiscus' (the North Yorkshire Police (NYP) investigation into Jaconelli and Savile) and 'Operation Conifer' (the Wiltshire Police (WP) investigation into Sir Edward Heath). He also contributed to the book *In Plain Sight: The Life and Lies of Jimmy Savile* by Dan Davies, which won the 2015 Gordon Burn Prize for the best piece of non-fiction crime writing.

In 2019 he was commended by NYP for his assistance in the Claudia Lawrence murder investigation.

As a young man I followed the 'Black Panther' and 'Yorkshire Ripper' investigations with great interest. It was obvious to me at the time that the British police service was not capable of handling large, complex investigations across multiple forces.

When Sutcliffe died in 2020, Chris and I were appalled by the superficial nature of the media coverage of Sutcliffe, which simply covered the twenty attacks he was convicted of, but ignored the other attacks he committed.

The police are charged by society with providing justice for the victim and closure for the family. It is clear that the police have failed to do this, and the media has not held them to account for this failure.

Chris and I hope this work will help bring more of the facts into the public domain, tell the victims' stories and bring some closure for their friends and relatives. Most importantly, we hope that it will improve the way the police investigate serial killers.

Introduction

The authors have set out to conduct an antecedent investigation, to identify as many of Sutcliffe's victims as possible and the full range of his offending. So the full story is told as far as is achievable at this late date.

There is no openly available, comprehensive official list of suspicious disappearances and unsolved attacks on women. As an example, the MPS maintained electronic records for murders and serious assaults only from April 1997 onwards when the Crime Report Information System (CRIS) came into operation. The MPS has a homicide list which has been maintained since April 1992, which includes a small number of homicides that were committed prior to April 1992 and solved after that date. There is no central database which can establish the presence of Sutcliffe in any investigation in the Metropolitan Police District (MPD). This is probably typical for all UK police forces. To identify if Sutcliffe had ever been a suspect in any murder or attempted murder and how he was eliminated, paper files would have to be retrieved from storage to enable manual retrieval of this information. The personal indexes (which hold information on when an individual has come to police notice) would then have to be checked manually and cross-referenced with the registry file.

Consequently, this book is only based on information in the public domain. When considering an attack, the authors gathered all of the information they could from appeals for information, freedom of information (FOI) requests and all available open sources. They then assessed if it could be an attack by Sutcliffe based on his movements, victim preferences, modus-operandi and the facts of the case. If there were not enough points of similarity, then the case was rejected. The authors have not graded the attacks with different degrees of certainty as to Sutcliffe's guilt; they have been included on the basis that Sutcliffe is a credible suspect. This cautious approach and reliance on information in the public domain means that there must be many other attacks the authors have excluded or are unaware of. So the true number of Sutcliffe's victims is certainly very much higher than set out herein.

As an example, the leading investigative journalist David Yallop has stated that Sutcliffe could have been responsible for the attempted murders of Barbara Miller (Bradford, March 1975) and Barbara Brearley (Doncaster, October 1976) and the murder of a twenty-one-year-old woman (Derby, 3 August 1979). Although Yallop's work is excellent, the authors felt there is not now enough evidence available to investigate these murders and identify if Sutcliffe is a credible suspect.

Fifteen antecedent investigations of one sort or another have been conducted to identify all the attacks committed by Sutcliffe but for which he was not convicted. The findings of the various antecedent investigations have never been released to the public in full and the papers on the Yorkshire Ripper murders are sealed until 2045. So this book will probably be the only assessment of the full extent of Sutcliffe's crimes and the failings of the investigation until then.

By painstaking analysis, the authors believe they have identified the attacks the antecedent investigations have attributed to Sutcliffe, which have never been fully released to the public. They are recorded below, along with the attacks he was convicted of.

Date	Name	Location	Antecedent Investigation	Resolution
22/04/66	Fred Craven	Bingley	OB1 TiC1	
22/03/67	John Tomey	Oxenhope	OB2 TiC2	
Aug 1969	Stone in Sock attack. Name withheld by WYP	Bradford		Cautioned, but not prosecuted
08/03/70	Jackie Ansell-Lamb	Cheshire	H1	
12/10/70	Barbara Mayo	Derbyshire	H2 CS1	
18/04/72	Marie Burke	Hertfordshire	H3, TiC3	
29/12/72	Bernadette Cassidy/ Wakefield Clerk Typist	Wakefield	B1	
22/02/74	Rosina Hillard	Leicester	H4	
01/03/74	Kay O'Connor	Colchester	H5	
10/04/74	Caroline Allen	Leicestershire	H6	
11/11/74	Gloria Wood	Bradford	B2	
05/07/75	Anna Rogulskyj	Keighley		Convicted
15/08/75	Olive Smelt	Halifax		Convicted
27/08/75	Tracy Browne	Silsden	CS2	Later admitted by Sutcliffe, but not prosecuted
30/10/75	Wilma Mccann	Leeds		Convicted
06/01/76	Rosemary Stead	Bradford	B4	
20/01/76	Emily Jackson	Leeds		Convicted
09/05/76	Marcella Claxton	Leeds		Convicted

Date	Name	Location	Antecedent Investigation	Resolution
29/08/76	Maureen Hogan	Bradford	B5	
05/02/77	Irene Richardson	Leeds		Convicted
22/03/77	Barbara Young	Doncaster	CS3 **B13?**	**Unclear**
Nov/Dec 1977	Doncaster sex worker. Name withheld by SYP	Doncaster	**B13?**	**which of these two cases is the 13th attributed to Sutcliffe by Byford**
21/04/77	Debra Schlesinger	Leeds	WYP1	Enough evidence to pass a file to the CPS, but not prosecuted
23/04/77	Patricia Atkinson	Bradford		Convicted
25/06/77	Jayne Macdonald	Leeds		Convicted
10/07/77	Maureen Long (1)	Bradford		Convicted
01/10/77	Jean Jordan	Manchester		Convicted
14/12/77	Marilyn Moore	Leeds		Convicted
22/01/78	Yvonne Pearson	Bradford		Convicted
31/01/78	Helen Rytka	Huddersfield		Convicted
02/03/78	Leeds Shop Assistant	Leeds	B6	
16/05/78	Vera Millward	Manchester		Convicted

Date	Name	Location	Antecedent Investigation	Resolution
28/11/78	Bradford Addressograph Operator	Bradford	B7	
17/02/79	Withheld by NYP	Harrogate	B8	
02/03/79	Ann Rooney	Leeds	B9	Later admitted by Sutcliffe, but not prosecuted
04/04/79	Josephine Whitaker	Halifax		Convicted
24/08/79	Wendy Jenkins	Bristol	H7	
01/09/79	Alison Morris	Ramsey	S2	
02/09/79	Barbara Leach	Bradford		Convicted
14/09/79	Dawn Webster	Grangemouth, Scotland	H8	
11/10/79	Yvonne Mysliwiec	Ilkley	B10 CS4 S1	
20/08/80	Maureen Long (2)/ Marguerite Walls	Leeds		Convicted
24/09/80	Upadhya Bandara	Leeds		Convicted
25/10/80	Maureen Lea	Leeds	B11 WYP2	Enough evidence to pass a file to the CPS, but not prosecuted
05/11/80	Theresa Sykes	Huddersfield	B12	Convicted
17/11/80	Jacqueline Hill	Leeds		Convicted

Date	Name	Location	Antecedent Investigation	Resolution
Unknown	Unknown 'Anita'	Unknown	W1	Victim interviewed by Detective Inspector (DI) Megan Winterburn, who reported that it was a Ripper attack, but was ordered to ignore it by WYMP Chief Constable Ronald Gregory

Key

TiC 1 – 3:	Taken In Consideration Form
B1 – 13:	Chief Constable Sir Lawrence Byford's Antecedent Investigation
CS1 – 4:	Assistant Chief Constable (ACC) Colin Sampson's Antecedent Investigation
H1 – 8:	Chief Constable Keith Hellawell's Antecedent Investigation
WYP 1 – 2:	West Yorkshire Police (WYP) 2002 Antecedent Investigation
OB1 – 2:	Detective Sergeant (DS) Desmond O'Boyle
S1:	Detective Superintendent John Stainthorpe
S2:	DC Mick Saunders
W1:	DI Megan Winterburn

This raises the question of how many attacks is Sutcliffe officially credited as being responsible for. This is set out below:

Category	Murders		Attempted Murders	
	Male	Female	Male	Female
Convicted		13		7
Confessed but not charged				2
WYP subsequently confirmed it has enough evidence to convict Sutcliffe		1		1
Police antecedent investigation has opined that Sutcliffe was responsible	1	9	1	12
Sub Total	**1**	**23**	**1**	**22**
Doncaster Sex worker*				1*
Total		**24**		**23 or 24***

* Depending on whether the attempted murder of the Doncaster sex worker or the murder of Barbara Young is the thirteenth case attributed to Sutcliffe by Chief Constable Sir Lawrence Byford

This book is not a biography of Sutcliffe. His life falls into thirteen phases, which are covered only in as much detail as is needed to establish his links to particular crimes. The authors have not covered the crimes Sutcliffe was convicted of or confessed to, or his trial and incarceration in great detail, because they have been covered extensively elsewhere. The issues surrounding Sutcliffe's mental state have been left for appropriately qualified commentators.

At the time, the police referred to Sutcliffe's victims who were not sex workers as 'innocent'. The implication being that the sex workers he killed were guilty of contributing to their own fate. The authors believe all of Sutcliffe's victims were innocent.

Four of the victims covered in the book have never been identified. Rather than referring to them by a flippant nickname like 'Nude in the Nettles' or as 'Woman', the authors have allocated them a female first name as a pseudonym, to give them dignity. There are no photographs of victims' bodies for the same reason.

Many people were deeply affected by Sutcliffe. These include not just survivors but also their children, witnesses, police officers, friends, family, suspects and professionals that were involved in the case. In a work of this size, the authors cannot cover the impact on the lives of each survivor in detail, so they have used individual cases as examples to show the collective impact.

The authors focussed on the crimes that were not publicly attributed to Sutcliffe. The cases are covered in chronological order except if cases have been linked, in which case they are considered together.

It is necessary at this point to say a few words about British policing in the 1960s and 1970s.

The small county, city and borough police forces established under the Victorian policing system were being merged into the larger forces we have today. In West Yorkshire, this process was ongoing and would have a major impact on the investigation. In 1968 the West Riding Constabulary (WRC) – the county force – merged with the borough forces for Barnsley, Dewsbury, Doncaster, Halifax, Huddersfield and Wakefield to form the West Yorkshire Constabulary (WYC). Then in 1974 WYC was amalgamated with the Leeds City Police (LCP) and Bradford City Police (BCP) to form West Yorkshire Metropolitan Police (WYMP), which became WYP in 1986.

With the exception of tyre tread analysis, forensic science was not much further advanced than it had been in Victorian times, being based primarily on fingerprints, hair, fibre, blood, identikit pictures, photography and pathology. Scene of the crime investigation was crude. Crime scenes were not preserved and evidence was not stored in order to take advantage of future improvements in forensic science.

Computers, Closed Circuit Television (CCTV), Automatic Number Plate Recognition (ANPR), mobile phones and deoxyribonucleic acid (DNA) were unknown. Criminal records were held on card indexes. Vehicle records were only computerised for the Driver and Vehicle Licensing Authority (DVLA) and Police National Computer (PNC) in 1974. Geographical profiling and forensic facial reconstruction had not been used prior to the Yorkshire Ripper investigation. The police had no doctrine or policy for media operations, which depended on the particular aptitudes and prejudices of the senior investigating officer (SIO) for each crime.

In the 1960s and 1970s authority was not questioned and the police service was inadequately scrutinised. Detectives could ignore evidence, withhold it from the defence and pervert the course of investigations. They routinely framed suspects by planting evidence and using violence or aggressive interviewing techniques to intimidate them into signing concocted confessions. In three attacks, an innocent man was convicted who was subsequently acquitted; a fourth was acquitted at trial; and Michael Hodgson was convicted of a murder the authors believe was committed by Sutcliffe. His conviction was never overturned and the authors have tried to expose the injustice he suffered. These men are included as victims.

Serial killers like to operate in areas they are familiar with because they feel comfortable and confident there. Their local knowledge of routes, people, patterns of activity, etc. helps them evade detection and they usually have a valid reason to be there if they are questioned by the police. Sutcliffe was a prolific, organised serial killer who travelled long distances on set routes, both for work and socially. It follows from this that analysing the clustering of attacks along these route packages is critical. The authors have performed this analysis and recorded it on maps for the first time. The maps are approximate and only for illustrative purposes.

Sutcliffe actively took countermeasures to confuse the police investigation. One of these was to vary his modus-operandi and areas of operation. Another was to conceal bodies. Caroline Allen was abducted in April 1974 and her body discovered in December 1975. 'Hope's' body lay undiscovered for two years. 'Hope' has never been reported missing. This is understandable. She was almost certainly a sex worker and probably estranged from her family. It is entirely possible that there are more victims of Sutcliffe who did not report his attacks, or whose bodies have never been discovered – some of whom may have not even been reported missing.

The police service believes it is the duty of the police and not journalists to investigate unsolved murders and perform antecedent investigations. Some forces have accused journalists investigating these matters of causing distress to the victims' families. The authors have considered this position carefully. This book shows that many of the investigations into Sutcliffe's crimes were not just incompetent, but were also contaminated by police corruption, self-interest and/or police politics. This resulted in multiple cover-ups from 1981 to the present day.

If the authors were to acquiesce to the police view that only the police should investigate or comment on failed investigations, it would conveniently overlook the inexcusable failure of many police forces to properly investigate Sutcliffe at the time and since. The public interest requirement is for an impartial investigation into these crimes to obtain justice for the victims, some element of closure for their families and for the mistakes made to be identified, so they are not repeated in the future. Under these circumstances, only investigative journalists that have the right skill base and are independent of the police can perform a credible investigation which is not tainted by any concern for the reputation of the police.

Now that Sutcliffe is dead, we will never know the full truth or the true number of his victims. The authors hope this book will go some way to establishing the true toll and fully identify the failures in the way the police investigated serial killers historically, which still continue today. The points of failure in these investigations and the issues that need to be addressed are also covered.

Acknowledgements

The authors would like to thank Don Hale, Michael Bilton, Gordon Burn, David Yallop and all the other journalists whose contemporaneous work gave the authors a rich source of material to conduct their investigation.

All the witnesses, victims and their families that came forward, including Diane, Child A, Child C, Child D, Alderman Norman Murphy, Witnesses 2, 3 and 4 in the murder of 'Hope', Witnesses 1 and 2 in the murder of Rosina Hilliard, Maureen Hogan, Woman A and Woman B, the witnesses from Preston and Sheffield, Irene Vidler, Stephen Downing and David Pollard.

Bob Bridgestock for his foreword. Keith Tordoff, for his heartfelt description of the impact of the case on the policemen involved. Detective Superintendent Bo Lundqvist for his comments on the murders of Teresa Thörling and Gertie Jensen. Richard Charles Cobb, for his excellent detective work on the murder of Marguerite Walls. Mick Saunders and Andy Laptew, and all the other retired police officers that came forward with information, who wish to remain anonymous.

Nigel Ward and Tim Thorne for allowing NYE articles and illustrations to be used. Our cartographer, Chris Routh, for his indefatigable attention to detail on the maps. Most of all, Chris's wife, Jeanne, for her friendship and support to both authors.

Jeanne, thank you for the past 21 years. I am lost without you, Chris.

Phase 1 and Phase 2

Phase 1. 1946 – 1961: Early life

Peter William Sutcliffe was born in Bingley in West Yorkshire on 2 June 1946. His parents were mill worker John Sutcliffe and his wife Kathleen.

Sutcliffe was a sickly child, had difficulty in walking at first and was very closely bonded with his mother. He went to school at the age of four, where he was withdrawn, avoided other boys and was bullied because of his weak frame. He stopped going to school altogether by pretending to leave home for school, then hiding in the loft of his home. When this was detected, he was put under closer supervision and returned to being a regular attender. The Sutcliffe family lived at 57 Cornwall Road, Bingley.

Sutcliffe left school in the summer of 1961 aged fifteen with no qualifications. This does not mean he was unintelligent, just that he was unsuccessful in school. He was a regular church-goer at school and for about two years afterwards. Other than being shy, physically weak and the hiding in the loft episode, he was unremarkable and did not demonstrate any propensity for crime.

Phase 2. 1961 – 1969: Thief, necrophiliac and emerging serial killer

Sutcliffe started work in Bingley as an apprentice fitter in 1961. He left this employment in 1962 and worked in a mill for a few months, until he was employed just outside Bingley, travelling to work on a motorcycle. His father was convicted of burglary for trying to steal from a neighbour's house on Christmas Eve, 1961. Although, so far as the authors can ascertain, this was his only conviction, Sutcliffe Senior may have been committing burglaries and thefts locally, and may have inculcated his son into this type of crime.

As he approached eighteen, Sutcliffe started to harden up and put himself on a course of 'bulk builder' supplements. His daily routine involved hours alone training with a 'bull worker', developing immense upper body strength.

Sutcliffe obtained employment as a gravedigger at Bingley Cemetery. The manual labour increased his strength. His family noticed he spent long periods in the bathroom, gazing at his hair in the mirror and trimming it with the occasional snip. He would later use this hairdressing skill to vary his appearance by changing his hairstyle, beard and moustache.

Peter Sutcliffe took a macabre interest in handling and washing bodies in the cemetery's Chapel of Rest. He particularly enjoyed washing the soiled surgical instruments after post-mortems and discussing the gory details of his job with his friends. He derived macabre pleasure in playing with old skeletons that were dug up whilst creating new grave spaces. He also talked about necrophilia. Touching corpses appeared to give him great pleasure; he examined almost every dead body that came in. On one occasion, he enjoyed examining the bags of flesh which were the remains of a person who had been hit by a train.

Sutcliffe also robbed the corpses. As soon as the mourners had left a burial, he would take the coffin lid off and search the bodies for jewellery. If a ring was stuck on the deceased's finger, he would get a pair of sharp shears and snip the finger off. He also prised mouths open and yanked teeth with gold fillings out with pliers. He would then replace the soil in the grave on top of the coffin. He fenced his ill-gotten gains to a local jeweller, so he was never short of money when drinking in the pub with his workmates.

None of his colleagues reported his sickening behaviour. Some of them noticed he was noticeably modest about exposing his penis when urinating in company. Tellingly, Sutcliffe had used a mallet to savagely hit elderly cemetery worker Eddie Bishop on the head. This was an early example of one of his modus-operandi: lulling his victim into a false sense of security through conversation, then hitting them on the back of the head with a hammer.

In 1963 at the age of seventeen, Sutcliffe obtained a provisional driving licence. He was arrested in Keighley for driving a motor car whilst unaccompanied and failing to display L-plates. There was a similar case against him during May 1964 in Bradford. This confirms he had access to vehicles and was driving further afield than his local area. There was no red-light district (RLD) in Bingley or Keighley; the closest RLD was in Bradford, so the implication was that he was visiting the RLD there. Throughout his life, Sutcliffe enjoyed visiting RLDs, giving him a reason to visit many cities.

At this time, Sutcliffe was interested in motorbikes and associated with bikers until about 1969. He was also courting a young woman from Keighley, but never went beyond passionate kissing with her.

1. Steve

In 1964 Sutcliffe was on holiday in the Lake District with 'Steve', a male friend, who made a joke about sex as they were getting ready for bed. Steve's description of what happened next is important:

> Peter picked up a knife and jumped on me, shouting, 'I'm going to cut your dick off, you bastard!' I'm a big bloke, but he was like a mad thing and I just couldn't stop him. He seemed possessed of some sort of super strength.

Steve's penis needed stitches.

Sutcliffe's uncontrollable and irrational anger about Steve's joke, coupled with his unease about showing his penis when urinating and lack of intimacy with his girlfriend, are strong indicators that he was impotent. This would explain the attack in a frenzy and his 'super strength' caused by rage over this condition and his uncontrollable enjoyment from using a weapon to stab genitalia. Exactly as he would later attack his victims.

2. Margaret 'Vicky' Williamson

Vicky Williamson was a sixty-three-year-old spinster who was murdered on the evening of Wednesday 23 December 1964 at Branch Road, Barkisland, near Halifax, as she walked home from a bus stop along Branch Road while returning from Christmas shopping. Two council employees saw her walking less than half a mile from her home just before 7.00pm. She was being followed by a youth whom they described as aged eighteen to twenty years, five-foot six-inches to five-foot eight-inches tall, with hair over his collar, wearing a three-quarter length coat and black 'winklepicker' shoes (these had notably sharp, long pointed toes, and were fashionable with Teddy Boys from the 1950s). This was the last sighting of Vicky alive.

Vicky's body was found on Christmas Day in a field off Branch Road. She had been attacked virtually opposite the entrance to her home, bundled over a wall, then strangled. Her body was then carried or dragged 200 yards over rough ground to an area known as Zachariah Wood. Robbery was ruled out as a motive because nothing was taken. The body was partially undressed and had been violated after death, indicating that her assailant was a necrophiliac.

Sutcliffe is known to have had an interest in necrophilia at this time and to have interfered with the body of an elderly woman who was a magistrate who had previously sentenced him. So Vicky was within the age range of Sutcliffe's preferences.

The description of the unknown youth fits Sutcliffe. He was five-foot seven-inches tall, aged eighteen in 1964 and clean shaven until 1967. Sutcliffe was a 'Teddy Boy'

Map 1 - The Bingley Cluster 1964 - 1969

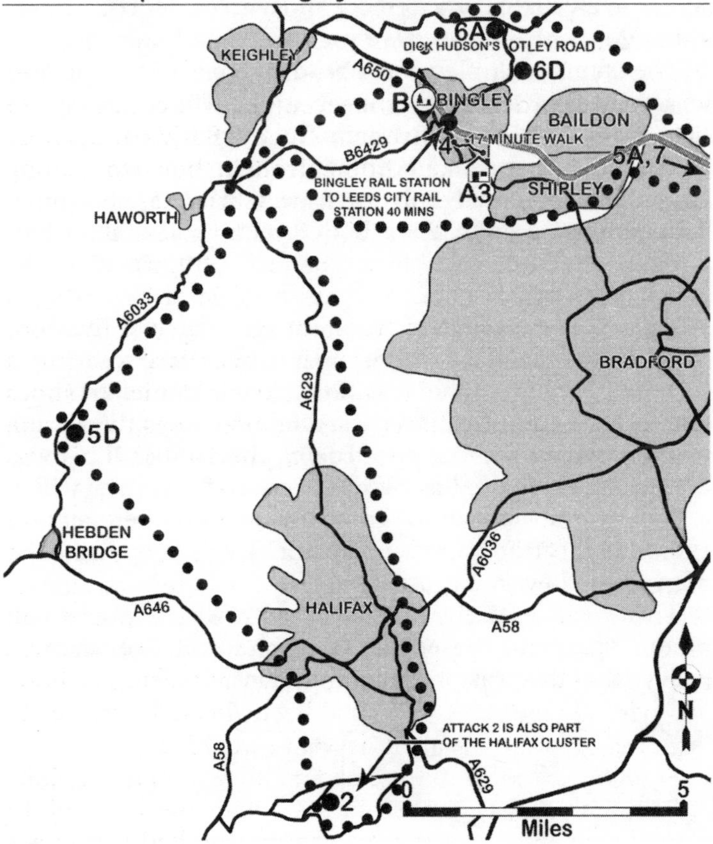

KEIGHLEY

A650

DICK HUDSON'S OTLEY ROAD

6A

6D

B BINGLEY

BAILDON

17-MINUTE WALK

B6429

4

5A, 7

BINGLEY RAIL STATION
TO LEEDS CITY RAIL
STATION 40 MINS

A3

SHIPLEY

HAWORTH

A6033

BRADFORD

A629

5D

A6036

HEBDEN
BRIDGE

A646

HALIFAX

A58

A58

ATTACK 2 IS ALSO PART
OF THE HALIFAX CLUSTER

A629

N

2

0

5

Miles

31

during this time and wore a three-quarter length 'finger-tip' drape jacket/coat and 'winklepicker' shoes.

The attack took place within sixteen miles of Sutcliffe's home at 57 Cornwall Road, Bingley, within his known area of offending. He is known to have visited pubs and coffee houses in Halifax during 1964. He had a motorbike and access to a Vauxhall Wyvern car and a green Morris Minor, although these vehicles were unlicensed and uninsured.

The attack took place on a road flanked by a stone wall in a rural spot between built-up areas, which was out of sight from dwellings, thus hiding a woman walking alone in darkness. Vicky had been quickly thrown over a wall, an action that could only have been done by a man of considerable strength. As a body builder and gravedigger, Sutcliffe would be capable of this. It is very similar to the attack on Tracy Browne.

Vicky's body was carried or dragged for two hundred metres from the place where she was murdered to another secluded location. This was so that the murderer could obtain sexual gratification from undressing and interfering with the corpse, without fear of being observed or disturbed. The crime therefore has two separate crime scenes, which is highly unusual, although many of Sutcliffe's attacks exhibited this feature. It is unclear if Vicky's body had been masturbated over or mutilated.

This is all entirely consistent with Sutcliffe's known modus-operandi. Based on this analysis, the authors believe that this was probably Sutcliffe's first kill.

No	Name	Date	Cluster(s)	Route Package
A	57 Cornwall Road			
B	Bingley Cemetery			
2	Vicky Williamson	23/12/64	Bingley, Halifax	
3	Child F	1965	Bingley	
4	Fred Craven	22/04/66	Bingley	

No	Name	Date	Cluster(s)	Route Package
5A	John Tomey Abduction Point	22/03/67	Bingley	Bingley-Leeds by rail
5D	John Tomey Deposition Site	22/03/67	Bingley	
6	George Ellis	1967	Bingley	
7	Mary Judge	26/02/1968	Bingley, Leeds (Not shown)	Bingley-Leeds by rail

During a Sunday night in March 1965, aged nineteen, Sutcliffe was seen with another youth trying door handles of several unattended motor vehicles in Old Main Street, Bingley. Both were arrested for attempting to steal from an unattended motor vehicle. He was fined £5 at Bingley Magistrates Court on 17 May 1965, then photographed, fingerprinted and a criminal record card was completed. He gained more motoring convictions during 1965 and 1966.

3. Child F
In 1965, aged nineteen, Sutcliffe pushed one of his younger sister's ten-year-old friends down a flight of stairs when she was playing at their home. Terrified, she looked back up the stairs and saw him grinning.

The authors believe this was a highly significant event in Sutcliffe's life. He realised that hurting females gave him great pleasure. He was to attempt to abduct and murder schoolgirls throughout his life.

After losing his job at the cemetery for poor timekeeping in 1965, Sutcliffe held a number of labouring positions. In 1966 he obtained employment with the local water board, digging up old pipework and making trenches. He also met Sonia Szurma. The couple hit it off straight away and became friendly with Trevor Birdsall. To quote Chief Constable Byford:

During his late teens he developed an unhealthy interest in prostitutes and spent a great deal of time, often in the company of his friend Trevor Birdsall, watching them soliciting on the streets of Leeds and Bradford. There is no evidence that he used their services at this stage although it is clear that he was fascinated by them and spent a considerable amount of time acting as a voyeur.

4. Fred Craven
(Attributed to Sutcliffe by DS O'Boyle and believed to be attributed to him in the original Taken in Consideration investigation)

Fred Craven, aged sixty-six, lived at 23 Cornwall Road – 150 yards from Sutcliffe at number 57. He was married with four children who he raised on his own. He was a bookie who operated from a small office on Wellington Street, Bingley, above an antiques shop.

On Friday 22 April 1966, shortly after 11.30am, Fred was found dead in his betting office, with the back of his head split open. He had defensive injuries to his left arm from trying to ward off the blows, as well as fractured ribs where he had been kicked in the chest. His wallet, which was believed to have contained £200 in cash, was missing. The weapon had been removed.

The SIO was Detective Superintendent George Oldfield and he was assisted by Detective Sergeant Dick Holland of the WRC. Both would become household names during the Yorkshire Ripper investigation. They established that Fred had gone into his office to pick up some papers and had made a telephone call to a relative shortly before his body was discovered.

They issued descriptions of two men who had been seen looking in the window at the antique shop prior to the murder. Both appeared to be men in working clothes. The first suspect was aged about forty, five-feet four-inches in height, wearing a dark jacket and cloth cap, and who appeared to need a shave. The second suspect was aged about twenty, clean shaven, five-feet five-inches in height, of slim build, wearing a dark jacket, light-coloured trousers and a blue denim cap.

Detective Superintendent Oldfield concluded that it was an opportunistic robbery, committed by local workmen who knew Fred and saw him enter the side-door entrance to his office above the antique shop. They followed him into the office and entered just as he finished his call. Sutcliffe's sixteen-year-old brother was arrested and held for questioning for forty-eight hours because he had a reputation for being a tearaway, wore a blue denim cap and had been seen in the area at the time of the murder. However, he had an alibi and was eliminated.

Fred's daughter Irene Vidler recalled Sutcliffe as a 'nasty piece of work' who pestered her sister for dates and taunted her father. She explained:

> My dad was only four-foot seven-inches tall because he had TB of the spine when he was a youngster. Peter Sutcliffe lived near us and my sister remembered him following her and dad once to the bus stop. He was walking behind them, mimicking the way my dad walked. Sutcliffe worked as a gravedigger and got paid extra for washing bodies. He used to take his mates up to see the dead bodies and would run around with skulls to frighten people. When he was caught and we heard the way he operated, we all thought it was him who'd killed my dad. He would have seen him as an easy target. We felt there can't be many people killing with a hammer, let alone in one small town. We phoned the police and my sister was told by George Oldfield, 'he only kills women'.

The authors believe the police were right that the murderers were local men who knew Fred, knew he carried money on him and saw him go into the shop. Because of the short timescale, the two men seen looking into the antiques shop are almost certainly the murderers. They were peering into the antiques shop prior to burglarising it, when they saw Fred go into his office, leaving the door open. They followed him into his office. There was no way they could leave Fred alive to identify them later, so they murdered him and stole the money he had on him. It was an opportunistic attack, so the murderers did not have a weapon like a cosh with them, but did have a hammer and other tools to break into the antiques shop.

The two murderers were Sutcliffe – the younger man – accompanied by an older man. Sutcliffe knew that Fred would be unable to resist because of his disability. He had animosity towards Fred, as demonstrated by his despicable mimicking of him, and may also have resented his rejection by Fred's daughter.

Fred's injuries were consistent with a hammer blow to the back of the head. He had been kicked and the weapon was removed from the scene. This is all consistent with many of Sutcliffe's later attacks.

As with Sutcliffe's theft-from-an-unattended-vehicle conviction, there were two men involved. The authors believe that at this stage of his criminal career Sutcliffe lacked confidence and preferred to be accompanied when committing crime. Sutcliffe was aged twenty, clean shaven, of the right height and build, and also wore a blue denim cap. He fitted the description far better than his younger brother did.

Both men would have been covered in blood, yet neither was seen walking or running through Bingley. So they either had a vehicle to get away in, or alternatively went a short distance home on foot. Possibly they used the more secluded route along the canal to avoid being seen. These factors would all be applicable to Sutcliffe, who lived sixteen minutes' walk away and is known to have had access to a car and a motorbike.

The authors have not been able to identify who Sutcliffe's accomplice was, but have identified some suspects, some of whom they have been able to eliminate:
- Sutcliffe's brothers were both too young and, at six-foot and six-foot four-inches respectively, too tall.

- Sutcliffe's father was also over six foot in height and therefore also too tall.
- Sutcliffe mixed socially with a younger crowd, so the second, older man is unlikely to be from his social circle. Eric Robinson (his accomplice when he was breaking into cars) was too young; his friend Trevor Birdsall was too tall.
- Some of Sutcliffe's workmates at the cemetery were older; they were all local workmen and therefore fitted the description of the older man. None of Sutcliffe's workmates at the cemetery were outraged at his routine theft of jewellery from the corpses and did not inform on him. Some of them may also have been stealing from the corpses. Could one of them have accompanied Sutcliffe to burgle the antiques shop, steal jewellery and sell it to Sutcliffe's fence, when they spotted Fred?
- Sutcliffe mixed with bikers. Could his accomplice have been a local biker, looking for easy money? Did they escape on a motorbike?

5. John Tomey

(Attributed to Sutcliffe by DS O'Boyle and believed to be attributed to him in the original Taken in Consideration investigation)

On 22 March 1967, taxi driver John Tomey, aged twenty-six, picked up a young man in Leeds who asked to be driven to Burnley in Lancashire. At Saltaire, on the outskirts of Shipley, he changed his mind and asked to go to Bingley. John stopped under a streetlamp near Bingley and showed his passenger the fare card. He had a clear look at his passenger and remembers that he was getting very agitated. The man told John that he hadn't got any money but said that he had an aunt at Nelson who would pay the fare, so John drove on to Nelson.

At about 11.20pm, John stopped the car near Oxenhope in an area of moorland. When he stopped to consult a map, John was struck about the head with a hammer. As the blows rained down, he put up his hands to defend himself, but fell forward, momentarily unconscious.

When he awoke, the passenger had smashed every light on the vehicle, including the number-plate light, headlights and the illuminated taxi sign on the roof. His assailant was outside the vehicle, smashing the driver's window with the hammer to try and get into the front. John's habit of locking the driver's door saved his life. He managed to start the engine and drive to a nearby cottage, where an ambulance was called.

John was found to have crescent-shaped lacerations to his scalp, identical to those found on Sutcliffe's later victims. The car interior had clear cup-shaped indentations caused by a ball pein hammer striking the car's roof interior headlining, made with enormous force as the attacker rained down frenzied blows on John's head.

This was not an opportunistic attack or a robbery gone wrong. Cabbies at the end of their shift carry a lot of money on them and are an easy target. The assailant had armed himself beforehand, so it was a planned attack on a defenceless man carrying a lot of money, which used violence far in excess of that required simply to intimidate or subdue the victim and steal his takings. John had a good look at his assailant's facial features in a well-lit area. The implication of this is that, as with Fred Craven, John's assailant did not care that his intended victim could identify him, because he did not intend to leave his victim alive to give evidence against him.

John described his attacker as in his twenties, five-feet eight-inches tall, with darkish skin, dark hair and a noticeable moustache and beard, with a local accent. A perfect fit for Sutcliffe, who was growing a beard at this time. As was the photofit he prepared for the police.

John subsequently identified Sutcliffe as his attacker from a line-up of photographs, including the one of Sutcliffe taken when he was convicted in 1969 (Illustration 1). John never drove again, only managed to work for another five years, never married and never had a family. He has since appeared in several documentaries, positively identifying Sutcliffe as the man who attacked him and destroyed his life. When interviewed in 2014 he said: 'I wish they could hang the bastard.'

The authors have no doubt that the man who tried to murder John for his takings was Sutcliffe.

He used a ball pein hammer, Sutcliffe's weapon of choice, and struck his victim in the back of the head with it. The weapon was removed from the scene. The attack was sudden and unprovoked. The attacker skilfully concealed the weapon, and engaged John in conversation to put him at ease. He was calm and gave no cause for alarm or suspicion, then when he was ready, instantly flew into a frenzy, catching John completely unawares: all classic indicators of a Sutcliffe attack. The assailant's actions and accent are consistent with someone that lived in Bingley.

Sutcliffe may have intended to murder John, leave his body by the side of the road, steal his cab, drive to a place close to home and abandon it. However, the authors believe this is unlikely. Quite apart from the fact that it would be very conspicuous and if stopped in a blood-stained stolen cab he would inevitably be arrested. What's more, abandoning the cab within walking distance of his home would alert the police to the area he lived in.

The authors believe Sutcliffe went to Leeds by train, intending to get picked up by a taxi driver who would have cash on him and would be a suitable victim for an armed robbery. He initially asked John to go to Bingley, then extended the distance, so he could initiate the attack on a route that would take him home, but would be far enough away to disguise his origin. Sutcliffe finally attacked his victim about ten miles from Bingley.

When John drove off, his assailant was left in the middle of windswept moorland, splattered in blood, clutching a bloodstained hammer, miles from anywhere, late at night. This raises the question of how Sutcliffe left the crime scene. The authors have used a standard exfiltration matrix to assess this. The options are:

1. Sutcliffe walked or hitchhiked about ten miles back to Bingley. This was a very risky prospect, with the possibility of being spotted on the road by a passing motorist, or the police

cars that he must have believed were rushing to the scene. It is highly unlikely that a driver would pick up a bloodstained man hitchhiking in the dark on a deserted area of moorland at night. Furthermore, no driver, bus driver, the ambulance crew, or the police cars that attended reported seeing a man walking or hitchhiking on the A6033, nor did anyone pick up a hitchhiker.

2. Sutcliffe marched eight miles cross country across the moors to Bingley. This requires a certain amount of local knowledge, navigational skill and endurance. It would be a daunting task without a map, compass, warm clothing and good footwear. Sutcliffe had never been a Scout or a walker, did not have cross country navigational skills and may not have had adequate footwear. He was happier in an urban environment and would have avoided the moors and stayed on the road.

3. Sutcliffe walked or hitchhiked to a phone box and called a cab to pick him up. This can certainly be eliminated. The next day, every local cabbie would know John had been attacked and any cab driver would certainly have reported picking up a fare who was covered in blood.

4. Sutcliffe walked cross country to Mixenden, Wainstalls, Hebden Bridge or Mytholmroyd (about two to five miles away from the crime scene but in the wrong direction for Bingley) and returned home on public transport. However, there were no reports of a bloodstained man on a local bus or train.

5. Sutcliffe walked to a phone box and called a friend to pick him up. He drove locally, so he would have known where the phone boxes were.

6. Sutcliffe did not go to Leeds by train. Instead, an accomplice dropped him off in Leeds and followed the cab

in a car or on a motorbike, and then picked up Sutcliffe and took him home after the attack. The authors have not been able to identify this potential accomplice, other than to say it was someone Sutcliffe trusted, probably the man who accompanied him when he murdered Fred Craven.

6. George Ellis, known as 'Old Ellis'
George Ellis worked with Sutcliffe at Bingley Cemetery. He was found dead by the side of the Otley Road sometime in 1967. WRC recorded his death as a hit-and-run accident, caused when he was walking home along the Otley Road from Dick Hudson's pub in the dark.

George's colleagues, including Sutcliffe, viewed the body in the chapel at Bingley Cemetery.

Extract from *Somebody's Husband, Somebody's Son: The Story of the Yorkshire Ripper*, by Gordon Burn:

> ...they were expecting the old man would be a bit of a mess. Amazingly, though, they found Ellis lying on the slab as though he was just resting: Trevor Mitchell raised his head gently to show them how the single blow had killed him almost instantly, fracturing the back of the skull like an egg.

He had no injuries, grazes, bruises or skid marks on him other than on the back of his head, arising from a fractured skull. These men had seen many victims of car accidents and expected to find the body had been mangled by the force of the impact with the vehicle and landing on the ground. Instead, the body was intact and the clothes in the same condition as when they last saw George at work on the day of his death. His colleagues expressed scepticism that he had been killed in a Road Traffic Accident (RTA). Unfortunately, in the 1960s you did not question the police.

The police version of events assumes that George – an elderly man – chose to walk three miles to Dick Hudson's pub and then walk three miles back over a cold, unlit, windswept moorland road after a night of drinking. This was despite there being plenty of pubs in Bingley for him to drink in, which did not require a six-mile hike. This is incomprehensible.

Using his experience from attending many fatal RTAs, Chris's conclusions about George's death are:

It is impossible for George to have been hit by a car and killed. Such an impact delivers multiple injuries all over the body, initially from the impact with the vehicle, which will catapult the body forward, and then when the body hits the ground and comes to a stop having rolled or bounced.

I would also expect the clothes to be ripped and soiled from the impact of the vehicle and then hitting the ground and rolling over until the body came to a halt.

It is inconceivable that a vehicle travelling at any speed could inflict a localised injury solely on the skull sufficient to kill a man of average height. The same injuries are apparent in the murders of Judith Roberts, Yvonne Pearson and Carol Wilkinson. Sutcliffe admitted using a walling hammer on Yvonne Pearson.

Sutcliffe regularly drove to Dick Hudson's to drink with friends. I believe that Sutcliffe offered George a lift there and back. Hence George's decision to drink in a pub so far from home.

When George got into Sutcliffe's green Morris Minor for the return journey, Sutcliffe stopped, probably on the pretext of needing to urinate. Having learned from his attack on John Tomey the previous March, he then dragged George out of the car and killed him with a blow to the head with a hammer. Probably a lump or masonry hammer.

The scene of George's death is open moorland on the Otley Rd. It is the same as the location of the attack on John Tomey, which is about ten miles away. Sutcliffe had recently had an altercation with George at work over a prank and may have had a grudge against him. However, I suspect the motive was robbery. The sources I have accessed do not record George's age or the date of his death. I cannot therefore identify if it was a Friday when he would have been paid. Nor do the sources record if George's wallet was missing, or was found empty.

Murder and attempted murder during an armed robbery were practically unheard of in 1960s Bingley. Yet there were two between April 1966 and the end of 1967. All on lone men with access to large amounts of cash at locations Sutcliffe was completely familiar with. John Tomey has identified Sutcliffe as his attacker. Sutcliffe knew Fred Craven and George Ellis, and had grudges against them. The attack on Eddie Bishop showed Sutcliffe was already attacking victims with blows to the head with a hammer and was prepared to use a weapon on men whom he knew and did not like. Only John Tomey was a young man. Fred, Eddie and George were all elderly and – like Sutcliffe's female victims – fitted his preference for lone victims who were unable to defend themselves.

Sutcliffe left Bingley Cemetery in November 1967 to work for the Water Board, then in 1968 he worked as a textile worker in Bingley. He was sacked from both jobs for bad timekeeping. Being late for work would blight all his future employments. His nocturnal prowling through RLDs from his late teens onwards may explain why he found it hard to get up in the morning.

7. Mary Judge

On Monday 26 February 1968 Mary Judge, aged forty-three, was attacked and beaten to death on waste ground beneath railway arches in Leeds. She was a housekeeper to a seventy-five-year-old man, who had no idea she was also a sex worker. Her head had been placed on a wall and beaten with a weapon, which police said was probably a brick. Her face was unrecognisable and she was identified by fingerprints from her criminal record.

Enquiries by the LCP revealed that Mary was outside the Regent Hotel Inn, situated at 109 Kirkgate, at 10.10pm on the night that she was murdered. Shortly afterwards, the Verger of Leeds Parish Church heard sounds of banging coming from near the railway arches but thought nothing of it. A boy travelling in a railway carriage into Leeds saw Mrs Judge being attacked at about 10.18pm. He described her assailant as a slim, youngish man with long dark hair. He did not see a car.

The SIO was Detective Superintendent Dennis Hoban, Head of LCP CID, who would feature prominently in the Ripper investigation.

Mary was a sex worker, which fits with Sutcliffe's victim preferences. It appears she had contracted with her assailant to have sex and taken him to the arches for this purpose. She had been beaten about the head, which is all consistent with Sutcliffe's modus-operandi. The weapon used was never identified, but if it was indeed a brick, this is consistent with Sutcliffe's later 'stone in the sock' attack. The weapon – which could also have been a hammer – was removed from the scene, which is a classic Sutcliffe indicator, and Sutcliffe fits the description of the man seen attacking her.

Mary was found nude; her clothes had been scattered around and none had been taken as a trophy. Her killer probably did not realise he had been observed from the train, which explains why he took the time to enjoy himself fully undressing the body.

At this time, Sutcliffe was routinely using sex workers and was regularly travelling from Bingley, which did not have a RLD, to Leeds, which did. The scene of the crime is about eleven minutes' walk from Leeds City Station. The deposition site is accessible by car, but one was not seen. Indicating that Mary was not picked up in a car and driven to the place where she was murdered. The attack occurred between 10.10pm and 10.25pm, leaving time for Sutcliffe to walk to Leeds City Station, catch a train to Bingley, then walk half a mile from Bingley Station to home. The attack on John Tomey was probably initiated after a train journey to Leeds. The authors believe that Sutcliffe regularly went to Leeds by train for assignations with sex workers, sometimes having sex with them prior to attacking them. But because of police attitudes towards sex workers, these attacks went unreported.

Map 2A below is reproduced from the Byford Report and shows the locations of the twenty attacks Sutcliffe was convicted of, which were all originated from Sutcliffe's homes by car only.

Map 2B extends this analysis to show the attacks the authors believe Sutcliffe committed from his family home at 57 Cornwall Road, Bingley (A), his wife's family home at 44 Tanton Crescent, Bradford (B) and their marital home at 6 Garden Lane, Bradford (C) using a car, or in two cases the rail network. Other than the attacks at Manchester and Sheffield, they are all within twenty miles of these three addresses. They are in twelve distinct clusters and sub-clusters, which the authors have designated as Home Clusters.

Map 2A – The Attacks Sutcliffe was Convicted of 1975 – 1980. Source: The Byford Report

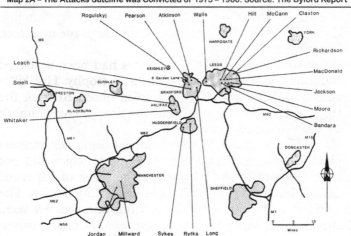

45

Map 2B – Byford Extended: Attack

NORTH WEST (NW) AND NORTH EAST (NE) CLUSTER ATTACKS

THE ATTACKS AT HARROGATE AND ILKLEY ARE BOTH IN THE APEX RECONNAISSANC
CLUSTER ATTACKS, BUT WERE NOT LAUNCHED FROM HOME USING A CAR:
58. THE ATTACK ON THE HARROGATE SCHOOLGIRL WAS PROBABLY FROM A LORRY
    ON THE RETURN JOURNEY FROM THE NE CLUSTER.
66. THE ATTACK ON YVONNE MYSLIWIEC AT ILKLEY WAS FROM A LORRY ON THE
    RETURN JOURNEY FROM THE NE OR NW CLUSTER.
THEY THEREFORE FORM PART OF THE NE AND NW CLUSTERS, NOT THE
HOME CLUSTERS.

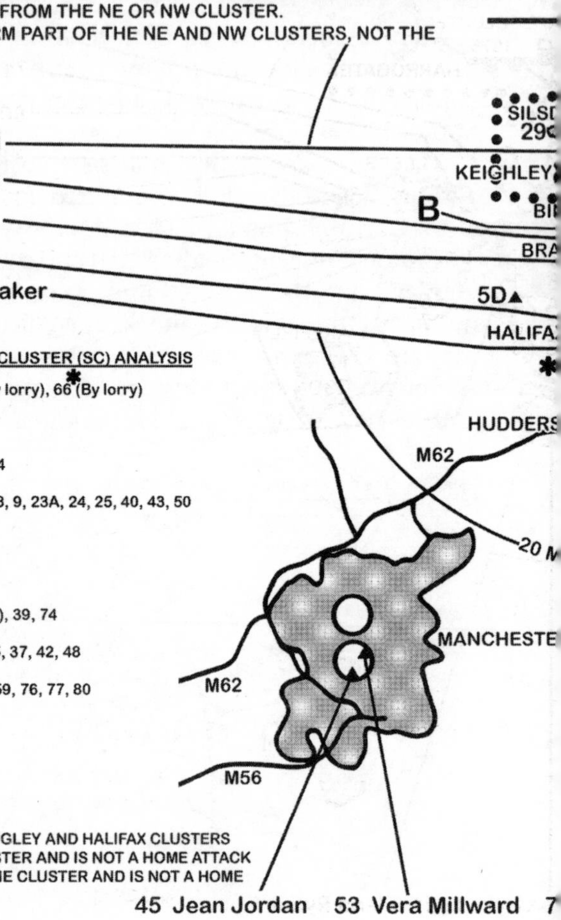

27 Anna Rogulskyj ──────────────────────────

50 Yvonne Pearson ──────

64 Barbara Leach ──────────

28 Olive Smelt ──────────

60 Josephine Whitaker ──────────

SILSD
29

KEIGHLEY
B ── BI
BRA

5D▲
HALIFA

HOME CLUSTER AND SUB CLUSTER (SC) ANALYSIS

APEX: 27, 29, 58 *(Probably by lorry), 66 *(By lorry)

BINGLEY: 2*, 3, 4, 5D, 6

BRADFORD: 33, 36, 46, 56, 64

BRADFORD BELLE VUE SC: 8, 9, 23A, 24, 25, 40, 43, 50

HALIFAX: 2*, 28, 60

HUDDERSFIELD: 51, 78

LEEDS: 5A (By rail), 7 (By rail), 39, 74

LEEDS GAIETY SC: 31, 34, 35, 37, 42, 48

LEEDS UNIVERSITY SC: 52, 59, 76, 77, 80

MANCHESTER: 45, 53

SHEFFIELD: 81

WAKEFIELD: 17, 23D

HUDDERS

M62

20 M

MANCHESTE

M62

M56

* CASE 2 IS IN BOTH THE BINGLEY AND HALIFAX CLUSTERS
CASE 58 IS IN THE NE CLUSTER AND IS NOT A HOME ATTACK
CASE 66 IS IN THE NW OR NE CLUSTER AND IS NOT A HOME
ATTACK

45 Jean Jordan   53 Vera Millward   7

THE ATTACKS IN THE HOME CLUSTERS WERE LAUNCHED
BY CAR FROM SUTCLIFFE'S HOMES AT:
A 57 CORNWALL ROAD, BINGLEY
B 44 TANTON CRESCENT, BRADFORD
C 6 GARDEN LANE, BRADFORD

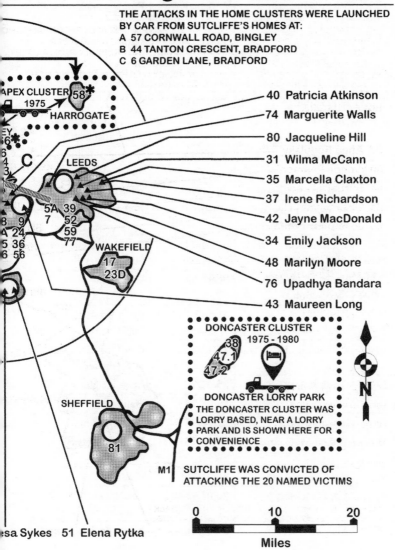

40 Patricia Atkinson
74 Marguerite Walls
80 Jacqueline Hill
31 Wilma McCann
35 Marcella Claxton
37 Irene Richardson
42 Jayne MacDonald
34 Emily Jackson
48 Marilyn Moore
76 Upadhya Bandara
43 Maureen Long

APEX CLUSTER 58
1975
HARROGATE

LEEDS

5A 39
7   52
     59
     77

WAKEFIELD
17
23D

DONCASTER CLUSTER 1975 - 1980
38
47.1
47.2
DONCASTER LORRY PARK
THE DONCASTER CLUSTER WAS
LORRY BASED, NEAR A LORRY
PARK AND IS SHOWN HERE FOR
CONVENIENCE

N

SHEFFIELD
81

M1 SUTCLIFFE WAS CONVICTED OF
ATTACKING THE 20 NAMED VICTIMS

0   10   20
Miles

…sa Sykes   51 Elena Rytka

47

No	Name	Date	Cluster(s)
A	**57 Cornwall Road, Bingley, until 10 August 1974**		
2	Vicky Williamson	23/12/64	Bingley, Halifax
3	Child F	1965	Bingley
4	Fred Craven	22/04/66	Bingley
5	John Tomey	22/03/67	Bingley
6	George Ellis	1967	Bingley
7	Mary Judge	26/02/1968	Leeds
8	Stone in sock attack	Aug 1969	Bradford, Belle Vue Sub-Cluster
9	Equipped for theft	30/09/69	Bradford, Belle Vue Sub-Cluster
17	Bernadette Cassidy	29/12/72	Wakefield
B	**44 Tanton Crescent, Bradford, 10 August 1974 until 26 September 1977**		
23A	Child D, Child E, Abduction	06/11/74	Bradford, Belle Vue Sub-Cluster
23D	Child D, Child E, Deposition	06/11/74	Wakefield
24	Child G	Mid Oct 1974	Bradford, Belle Vue Sub-Cluster
25	Gloria Wood	11/11/74	Bradford, Belle Vue Sub-Cluster
27	Anna Rogulskyj	05/07/75	Apex Keighley
28	Olive Smelt	15/08/75	Halifax
29	Tracy Browne	27/08/75	Apex Silsden
31	Wilma McCann	30/10/75	Leeds, Gaiety Sub-Cluster
33	Rosemary Stead	06/01/76	Bradford
34	Emily Jackson	20/01/76	Leeds, Gaiety Sub-Cluster
35	Marcella Claxton	09/05/76	Leeds, Gaiety Sub-Cluster

No	Name	Date	Cluster(s)
36	Maureen Hogan	29/08/76	Bradford
37	Irene Richardson	05/02/77	Leeds, Gaiety Sub-Cluster
39	Debra Schlesinger	21/04/77	Leeds
40	Patricia Atkinson	23/04/77	Bradford, Belle Vue Sub-Cluster
42	Jayne MacDonald	26/06/77	Leeds, Gaiety Sub-Cluster
43	Maureen Long	10/07/77	Bradford, Belle Vue Sub-Cluster
C	**6 Garden Lane, Heaton, Bradford, 26 September 1977 until arrest**		
45	Jean Jordan	01/10/77	Manchester
46	Carol Wilkinson	10/10/77	Bradford
48	Marilyn Moore	14/12/77	Leeds, Gaiety Sub-Cluster
50	Yvonne Pearson	22/01/78	Bradford, Belle Vue Sub-Cluster
51	Elena Rytka	31/01/78	Huddersfield
52	Leeds Shop Assistant	02/03/78	Leeds, University Sub-Cluster
53	Vera Millward	16/05/78	Manchester
56	Carole Montgomery	28/11/78	Bradford
59	Ann Rooney	02/03/79	Leeds, University Sub-Cluster
60	Josephine Whitaker	04/04/79	Halifax
64	Barbara Leach	02/09/79	Bradford
74	Marguerite Walls	20/08/80	Leeds
76	Upadhya Bandara	24/09/80	Leeds University Sub-Cluster
77	Maureen Lea	25/10/80	Leeds, University Sub-Cluster

No	Name	Date	Cluster(s)
78	Theresa Sykes	05/11/80	Huddersfield
80	Jacqueline Hill	17/11/80	Leeds, University Sub-Cluster
81	Olivia Reivers	02/01/80	Sheffield

Doncaster Cluster (Attacks by lorry from work and shown on Map 2B for convenience only)				
No	Name	Date	Cluster(s)	Route Package(s)
38	Barbara Young	22/03/77	Doncaster	All routes from Harwich, Peterborough, Dover, London and the South East go via or close to Doncaster
47.1	Doncaster sex worker	Nov/Dec 1977	Doncaster	
47.2		Jan/Feb 1978	Doncaster	

Sutcliffe seems to have been comfortable having a secure base to launch an attack from and return to. The authors believe he likewise used his sister-in-law's home in Alperton, West London, his sister's home in Duxford, Cambridgeshire and his girlfriend's home in Holytown, near Glasgow, to launch attacks.

8. 'Stone in the sock' attack
(Cautioned but not prosecuted)
During the second half of 1969, Sutcliffe became aware that Sonia – who had been his girlfriend for three years – was seeing another man. This carried on until the end of 1969. During this time, Sutcliffe still had a motorbike and he would roam on 'runs out' with it. It is not known where he went or for what purpose.

Sutcliffe, feeling betrayed and utterly devastated, confronted Sonia in about July 1969. She refused to answer any of his questions or confirm if their relationship was over. He decided to take revenge by going with a sex worker that night. Driving down Lumb Lane in Manningham (Bradford's RLD), he saw a sex worker soliciting at a petrol station. Having confirmed she was 'doing business', they agreed on a price of £5.

This is Sutcliffe's description of what happened:

I thought that I would have intercourse with the prostitute but changed my mind when it got to the stage where we had got to do it. We were on the way to her place and were talking and I realized what a coarse and vulgar person she was. We were practically there and I realised that I did not want to do anything with her. Before getting out of the car I was trying to wriggle out of the situation but I felt stupid as well. I picked up the girl outside a garage and I realised later that the men who worked there were her protectors. I'd given her a £10 note and she said she'd give me my change later. We got to her house and went inside. There was a huge Alsatian dog on a mat in front of the fire downstairs. She started going upstairs and I realised I just didn't want to go through with it. The whole thing was awful. I felt disgusted with her and myself. I went upstairs behind her and into the bedroom. I even unzipped her dress, but I told her straight out I didn't want to do anything with her. She could keep the money, just give me my change. She said she'd have to go back to the garage where I'd picked her up, to get some change, so I drove her there. I just wanted to get away. I felt worse than ever about Sonia and everything.

We went back to the garage by car and she went inside and there were two chaps in there. I don't know whether she did this regularly, but she wouldn't come back out. One of the men came banging on the car roof when I refused to go away. He said, 'If I were you, I wouldn't get out of that car. You'd better get going.' I would have had a go at him, but he was holding the wrench in a menacing sort of way. Then I saw the girl come out with another big-built bloke. They walked off together, having a laugh. I just felt stupid, I drove home more angry than ever. I felt outraged and humiliated and embarrassed. I felt a hatred for the prostitute and her kind.

Three weeks later, Sutcliffe saw the same woman in a pub in Manningham:

I went and approached the one I had been with three weeks previously and told her I hadn't forgotten about the incident and that she could put things right so there would be no hard feelings. I was giving her the opportunity to put things right and give back the payment I had made to her. She thought this was a huge joke and, as luck would have it, she knew everybody else in the place and went round telling them. Before I knew what was happening, most of the people were having a good laugh.

Shortly after this second encounter, Sutcliffe and Trevor Birdsall were sitting in Trevor's Austin Mini in St Paul's Road, Manningham. Sutcliffe had been looking for the woman who had stolen £10 from him but to no avail. Sutcliffe suddenly left the vehicle and walked out of sight. He came back about ten minutes later out of breath as though he had been running and told Trevor Birdsall to drive off quickly. As they headed towards Bingley, Sutcliffe claimed that he had followed an 'old cow' to a house somewhere and had hit her on the back of her head with a stone in a sock. He explained that the sock had fallen apart and the stone had fallen out. He removed the sock from his pocket and dumped its contents out of the window. This became known as the 'stone in the sock' attack, although the sock actually contained a brick.

The woman he had attacked – who did not resemble the woman who stole his money – noted Trevor Birdsall's car's registration number, and the next day two detectives questioned him. He directed them to Sutcliffe. They interviewed Sutcliffe at his home and he admitted hitting the woman but claimed it was only with his hand. The woman did not want to press charges because she did not want her husband – who was in prison – to know she had been doing sex work. So the police could only caution Sutcliffe.

This was intelligence that Sutcliffe committed offences of aggravated assault with a weapon against a sex worker and it should have been indexed in the collator system and passed to the Force and Regional Intelligence Collators for future use, but was not. This was the first major point of failure (MPoF) in what was to become the Yorkshire Ripper investigation.

9. Going equipped for theft
(Convicted)

During the early hours of Tuesday 30 September 1969, Sutcliffe was observed by the police in the Manningham area of Bradford sitting in his vehicle with the engine running quietly and the lights off. When a BCP constable approached the car, Sutcliffe drove off at high speed. Sutcliffe's car was again spotted a short distance away, this time parked and unattended with the lights on and the engine running.

Sutcliffe was discovered hunched behind a privet hedge within a private garden with a hammer in his hand. He told the constable that a hubcap had flown off his front wheel and that he had been looking for it and the hammer was to help him secure it in place. The policeman arrested him for going equipped for theft, neglected to search him (MPoF) and called up a police van to take him to the police station. While he was in the back of the van, Sutcliffe slipped a long-bladed knife down a gap between the side of the vehicle and the wheel arch cover.

Here Chris uses his experience from his service in Uniform Branch to comment on the conduct of the arrest:

Searching a suspect at the scene was a routine task and this was instilled at Training School. Under the circumstances that Sutcliffe had been found in, most coppers would have arrested him for being in possession of an offensive weapon and searched him at the scene before he got into the police van as a matter of routine. Astonishingly, Sutcliffe wasn't searched at the scene to obtain evidence of crime and prevent injury to the officer or offender.

Sutcliffe was taken to Bradford Police Station and charged with going equipped for theft. If he had been searched before he was put in the van, the knife would have been found and he would have been charged with being in possession of an offensive weapon. Sutcliffe was charged, photographed (see Illustration 2) and fingerprinted, then released on bail. He was fined £25 at the Magistrates Court two weeks later.

Sutcliffe had obviously intended to attack a sex worker, but had changed his modus-operandi. Following the failure of the 'stone in the sock' attack, he had abandoned using a brick or an improvised cosh made from one. Chris continues:

> As was routine at the time, a local and national check should have been made to see if there was anything known about him and that should have thrown up the local caution a couple of weeks earlier. Given that both offences were committed in the RLD and that the first involved a sex worker, a huge opportunity was missed to link him to the caution for the 'stone in the sock' assault and this offence.
>
> The Custody Sergeant looking at the two cases would then have had the option of charging him with carrying an offensive weapon and Sutcliffe would have then been identified as a danger to women and recorded at Force Headquarters and in the Scotland Yard 'Method Index'. This would have

then catapulted him to the top of the suspects later in 1975 when the 'Yorkshire Ripper' attacks began and inevitably would have led to his early arrest.

Sutcliffe's conviction for this offence was recorded at the WYC Criminal Record Office (CRO) and with the BCP Intelligence Collator. But both records made no reference to a hammer. Whereas the Scotland Yard CRO, which had the same copy of the conviction, recorded it as 'Equipped for stealing (hammer)' and under 'Method', the words 'In possession of housebreaking implement by night namely a hammer'.

This inattention to detail was to have catastrophic consequences for the Yorkshire Ripper investigation (MPoF).

10. Lucy Tinslop

Lucy Tinslop was murdered on Monday 4 August 1969, at around 11.30pm in St Mary's Rest Garden in Bath Street, Nottingham, on her twenty-first birthday. Lucy had been strangled. Her killer, having an obvious sexual motive, had disembowelled her and stabbed her vagina over twenty times. It is unclear if there was one entry wound with multiple stabbing through the same wound, or if the murderer had masturbated over her.

A FOI request has confirmed that all records of this crime were destroyed by Nottinghamshire Police.

Sutcliffe should be considered as a suspect for this murder, because he had access to a motorbike and other vehicles at this time. It takes about two hours to travel from Bingley to Nottingham. He could also have travelled by rail via Leeds. He was still bitter about Sonia's betrayal and this may have further motivated him to attack another woman. He was also apparently enjoying mutilating his victim's body for the first time. Lucy was strangled, just as Vicky Williamson was. Since his relationship with Sonia was on hold, Sutcliffe now had more time to roam. The authors believe Sutcliffe visited Nottingham and murdered Lucy while on a 'run out'.

Had this attack occurred in the period 1975–1980, it would immediately have been categorised as an attack by the Yorkshire Ripper, because it contained the main elements of his modus-operandi. The connection was not made at the time because the Yorkshire Ripper was believed to only operate in West Yorkshire and Manchester.

An extract taken from the report by ACC Colin Sampson in October 1981 confirms:

A number of attacks on women since 1966 in West Yorkshire remain undetected. Sutcliffe has now been interviewed about these and other cases which occurred elsewhere in the country but has denied responsibility.

ACC Sampson obviously suspected Sutcliffe of committing other attacks from 1966 onwards outside West Yorkshire. Lucy's murder is probably one of them. It is one of the Central Cluster of attacks committed on 'runs out' or while he was travelling on route packages to or from Bingley or Bradford, to the Alperton, South East, Duxford or South West Clusters.

No	Name	Date	Cluster	Route Package
A	Bingley and Bradford			
H	Maureen's home at Duxford			
10	Lucy Tinslop	04/08/69	Central	
12D	Jackie Ansell-Lamb Deposition site	08/03/70	Central	2.1. Alperton-Bingley
13D	Barbara Mayo Deposition site	12/10/70	Central	2.2. Alperton/ Deptford-Bingley
15	Marie Burke	18/04/72	Central	2.1. Alperton-Bingley

No	Name	Date	Cluster	Route Package
16	Judith Roberts	07/06/72	Central	2.3. Bexley-Bingley
18	Wendy Sewell	12/09/73	Central	3.1. Duxford-Bingley
19	Rosina Hilliard	22/02/74	Central	3.1. Duxford-Bingley
21A	Caroline Allen abduction point	10/04/74	Central	3.1. Duxford-Bingley
21D	Caroline Allen deposition site	10/04/74	Central	3.1. Duxford-Bingley
62	Wendy Jenkins	27/08/79	South West	Not part of the Alperton route packages. Shown here for convenience only

Between 1961 and 1968, Sutcliffe had been in trouble with the police over driving offences – in itself not unusual or giving any cause for alarm. He had made his first attack on a female and his first attack with a knife, which was on a man, both of which he enjoyed. Although he only had one theft conviction, he may have been routinely involved in offences of theft from 1965 onwards. This was possibly to make up for the shortfall in his income caused by his irregular employment and not being able to sell stolen jewellery after losing his job at Bingley Cemetery.

At some point Sutcliffe stopped using an accomplice, probably after Trevor Birdsall informed on him for the 'stone in the sock' attack. He also realised that attacking women gave him sexual pleasure and so specialised in attacking women. He had also started to experiment and change his modus-operandi by alternating his choice of weapons, variously using a knife and a hammer. This was a trend that was to continue throughout his life.

Sutcliffe had started his criminal career as a thief, stealing from corpses and cars, but graduated to armed robberies and murder. His work at the cemetery aroused his interest in necrophilia and he probably indulged in this practice while working there. He was a dangerous man and the authors have no doubt that he committed many other attacks on women and violent robberies during this period that remain undetected.

In 1968 the records of previous convictions would have been transferred to the MIRIAM system. A new index card should have been raised from his original criminal record, converting the nominal index filed under Peter William Sutcliffe DOB 02 June 1946 containing a CRO number and CRO 74 antecedent history, along with associates for his previous convictions gained in 1965 for attempted theft.

A copy of the information gained from the interview for the 'stone in the sock' attack and the 'Going equipped for theft' conviction should have been forwarded to the BCP collator for updating on his record card and forwarded to the central WYMP Intelligence Bureau and combined CRO. This did not happen, so the Yorkshire Ripper investigation did not have an accurate CRO antecedent history for Sutcliffe (MPoF).

Phase 3. 1969 – 1975: Developing as a serial killer

By the end of 1969, Sutcliffe had killed multiple times and specialised in attacking unaccompanied women. He was

Map 3 - The Bristol, Alperton, Deptford & Bexley, To Bingley & Bradford Route Packages

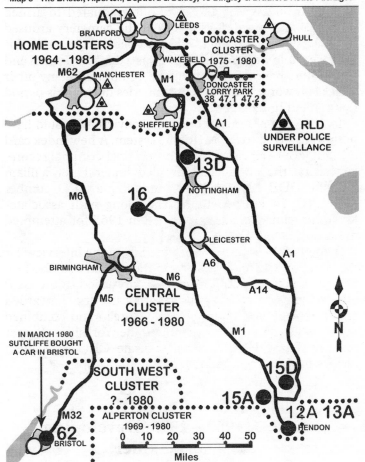

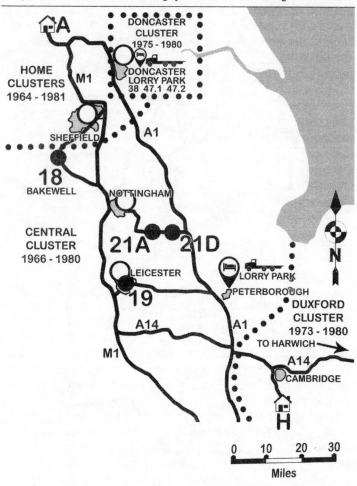

Map 5 - The Central Cluster 1966 - 1980

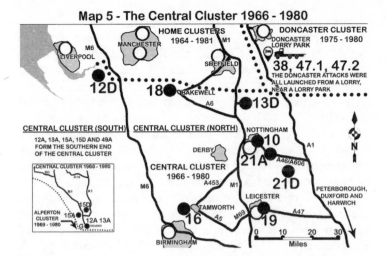

experimenting with different modi operandi to confuse the police investigation, which had still not recognised that these attacks were connected to one perpetrator. He was no longer using an accomplice and had stopped committing crimes in Bingley, to prevent the police from linking these offences to a local man.

During 1969 or 1970 Sutcliffe's younger sister Maureen became friendly with a regular soldier, Robin Holland, who would often go out drinking with Sutcliffe. Robin has confirmed that sex workers were always on Sutcliffe's mind. He would brag about his exploits with them and would often nip out for a 'quickie' with one. However, while at home, Sutcliffe would preach about the immorality of men who two-timed their wives.

Maureen and Robin married in early 1973 and settled in married quarters at Duxford. They had a child on 1 April 1974. Sutcliffe loved Maureen and was a devoted uncle. He visited them frequently, travelling via the M1 and Midlands crossover to the A1, giving him regular access to the Midlands.

11. Ann Smith

On 28 January 1970, the body of twenty-year-old Ann Smith, who lived at Crockerton Road, Tooting, London, was found in a three-foot ditch off Burgh Heath Road. This was a 'lovers' lane' on the edge of Epsom Downs, Surrey, which at the time fell within the jurisdiction of the MPS.

Ann had been dead for two or three days when she was found. She was wearing only a miniskirt, her underwear was near the body and she was not wearing footwear. Her body was posed with one hand behind her head.

She had multiple injuries. The cause of death was ligature strangulation. The degree of violence she had been subjected to was described by the SIO, Detective Chief Superintendent (DCS) Keith Etheridge, as 'excessive'. A police spokesman described the savage murder as the work of a demon.

It later emerged that Ann was estranged from her husband and had a two-year-old son. She had fled from a vice gang in Liverpool and had worked in a sweet shop in Brixton prior to moving to Tooting. Ann then returned to prostitution, soliciting clients in cars at Acre Lane, Brixton, and Clapham Common.

The investigation identified that Ann had been murdered near Clapham Common by one man in an office, shop, or factory and then taken to Epsom Downs.

Ann was a sex worker lured into a car to drive to another location to have sex. Death by ligature strangulation after a massive blow to the head, the savagery of the attack, posing of the body and the scattering around of clothes are all consistent with Sutcliffe's modus operandi.

From about 1969 onwards, Sutcliffe and Sonia started visiting Sonia's sister Marianne, who lived at three addresses in West London. Two were at Alperton, which was situated close to the A406 North Circular Road that led to the start of the M1 at Hendon. All three addresses are referred to generically as being in Alperton. Sutcliffe and Sonia attended Marianne's piano recitals and watched the opera and ballet together in London and other venues. He was therefore travelling around London at night and could have committed attacks after he had dropped off Marianne and Sonia.

Clapham Common and Acre Lane are the closest RLDs to Alperton and are about an hour's drive away. Epsom Downs is about an hour from both locations and has a fast exit route back to the A406 North Circular Road, via the A24.

Sutcliffe was itinerant in his employment at this time and may have been working as a mechanic in a garage. If so, this would explain brick dust and engine oil being transferred to Ann's body – as with the murder of Gloria Booth – leading the police to conclude that Ann had been murdered in commercial premises. It is unclear if Sutcliffe was ever considered as a suspect in this murder.

No	Name
A	Marianne's home in Alperton
B	Start of M1 at Hendon/Brent Cross.
11A?	Probable abduction point for Ann Smith
11D	Deposition site for Ann's body

The authors believe that Ann's murder was launched from Marianne's home, becoming the first of the Alperton Home Sub-Cluster.

Between 1973 and 1975, Sutcliffe visited Marianne at Alperton, sometimes travelling on across London from Alperton to visit Robin and Maureen in Duxford. The authors believe that three murders were committed while Sutcliffe was travelling from Alperton to Duxford, Bingley or Bradford, thus forming the Alperton East Sub-Cluster.

Diagram 1 - Murder of Ann Smith

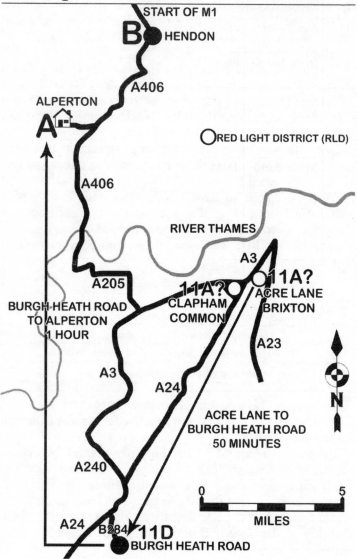

No	Name	Date	Cluster	Route Package
F	Marianne's house at Alperton			
R	Conquering Hero Pub			
11	Ann Smith	26/01/70	Alperton Home SC	
12A	Jackie Ansell-Lamb	08/03/70	Central	2.1. Alperton-Bingley
13A	Barbara Mayo	12/10/70	Central	2.2. Alperton/Deptford-Bingley
14	Gloria Booth	13/06/71	Alperton Home SC	
15	Marie Burke	18/04/72	Central	2.1. Alperton-Bingley
26	Eve Stratford	18/03/75	Alperton East SC, Duxford	2.4. Alperton to Duxford, 2.5. Alperton-Bradford
30	Lynne Weedon	03/09/75	Alperton Home SC	
32	Margaret Lightfoot	24/11/75	Alperton East SC, Duxford	2.4. Alperton to Duxford, 2.5. Alperton-Bradford
44	Elizabeth Parravicini	08/09/77	Alperton Home SC	
49A	Child A and Child B	1977/78	Central abduction, North East deposition	6.1. London/South East-Bradford/Sunderland Docks
57	Lynda Farrow	19/01/79	Alperton East SC	
71	Patricia Morris	16/06/80	Alperton Home SC	

Map 6 - The Alperton Cluster and Convergen

LOUGHTON

32

26 AND 32 ARE
IN BOTH THE
ALPERTON AND
DUXFORD
CLUSTERS

S THE
RAL,

ERS

A10

A406

WOODFORD
GREEN

57

**DUXFORD
CLUSTER**
1973 - 1980

A1400

A12

26
LEYTON

A12

A406

A13

SMITHFIELD
MARKET

A1202

A3

DEPTFORD

A2

LEP DEPOT
CHARLTON

BRIXTON

BEXLEY

A2

SUTCLIFFE LIVED AT
DEPTFORD FROM
SEPTEMBER 1970 TO
SEPTEMBER 1971 WHILE
SONIA WAS AT TEACHER
TRAINING COLLEGE THERE.
FROM SEPTEMBER 1971 TO
MAY 1972 HE VISITED HER
ON WEEKENDS

CRE
ANE

R

A23

SOUTH EAST CLUSTER
1970 - 1980

N

SUTCLIFFE VISITED SONIA AT
BEXLEY PSYCHIATRIC HOSPITAL
EACH WEEKEND AND ON HOLIDAYS
FROM MAY 1972 – 1973, STAYING
LOCALLY OR AT ALPERTON

0   5   10

Miles

12. Jacqueline 'Jackie' Ansell-Lamb, 13. Barbara Mayo (Both believed to have been attributed to Sutcliffe by both ACC Hellawell and ACC Sampson)
15. Marie Burke (Believed to have been attributed to Sutcliffe on the original Taken in Consideration investigation and by ACC Hellawell)

The murders of Jackie Ansell-Lamb and Barbara Mayo are considered together because they have been linked in the media. The murder of Marie Burke was not linked at the time, but should have been.

JACQUELINE 'JACKIE' ANSELL-LAMB

In the afternoon of Sunday 8 March 1970 at 2.30pm, David Sykes dropped off eighteen-year-old Jackie Ansell-Lamb at the start of the M1 at Hendon so she could hitchhike to her flat in Manchester. The next day her flatmate reported her missing.

On Saturday 14 March 1970, Jackie's body was found spread-eagled face down in Square Wood, Mere, near Knutsford in Cheshire, some half a mile from the Chester-to-Manchester Road. She had been partially undressed; her miniskirt had been removed and her clothes placed neatly next to her. Her maxi-length coat had been removed with force, but had been used to cover the body. The buttons of her coat were missing – torn off, as in the later murder of Wilma McCann.

The post-mortem identified that Jackie had been severely beaten around the back of the head and sexually assaulted. The cause of death was ligature strangulation with a garrotte.

A garrotte is a handheld ligature used to strangle a victim. It can be made with any light cord or rope of good tensile strength about two to three feet long. A loop is made at each end for grip and two knots tied a few inches apart in the centre.

To use it, the assailant approaches the victim from the rear with a hand on each end of the garrotte, holding it taut.

The assailant throws the garrotte over the victim's head and either loops it or crosses the hands at the rear of the neck. He then pulls both ways. This cuts off air and the two knots crush the larynx. Strangulation is quick and silent.

Cheshire Constabulary tracked Jackie's movements as far as a café just off Junction 20 of the M6 near Warrington at 10.00pm. She was seen talking to a smartly dressed man who looked like a sales rep. They left and got into a car together.

Jackie's journey from Hendon to Mere via the M1/M6 was a 176-mile, three-hour journey. She left Hendon at 2.30pm. Even adding an hour on, she should have been in the area of her deposition by around 6.30pm. So the café sighting of between 9.00pm and 10.00pm is probably erroneous.

There are multiple Sutcliffe indicators. The body was found in a secluded rural area, partially undressed with the clothes nearby. It was posed, had been sexually assaulted and covered by a coat. The victim had been severely beaten about the back of the head, possibly with a hammer, and then strangled with a garrotte.

By now, Sutcliffe was varying both his modus operandi and geographical area of operations to confuse the police. The authors believe Jackie was the first victim he killed with a garrotte. When he was arrested in 1981, he was in possession of a garrotte in the form of a three-foot piece of blue-and-red plaited nylon rope knotted at each end for gripping, with two knots a couple of inches apart in the middle. Garrottes were used in the murders of Kay O'Connor, Gloria Booth, Wendy Sewell, Marguerite Walls and in the attempted murder of Upadhya Bandara.

Child D has confirmed that Sutcliffe picked up hitchhikers in his car. The authors believe that Sutcliffe was returning home to Bradford after visiting Marianne, saw Jackie at Hendon or at some other point on the M1, and offered her a lift. When she said she was going to Manchester, he said he was also going there, and she got into his car.

Sutcliffe had a very good knowledge of the road network and probably knew Manchester from visits to the RLDs there. He would have been able to plan a route to Manchester, identify a place to make his attack, and identify an exit route while he was driving. He could then drive to Bradford via Manchester, passing the deposition site, which he may have selected in advance while travelling.

Sutcliffe probably stopped at Square Wood, telling his victim that he needed to urinate. It is consistent with Sutcliffe's preference for a location that allows a fast exit from the scene of the crime to a motorway. The M62 is the fastest route from Square Wood to Sutcliffe's home.

Jackie's murder was the first of the Central Cluster of attacks. These occurred along the various routes from London and Duxford to Bingley and Bradford, or when Sutcliffe was roaming on 'runs out'.

BARBARA MAYO

Barbara Mayo, aged twenty-four, was a student teacher living with her boyfriend, David Pollard, in London. On Monday 12 October 1970, she went to Hendon at about 8.30am to hitchhike to Catterick to collect a car from there. David reported her missing that day.

On Sunday 18 October, Barbara's body was found in a secluded wood some twenty yards down a track, near Ault Hucknall, Derbyshire, just off the M1. She was face down, covered by leaves, fully clothed but with her clothing in disarray and her jacket spread over her. She had been beaten about the head and strangled with a ligature. The buttons from her coat were missing. It was never established if she had been murdered at the deposition site or elsewhere, and the police did not reveal if she had been sexually assaulted.

In accordance with standard practice, Derbyshire County and Borough Constabulary (DCBC) called in Scotland Yard, which had a pool of experienced detectives to assist the smaller county forces in leading major investigations. Detective Superintendent Charles Palmer from the MPS led the investigation, assisted by a detective sergeant (DS) who ran the incident room. He said about the killer:

> He is an evil and calculating killer, he may have killed before, he may certainly kill again...

It is clear from these remarks that, with hindsight, Detective Superintendent Palmer was talking about the emergence of what we now call a national, organised serial killer, a decade before Sutcliffe was arrested.

The investigation focussed on David Pollard, who was involved in the London drugs scene. Detective Constable (DC) Andrew Laptew confirmed in correspondence with Chris that:

> I had occasion to visit the Barbara Mayo Incident Room in Derby [in connection with another enquiry]. The consensus of opinion was that Barbara was murdered as a result of a drugs dealing dispute. Therefore, the circumstances surrounding her death were never linked to Sutcliffe.

This diverted the investigation away from what was clearly a sexually motivated attack. David Pollard was eliminated and the investigation, which became the largest investigation in the history of the police service up to that time, did not identify Barbara's killer. A major factor in its failure was that it focussed on two sightings of Barbara that were probably erroneous. A local butcher said that a woman fitting Barbara Mayo's description had bought some faggots from his shop in Kimberley, which is one mile from the M1 and about twenty miles from Ault Hucknall. Another witness said she had seen a woman fitting Barbara Mayo's description getting into a Morris Minor 1000 Traveller driven by a clean-shaven man at about 4.00pm at Kimberley, Nottinghamshire.

Barbara's journey from Hendon to Ault Hucknall is a 140-mile journey which takes about two hours and fifteen minutes. Even adding an hour, she would have been in her deposition area by 12.30pm. So the Kimberley sighting at 4.00pm is outside the time parameters. Nevertheless, an enormous amount of police time was wasted tracking down over 100,000 Morris Travellers and interviewing their drivers. David Pollard wrote to Chris:

> As you know, the most concerning aspect of Barbara's murder is the massive hunt for the Morris Traveller and its driver which, as best it is possible to see, was entirely misdirected. This skewed the whole of the investigation and perhaps a number of others.
>
> Where there is evidence is in the presumed sighting with the Morris Traveller in Kimberley. If there is a plausible scenario for this, I haven't been able to find it. Setting off at maybe 8.30 in the morning it doesn't take a pretty young woman hitching on a busy motorway in bright daylight until after 4 o'clock in the afternoon to travel 120 miles.
>
> Even if there were to be some explanation for this, how would she have reached Catterick from Kimberley before the garage closed?
>
> Why would she have taken a detour to buy a couple of faggots? It is well-nigh impossible that the Kimberley sighting was of Barbara. There were no faggots in her stomach contents, only the breakfast she had before leaving home.
>
> But this supposed and highly publicised sighting certainly gave the murderer a clear run. Public attention was directed to the wrong time, the wrong place, the wrong vehicle and the wrong photofit.

Sutcliffe was wrongly eliminated as a suspect in 1981 because the van driver was clean-shaven.

During September 1970, Sonia Sutcliffe began a three-year teacher training course in Deptford, living in a hall of residence which prohibited male visitors. Initially, Sutcliffe visited Sonia at weekends and holidays, travelling down straight after work. He stayed with Marianne, or slept in his car or in a tent, before driving back in time to start work. He also lived in a bedsit near Alperton as well as in bed-and-breakfast accommodation in Deptford, surviving on what he could earn as a mechanic at a local garage and drinking at the Conquering Hero pub. He would have developed a good knowledge of the area and may have committed attacks there which went unrecorded or were not linked to him after his arrest.

Sutcliffe was regularly driving up the M1 to Bradford. He had his tool bag with him, with the hammers and screwdrivers he used to attack women. Sutcliffe could easily have been returning home up the M1 and been at Hendon at the same time as Barbara, or could have picked her up en route.

Barbara's body had been posed, her clothes were found nearby and she had been partially covered. She had been severely beaten about the back of the head, possibly with a hammer, and strangled with a ligature. Scotland Yard emphasised that the murderer may have killed before and would certainly go on to kill again. The police referred to both Jackie and Barbara as having been brutally raped, however, there were no semen samples. The implication of this was that they were not penile raped, but – as in Josephine Whitaker's case – they were raped with an implement. All these factors point to Sutcliffe's guilt.

MARIE BURKE
Marie Burke was a drifter who was last seen at 6.30pm on Tuesday 18 April 1972 thumbing a lift from a lorry driver on the M1 at Brent Cross. She was seen later hitching a lift at a pub at Leverstock Green close to the interchange of the M1 and A414. She was found severely injured in a layby on the A414 Hemel Hempstead Road on the outskirts of St Albans. She was unconscious but still breathing, her body covered with her coat.

She had been hit around the back of the head with a blunt instrument several times. She lay in a coma for three weeks, hovering between life and death. The attack upon her was described as 'particularly savage', leaving serious head injuries.

Marie was so badly injured that she couldn't remember who picked her up from the pub in Leverstock Green. Marie returned to her itinerant lifestyle, and although she regularly rang the incident room for updates on the case, contact ceased in 1980.

The attack was written off as a traffic accident (MPoF), which ensured it was not linked to the murders of Jackie and Barbara in 1970. The file was then destroyed or lost in a force reorganisation.

In 1972, Easter Monday fell on 3 April. Sonia had a two-week Easter break from teacher training and returned to Bradford. Two weeks later, Sutcliffe drove Sonia back to stay with Marianne at Alperton. His return journey to 57 Cornwall Road could have been on 18 April.

The A414 links the M1 to the A1(M). The M1 is the fastest route from Alperton to Bingley, but the A1(M) is only marginally slower. It would have been easy for Sutcliffe to turn off the M1 to the A414 on the premise that he wanted to urinate, or to have consensual sex with his passenger at the layby (which was used by courting couples), then attack Marie once she was out of the car. The deposition site allowed a fast exit from the area using a motorway.

Marie had been severely beaten about the back of the head with a blunt instrument. A retired detective who worked on the case has confirmed to Chris that her injuries are consistent with the use of a hammer. A Ripper signature.

In summary, the most likely abduction points for all three victims were within twenty miles, and the attacks took place within two years of each other. Marie Burke had extensive head injuries; Jackie and Barbara also had head injuries and were moved from the first blitz attack on a lane to a secluded spot in a wooded area, had been raped (probably using an instrument) and strangled. As with confirmed Ripper victims Wilma McCann, Emily Jackson, Irene Richardson, Vera Millward, and Josephine Whitaker, they were posed covered with their coats. All were found in secluded rural locations near motorways.

All three attacks matched Sutcliffe's modus operandi in several attacks he was convicted of. Strangulation is the cause of death in only 15 per cent of homicides. The posing of a body after death occurs in less than one per cent of homicides. Tellingly, there are no other UK offences from the 1970s where a stranger-murder involved a garrotte other than those perpetrated by Sutcliffe.

Sonia stayed with Marianne while she did her teacher training and Sutcliffe often visited them.

14. Gloria Booth

On Saturday 12 June 1971, twenty-nine-year-old typist Gloria Booth, who also worked part-time as a barmaid, left work at the White Hart public house, Yeading Lane, Northolt, at around 11.30pm. She was seen by witnesses walking north along Yeading Lane and Ruislip Road towards the A40 roundabout and the Polish War Memorial. She made a telephone call from a phone box at around 11.50pm to the barman at the Viking public house on West End Lane, as they were meant to go to a party together, but the connection was broken.

She was then seen waiting around outside the Viking at 12.30am on the Sunday morning, apparently waiting for the barman to finish work from a 'lock-in', talking to a man who was described as being of 'shortish' height, wearing dark clothing.

At 8.00am on the morning of Sunday 13 June, Gloria's near-naked body was discovered dumped on a bramble patch in Stonefield Park, South Ruislip. No attempt had been made to hide the body, and her clothes were strewn around her. The only clothing on Gloria was her blouse and bra, which were both pushed up to the top of the chest, indicating the body had been posed.

The cause of death was asphyxia due to compression of the neck. There were two small bruises either side of the Adam's apple and one on the right side of her neck, indicating that she had been garrotted. There was oil and brick dust on her body. Both of Gloria's nipples had been bitten off. There were numerous bite marks over both of her breasts and a further single bite mark on her body to the right of her navel, all of which had occurred after her death. A blunt instrument had been repeatedly pushed into Gloria's vagina in a frenzied attack. She had not been raped, but the offender had tried to have necrophilic sex with the corpse indicating that her attacker was impotent.

The investigation concluded that Gloria had waited so long for the barman to finish work that she missed her last bus back to Ealing. She may have accepted a lift from a stranger, or decided to walk back to Ealing and been abducted. The officers that conducted house-to-house enquiries were instructed to identify if any of the men interviewed had a gap between their front teeth.

Sutcliffe may have been visiting Sonia and Marianne at Alperton, which is only seven miles from the deposition site. The authors believe he followed Gloria on foot from where she was last seen, possibly engaging her in conversation. Nairn Road was un-adopted, and there was a footpath running along the hedge outside the recreation ground which Gloria may have used as a shortcut. There was mud staining on her legs, left arm and thighs and numerous scratch marks on her body, together with bruising on the right middle forearm, consistent with having been dragged by her right arm to her final location. The authors believe she was attacked after taking the shortcut, or was attacked near Nairn Road and dragged into the playing field. She was murdered at a crime scene closer to the path. Gloria's body was then dragged from the crime scene, where her clothes and possessions were found, to a secondary location where the killer posed her body. As he knelt on the victim to mutilate Gloria's genital area and masturbate over her, oil and brick dust transferred itself from his clothing onto Gloria's body.

The murder of Gloria Booth contains a number of elements common to other murders committed by Sutcliffe. Sutcliffe had a gap between his teeth. A tooth mark with a gap was left on one of Josephine Whitaker's breasts in April 1979. Her body also had traces of brick dust and oil on it. He scattered Jean Jordan's clothes over a wide area. His confession to murdering Barbara Leach replicates what happened to Gloria:

> I took hold of her by the wrists, or was it by the ankles, and dragged her up this entrance to the back of the house.

In November 1971, Sutcliffe obtained full-time employment on the nightshift at Baird's TV in Bradford.

During May 1972, Sonia suffered a nervous breakdown and was admitted to Bexley Mental Hospital in South-east London. Sutcliffe loyally supported Sonia, working the nightshift at Baird's then visiting her most weekends and holidays. She had a slow recovery, returning to the family home in Bradford as a voluntary outpatient at the Linfield Mount Hospital until May 1976. Throughout this period, she was in and out of circulation depending on her health, and Sutcliffe was free to roam.

16. Judith Roberts and Andrew Evans
(Miscarriage of Justice)
At around 6.00pm on Wednesday 7 June 1972, Judith Roberts, a fourteen-year-old schoolgirl, left her home at 155 Gillway Lane, Wigginton, near Tamworth, Staffordshire, to ride her cycle up Main Road then along Comberford Lane, which dissects the A513 and what used to be the A453, leading to the M1.

Judith was reported missing at 10.30pm and a search started that night. At 4.30pm on the Saturday, Judith's body was found hidden under grass cuttings, sacks and a corrugated asbestos sheet in a field close to the entrance from a local lovers' lane less than a mile from her home.

Judith was face down, naked below the waist with her anorak pulled up over her head. Her shoes were near her body and her underclothes were lying mostly underneath her. There had been no sexual assault.

Judith had been subjected to a frenzied attack and battered to death by being struck repeatedly around the head. The pathologist concluded that she had been killed before 7.30pm on 7 June. The first blow was to the back of her head, and it fractured her skull into eighteen pieces and rendered her unconscious. Further severe blows, particularly to the left side of her face, had been inflicted, and Judith was struck a number of times whilst lying prone on the ground. Only a piece of asbestos had her blood on it.

Several witnesses were traced. Seven different vehicles were seen using the lane at the material time, including a Morris Minor and a grey Ford Escort. A girl fitting Judith's description was seen wheeling a cycle and talking to a man who was wearing working clothes and wellington boots.

A fingerprint was found on Judith's cycle and as a result a massive fingerprint-taking operation of the local male population was undertaken but no matches were found. There is no proof the print belonged to Judith's murderer.

Judith's body was not mutilated and she had not been raped despite the obvious signs of a sexual motive. This may have been because the murderer was disturbed and had to hurriedly hide both the body and the cycle.

At this time, Sonia was a patient at Bexley. Sutcliffe regularly travelled down from Bingley along the M1 to see her. He owned an old Morris Minor at the time and also had access to Sonia's mother's grey Ford Escort.

The authors believe Sutcliffe was diverted from his normal method of operation by working night shifts, which forced him into committing a midweek daylight crime. So he diverted off the M1 looking for a victim whilst travelling to or from London to visit Sonia.

A heavy hammer, possibly a walling/masonry hammer, was probably used to kill Judith, administering one heavy crushing blow which caused the skull to cave in like an eggshell. Sutcliffe used a walling hammer when he murdered Yvonne Pearson, fracturing her skull into seventeen pieces. He always removed the weapon from the scene of the crime.

Sutcliffe hid the bodies of several victims. Yvonne Pearson's body was hidden under a settee on waste ground. Marguerite Walls's body was partially covered with grass cuttings and leaves. Helen Rytka was also covered with a piece of corrugated asbestos.

The facial injuries are consistent with Judith's killer dragging her quickly by her legs face down from the roadside and into the field out of sight of passers-by to a secluded area. Bruises and abrasions to Wilma McCann's face confirmed that she had also been dragged along the ground by her legs after being struck on the back of the head.

The blows to the left side of Judith's face had left a Y-shaped indentation. This is another Ripper signature. Sutcliffe had an old Phillips/Pozidriv screwdriver that was so worn that it could no longer grip the slot in a screw's head. He filed down one of the four projections that formed the tapering cross-shape, to use the screwdriver as a bradawl, which, when used as a weapon, left a distinctive Y-shaped indentation, which was found on the body of Josephine Whitaker. Judith's injuries are perfectly consistent with this weapon that was unique to Sutcliffe, and their position indicates that they were applied by a right-handed man striking to his right to the left side of his victim from slightly behind and to the victim's left. It is consistent with her walking and pushing her bike from the left while talking to her murderer who was on her left. When Sutcliffe attacked schoolgirl Tracy Browne, he walked with her for some distance, engaging her in conservation and winning her trust before attacking her.

ANDREW EVANS

A seventeen-year-old former soldier, Andrew Evans, who had been stationed near Lichfield, later confessed to the murder. When interviewed by the police, he was denied medical attention and a solicitor, and was not cautioned. There was no evidence to place him at the scene, it was not his fingerprint on the bike, no blood was found on his clothes and there were broad inconsistencies in his story of how he had killed Judith. He retracted the confession and pleaded not guilty, but was nevertheless convicted of Judith's murder in 1973. A search of his home had not found the murder weapon, so the prosecution alleged that the asbestos sheet was the murder weapon. The defence pointed out that it was doubtful whether the asbestos could have had the weight and strength to have inflicted the injuries on Judith's head and that the murder weapon had obviously been removed from the scene.

Andrew Evans successfully appealed against his conviction in 1997. He had mental health issues at the time which caused him to believe he was guilty and confess to the crime. Because the murder was recorded as detected, it was never considered in any of the antecedent investigations that were performed after Sutcliffe's arrest in 1981. Following his acquittal, Staffordshire Police said it had no plans to reopen the investigation. So Sutcliffe has never been considered as a suspect for this murder.

17. Bernadette Cassidy also known as (AKA) Wakefield Clerk Typist
(Believed to have been attributed to Sutcliffe by Chief Constable Byford)

On Friday 29 December 1972, Bernadette Cassidy, a nineteen-year-old clerk and typist, left a pub at the top of

Westgate, Wakefield, at around 10.30pm to make her way home. It was a foggy night, and she saw a man following her. He had staring eyes, dark, longish hair, and a beard and moustache.

As Bernadette reached the row of houses where she lived she was suddenly grabbed from behind. She started screaming loudly. Her attacker covered her mouth and told her several times to stop; she claimed that he had a local accent. After she screamed again, he punched her on the back of her head with his fist and shoved her into a low wall where she grazed her face.

Fortunately, a nearby resident who was a prison officer heard her screams, opened his bedroom window and, realising what was happening, ran out of the house. The assailant ran off with the prison officer in pursuit but was able to get away in the fog.

When interviewed, Bernadette said her attacker was in his mid-twenties, of medium build, five-foot ten-inches in height, with long dark hair, dark eyebrows, a beard and moustache that included a tuft between the chin and the mouth. She made a photofit (see Illustration 3) which is a perfect match for Sutcliffe, except that his hair was longer (which was fashionable in 1972).

This case did not appear in the local newspapers and Bernadette heard no more. When Sutcliffe's photo appeared in the newspapers after his arrest, she recognised him as her attacker.

The short distance from Sutcliffe's home in Bingley, the local accent, a striking resemblance to the photofit and the eyewitness identification make it certain that Bernadette was attacked by Sutcliffe. Had she not fought so bravely, coupled with the intervention of the prison officer, there is no doubt that Bernadette would have been murdered.

Sutcliffe left Baird's TV in April 1973 for a job with Anderton International as a furnace-man on the night shift.

18. Wendy Sewell and Stephen Downing
(Miscarriage of Justice)

At around 12 noon on Wednesday 12 September 1973, Wendy Sewell, a thirty-two-year-old married secretary, left her office in Bakewell. Before she left the building, her manager heard her talking with an unknown man in her office, who spoke with an abrupt, high-pitched voice.

At about 12.50pm she was seen by several people entering Bakewell Cemetery. These included seventeen-year-old cemetery worker Stephen Downing, who was going home for a quick break before returning some twenty minutes later.

Sometime between then and about a quarter of an hour later, Wendy was subjected to a frenzied attack, during which she was hit on the back of her head with a pickaxe handle at least eight times. The police alleged that the pickaxe handle came from an unlocked tool store in the cemetery.

Wendy was initially attacked on the footpath in the cemetery close to the consecrated chapel where a bloodstained and splintered pickaxe handle was found along with her bloodstained clothes. She had been struck on the head, then undressed whilst semi-conscious.

Wendy was found shortly afterwards by Stephen Downing when he returned to the cemetery. She had stood up and staggered around before collapsing and hitting her head on a gravestone. She was nearly naked from the waist down, her blouse and bra had been pushed up to reveal her breasts and she was covered in blood. However, she had not been mutilated or interfered with, probably because her attacker was disturbed by Stephen's return.

She was still alive, so Stephen tried to render first aid, getting her blood on his clothes in the process. He then got help from his workmates, who called the police. Her body was then dragged some twenty-five feet to a more secluded part of the cemetery in rough ground amongst old headstones. The authors believe the move to a second secluded location was to provide cover and time to perpetrate a necrophilic attack, and that Wendy had been undressed in preparation for being mutilated and violated. When Stephen returned with his colleagues, he found that Wendy had staggered about twenty-five yards and collapsed.

The police arrived, but did not render first aid, call an ambulance, or cordon off the crime scene. She was finally admitted to hospital at 2.40pm in a coma.

STEPHEN DOWNING

Officers from DCBC recovered a pickaxe handle from the scene and took Stephen to Bakewell Police Station. Ostensibly, this was to help them with their enquiries as a witness, but in reality it was because he had already been designated as the prime suspect.

Once in the police station, Stephen was not arrested or cautioned and was denied access to his parents – even though he was a minor with learning difficulties – or a solicitor, even though he asked for one twice. When his parents came to the police station they were told he did not need a solicitor and told to leave.

Having isolated him from any outside support, the police questioned Stephen aggressively and intensively for nine hours, during which time they allegedly took bets on how long it would take to get a confession. Stephen alleges the police officers assaulted him by pulling his hair and physically shaking him, to intimidate him and keep him awake. He was told that if he did not confess he would be kept there all night.

Unsurprisingly, given his age, intellect, submissive personality and the intimidation he was subjected to, Stephen capitulated and signed a confession. The police wrote the confession in pencil for him and he was told to write over it in ink, so it was in his handwriting. In this document, he confessed that he had beaten Wendy Sewell to death with two blows from a pickaxe handle which he had taken from the cemetery tool store and then had sexually assaulted her. He was then brought before the magistrates the next day and remanded in custody.

On 14 September 1973 Wendy died without gaining consciousness and Stephen was charged with her murder. The autopsy took place the next day.

Stephen had no history of offending, was naïve, had learning difficulties, was overly respectful of authority figures and eager to please, which made him easy to manipulate. The psychiatric report on him compiled before the trial assessed him as having a reading age of eleven and an IQ of 91. It concluded: 'It is highly unlikely someone with his passive personality would attack a female.'

Stephen went on trial in February 1974. There were serious failings in the prosecution case:

- The autopsy revealed that Wendy had been subjected to ligature strangulation with a garrotte, which was not mentioned in Stephen's confession.
- Wendy had been beaten with a pickaxe handle eight times, not the two specified in the confession.
- There was no evidence of the sexual assault he had confessed to.
- The prosecution was unable to establish a motive for such a savage attack.
- Stephen retracted the confession and gave evidence that the police had told him what to write. This was verified by the fact that the language used was far more sophisticated than Stephen could have possibly used because he had a reading age of eleven.
- A man was seen by at least one witness running out of the cemetery up Butts Road covered in blood. But this was not followed up by DCBC, because they had prematurely fixated on Stephen as the murderer.

Stephen was badly represented at the trial. The reference to the ligature was in an appendix to the autopsy and his barrister did not put it before the court. Had it been presented, the case concocted against Stephen would have collapsed, because the police did not find a ligature on Stephen or at the scene of the crime. This showed that Stephen's confession was bogus and that the ligature had been removed from the scene of the crime by a third party: the murderer.

However, the key weakness in the defence case was that a forensic scientist gave evidence that the bloodstains on Stephen's clothing: 'Was a textbook example...which might be expected to be seen on the clothing of the assailant.' This evidence ensured he was convicted and served twenty-seven years for a crime he did not commit.

Matlock Mercury editor Don Hale took up Stephen's case. Don traced the pickaxe handle used to beat Wendy Sewell and had it forensically examined. This revealed that Stephen's fingerprints were not present on the weapon, but a bloody palm print from a person unknown was present.

Interestingly, Don linked the murder of Wendy Sewell to those of Barbara Mayo and Jackie Ansell-Lamb, based on these common characteristics:

- Barbara and Wendy were very beautiful women of similar appearance and both had long black wavy hair.
- All three victims had been beaten about the head.
- Wendy, Barbara and Jackie had all been strangled. (Don did not have access to the autopsy report but had noticed the ligature marks on Wendy's body on a mortuary photograph.)
- All three bodies were found face down.
- All three victims were found naked from the waist downwards.
- Barbara's and Wendy's handbags and personal effects were stolen.

Don notified DCBC of his conclusions, but was ignored. Then in 2014 he teamed up with Chris and they took Don's analysis further.

DCBC's successor force was Derbyshire Constabulary, which refused to release the autopsy report, which is always the start point in any murder investigation. However, Chris obtained it from a confidential informant. This showed that Wendy had been garrotted before being attacked with the pickaxe handle. However, the pathologist made no mention of these substantial additional factors in his Observations & Conclusions. Neither DCBC nor the defence brought this to the attention of the court, although it would certainly have resulted in Stephen's acquittal, because his confession did not mention a ligature and none was found on him or at the scene.

Chris's reconstruction of what actually happened is as follows:

Wendy was originally attacked on the footpath by having a knotted garrotte looped over her neck and pulled tight to render her unconscious. This would explain the massive bruise in the region of her Adam's apple as well as the bruising to the deep cervical muscles in the back of her neck where the garrotte would be twisted in a tourniquet fashion. The result of this initial attack would have the effect of her dropping to her knees, where she was then rendered unconscious by repeated blows to the back of the head with the pickaxe handle, which we now know was brought to the scene by her murderer, and was not from the workman's store. She was also repeatedly kicked.

At that point she had her footwear removed and was quickly stripped of her clothes from the waist down and her bra and top clothing pushed up to her shoulders in classic 'Ripper' fashion to expose the torso, ready for mutilation with a knife or screwdriver.

The assailant dragged Wendy from the initial site of the attack. This explains the findings of the bruising found on her mouth, nose, cheek, nose and ear, all on her left side, coupled with bruises found between her left knee and ankle. This is consistent with Wendy having been dragged by her left calf area from the site of the attack to the secondary crime scene.

In January 2002 the Court of Appeal ruled that the coercive nature of the alleged confession – coupled with new forensic evidence that the bloodstains were consistent with giving first aid – rendered the conviction unsafe, and Stephen Downing was freed.

Don Hale was voted *The Observer*'s Man of the Year for 2001, Journalist of the Year and was made an OBE for his efforts and campaigning journalism. However, he paid a heavy price for his efforts to right the injustice done to Stephen Downing. He alleged that Derbyshire Constabulary 'made my life absolute hell for five or six years', forcing him to relocate from Derbyshire.

At this time, Sonia was still in hospital, which may mean that Sutcliffe had not been having conjugal relations with her for an extended period of time. He certainly had plenty of time to roam and there is no way of ascertaining what his movements were. Wendy and Judith Roberts were both murdered on a Wednesday.

Sutcliffe may have been visiting Bakewell socially on a day off, or on the way to or from his sister's at Duxford. It is easily accessible from the M1 via the A617 road and then the A619. The cemetery is about two minutes' drive from the A619. This would take about two hours from Bingley. The onward journey to Duxford via the M1 would take just under three hours. This is consistent with Sutcliffe's choice of a location that allows a fast exit from the scene of the crime to an A road, then usually to a motorway.

The crime scene was a secluded area. Sutcliffe had worked as a gravedigger and would have been comfortable in the environment of a graveyard. The attack was ruthlessly and efficiently executed, indicating confidence and practice. It probably took a few seconds. Just like Fred Craven, Kay O'Connor, Emily Jackson, Jean Jordan, Yvonne Pearson, Sally Shepherd and Marguerite Walls, Wendy was kicked.

Wendy had been undressed from the waist downwards and her blouse and bra had been pulled up, a form of posing particular to Sutcliffe.

Wendy's genital area had been stabbed repeatedly after death with a weapon that had been thrust in and out of her vagina several times. Again, this type of mutilation was specific to Sutcliffe and featured in the murders of Emily Jackson and Josephine Whitaker.

Wendy had been attacked from behind and the back of her skull was smashed in, another Sutcliffe indicator.

So far as the authors are aware, Sutcliffe had never used a pickaxe handle before. It is large and heavy and would need a strong man to wield it at shoulder height in order to execute the blows that Wendy Sewell sustained. Sutcliffe had used a pickaxe during his work; he was a body builder and had developed enormous upper arm strength. It is quite possible that he chose to use a pickaxe handle on this occasion.

It transpired some twenty-five years later that the six assorted pickaxes and handles used by the cemetery workers were all stamped BUDC (Bakewell Urban District Council) and were all accounted for in the store. Therefore, the murder weapon had been brought to the cemetery by Wendy's attacker, not taken from the tool store that Stephen had access to as the prosecution claimed. Sutcliffe had a history of theft; he may have stolen the pickaxe handle from one of his employers.

Two of Sutcliffe's surviving victims, John Tomey and Tracy Browne, both remarked that he had an insipid, high-pitched voice. Was he the man Wendy was talking with in the office?

Stephen's acquittal in 2002 was a major humiliation for Derbyshire Constabulary and it reopened the Wendy Sewell investigation. It emerged that in 1973 there were twenty-two other suspects that were not eliminated and there was a partial palm print and a partial fingerprint on the stock of the pickaxe handle which were not from Stephen Downing or any of the other suspects. In February 2003, Derbyshire Constabulary issued its report, which included the conclusion that: 'The Police are not looking for any other person for the murder of Wendy Sewell.'

In other words, it was refusing to accept that it had bungled the investigation and was still maintaining that Stephen was the murderer. Derbyshire Constabulary then restricted access to the files until 2032 under the thirty-year rule to prevent any further investigation or the need to justify this position.

The decision to maintain Stephen as the only suspect has ensured that Sutcliffe has never been considered as a suspect in Wendy's murder, although it is entirely consistent with his modus operandi and movements. The authors believe the man covered in blood seen running away is Wendy's murderer and it was Sutcliffe.

19. Rosina 'Rosie' Hilliard
(Believed to have been attributed to Sutcliffe by ACC Hellawell)

At 7.00am on Friday 22 February 1974, the fully clothed body of twenty-four-year-old sex worker Rosina Hilliard was discovered lying across a narrow road in a building site in Spinney Hill Road, Highfields, Leicester, just off the main Humberstone A47 road.

Leicestershire Constabulary mounted a major investigation, which revealed that Rosie worked the Charnwood RLD and had been seen by members of its Vice Squad at 1.30am that day at the junction of Berners Street and Melbourne Road. This is about half a mile from the deposition site.

Rosie had been killed by one massive blow to the head with a blunt instrument, possibly a hammer. An attempt had also been made to strangle her. Her injuries indicated that she had then been run over by a car. Plaster casts taken of the tyre impressions left at the scene of the murder indicated they may have belonged to a Ford Escort. Other sex workers identified a Morris Minor and a Ford Escort, which were not vehicles used by their regular clients.

Chris contacted the *Leicester Mercury* with details of Rosie's murder and the murder of Carolyn Allen. It published a two-page report, and as a result, two new witnesses contacted Chris.

The first new witness was a seventy-two-year-old man who told Chris that during 1974 he was seeing someone else's wife, whom he subsequently married. On the date of Rosina's murder, at around 2.05am, the man and his female companion were walking along Humberstone Road (next to the deposition site on Spinney Hill Road) when he heard strange noises from a high-revving vehicle engine coming from the building site. On looking over the compound he saw a saloon car in the dark going backwards and forwards, trying to free itself from where it had become bogged down in the mud on the site.

Neither of these witnesses came forward to the police for fear their affair would become public knowledge.

The second witness saw Sutcliffe in 1978 at a filling station on Uppingham Road, which is the A47 and on the route to the pick-up point for Rosina Hilliard at the junction of Melbourne Road and Berners Street. The A47 leads to the M1 and provides a fast getaway back to Bradford. This witness stated:

> In 1978 I returned to work as a cashier, at the Trocadero petrol station, Uppingham Road, just round the corner from Humberstone Drive. It was dark. Round about 8:00pm, a man came up to the kiosk to pay for his petrol. As he walked two or three feet to walk away, he turned and stared at me. I am sure it was the Yorkshire Ripper. He walked two or three more feet and turned and stared again before getting into his vehicle, which I'm sure was a car.

This shows Sutcliffe was familiar with Leicester (Child C's evidence also confirms this) and travelled through it, past Rosie's abduction point. Was Sutcliffe filling up at the service station ready for the journey home via the M1, prior to picking up a sex worker that night?

There was a 'Three-day Week' from 31 December 1973 until early March 1974 (businesses were forced by the government to close for two days a week because of electricity cuts caused by a shortage of coal), so many people could not work for those days. Sutcliffe was working as the night furnace operator at Anderton International in Bingley and would have been on short-time working or laid off. He had just bought a lime-green Ford Capri (registration number EUA 831K) with a sun grille in the back window. He had more time to roam, giving him time for extended 'runs out', and his movements are completely unknown.

Rosie was murdered at about 2am on Friday 22 February 1974 whilst Sutcliffe was on short-time working. Did he visit Maureen on the Thursday and Friday while he was laid off and then return to see Sonia at the weekend? The A14 from Coventry to Huntingdon was not completed until the mid-1970s and neither was the M11 south from Cambridge. So Sutcliffe's return route from visiting Maureen could have been the A1 from Duxford, Leicester cross-over A47 to the M1, passing both the abduction point and the deposition site at Spinney Hill Road.

Sutcliffe owned a Morris Minor and a lime-green Ford Capri which could have been mistaken for a Ford Escort in bad light. He also regularly borrowed Sonia's mother's Ford Escort.

Rosie was a sex worker, which fitted with Sutcliffe's victim preferences, and the crime scene was in Leicester's RLD. The victim was lured to a secluded site on the pretext of having sex and then attacked. The cause of death – attack with a blunt instrument, possibly a hammer – was a classic indicator of a Ripper attack. An attempt had also been made to strangle her. The authors suspect that a garrotte was used to strangle Rosie and the blunt instrument may have been a walling or lump hammer.

All of this fits perfectly with Sutcliffe's modus operandi. However, the body was not undressed and posed. This is obviously because Sutcliffe was disturbed by witness 1 and his lover, and he therefore followed his standard modus operandi of fleeing the scene in his car.

20. Kay O'Connor
(Believed to have been attributed to Sutcliffe by ACC Hellawell)

Barmaid Kay O'Connor, aged thirty-seven, walked from her home at Wickham Road, Colchester, Essex, to the shops and collected her mother's pension between 2.30pm and 3.30pm on Friday 1 March 1974.

Just after 4.00pm, a next-door neighbour heard strange noises coming from Kay's kitchen at the rear of 8 Wickham Road. When she peeped in through the window she saw Kay lying in a pool of blood on the floor. Her killer had forced open the back door which led to an alley. Kay had been strangled and then stabbed, kicked and punched in a frenzied attack. Some of her clothing below the waist, including one of her suede boots, had been ripped off. There was evidence of what detectives vaguely referred to as 'a sexual motive' at the time. She had been murdered brutally, efficiently and quickly, giving her no time to cry out, indicating confidence and practice. It probably took a few seconds.

Despite a major enquiry, the only piece of evidence to emerge was a photofit of a man seen in the area shortly after Kay was murdered. Multiple witnesses described him as tough looking, about five-foot six-inches tall, medium build, wearing heavy work clothes and having large bushy sideburns that nearly met the corners of his mouth.

The photofit of the man seen loitering in the area is very similar to photofits of Sutcliffe compiled by some of his other victims. He is not shown with a moustache or beard, but Sutcliffe also varied his facial appearance.

He variously sported a thin, wispy Mexican moustache, a sparse beard and no sideburns, a full beard and moustache, sideburns, no sideburns, reduced facial hair, or no beard and no moustache. Sometimes his hairstyle was thick and sometimes much shorter. Hence the reason that the photofit pictures of him by victims varied so widely. In his book *The Outsider*, the then-retired Chief Constable Keith Hellawell states that Yvonne Mysliwiec was adamant that when Sutcliffe attacked her, he did not have a beard or moustache, probably because he had shaved them off to vary his appearance.

Sutcliffe was employed as a furnace-man at the time, so he would probably have worn heavy working clothes, which fits the description of the clothes worn by the suspect.

Like the murders of Fred Craven, Eve Stratford, Lynda Farrow and Patricia Atkinson, the victim was attacked in her home. As with Gloria Booth and Lynne Weedon, the attack started from a secluded alleyway or lane. Unusually, the knife was found in the house – as with the murder of Lynda Farrow. Sutcliffe usually took great care to remove weapons from the scene. Kay O'Connor was kicked then strangled, possibly with a ligature or garrotte, then stabbed repeatedly after death. All these were key Sutcliffe indicators.

One of Kay's boots had been removed. The authors believe this was because Sutcliffe had started to undress the body from the waist downwards, intending to lift up Kay's blouse and bra then mutilate the body, but he was disturbed by the neighbour and fled.

Wickham Road is two minutes' drive from the A134, which connects via the A133 and the A12 to the M11 and then to the A1(M) for the return trip home, allowing a fast exit from the area using a motorway.

The murder took place during the 'Three-day Week' period and, like the murder of Rosina Hilliard, took place on a Friday. When Sutcliffe visited his sister in Duxford he

Map 7 - The Duxford Cluster 1973 - 1980

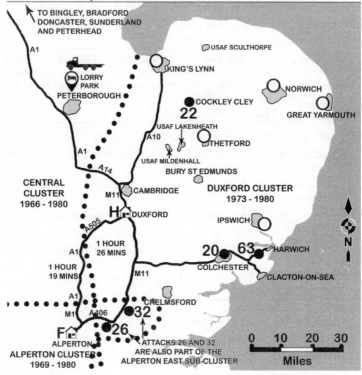

regularly took his four-year-old niece on seaside trips to Clacton-on-Sea. The route there would take him through Colchester, giving him local knowledge. It was to be the first of the Duxford Cluster from 1973 onwards, which were never linked by the police. They were centred around Maureen and Robin's married quarters at Duxford until Robin was posted to the British Army of the Rhine (BAOR) in Germany in 1975, and then along routes from Harwich to Bradford when Sutcliffe was working as a lorry driver the same year.

No	Name	Date	Cluster	Route Package
F	Marianne's house at Alperton			
H	Maureen's home at Duxford			
20	Kay O'Connor	01/03/74	Duxford	3.2. Clacton on Sea-Duxford
22	'Jane' AKA 'Cockley Cley Woman'	7 – 14/08/74	Duxford	N/A
26	Eve Stratford	18/03/75	Alperton, Duxford	2.4. Alperton-Duxford
32	Margaret Lightfoot	24/11/75	Alperton, Duxford	2.4. Alperton to Duxford, 2.5. Alperton-Bradford
63	Alison Morris	01/09/79	Duxford	3.3. Harwich-Bradford

21. Caroline Allen
(Believed to have been attributed to Sutcliffe by ACC Hellawell)
On Wednesday 10 April 1974, an elderly woman saw what she described as a lime-green Lotus sports car near the

A52/A606 roundabout at Edwalton. The driver talked to a teenage schoolgirl for about five minutes before she ran over to the lady, saying she was terrified. The girl stayed with the woman until a bus arrived.

That evening at about 8.00pm, seventeen-year-old schoolgirl Caroline Allen, who was working as a part-time nanny during her Easter holiday, left her employer's home in Walnut Drive, Bramcote, Nottinghamshire. Caroline said she intended to catch a bus home to Kinoulton, Nottinghamshire, fifteen miles away and was never seen again. She was known to hitchhike locally.

Nottinghamshire Constabulary identified that a hitchhiker fitting Carolyn's description accepted a lift from a lime-green Lotus Europa with a part registration number LTW or LTP. It was originally travelling northwards along the A606 from Leicester towards Nottingham. But it turned round when the male driver saw her hitching in the opposite direction at the A52/A606 roundabout at Edwalton, Nottinghamshire, which is about halfway between Bramcote and Kinoulton. The car then drove off southwards to the A46, towards Leicester, in the opposite direction it had come from.

There were further sightings of the lime-green Lotus in the car park of the Durham Ox public house at Six Hills on the A46 which was a short distance from the murder scene. However, it emerged during early January 1976 that the driver of a Lotus car actually picked up a male hitchhiker. Whether there were two different lime-green Lotus Europas operating on the same day in Leicestershire is unknown.

Caroline's body was found in woodland on 3 December 1975 at Old Dalby Wood, Little Belvoir, Leicestershire. Her remains were skeletal and had been disturbed by wildlife. The pathologist was unable to identify a cause of death, but was able to confirm that she had been beaten about the back of her head. Her jeans were missing, indicating a sexual motive.

Caroline was murdered during the Easter holiday when Sutcliffe would have been off work. His nephew had been born only nine days before. Caroline was hitching along the A52, which connects the M1 to the A1. Was Sutcliffe returning to Bradford using the route A1, A606/A52, M1, having visited his sister and seeing his new nephew in Duxford for the first time?

This would be a convenient route for Sutcliffe to travel to and from Duxford. He was surveillance aware and went to great lengths to avoid it. Was he varying his route by using the A52/A606 route to avoid the A47 and the site of the murder of Rosie Hilliard from two months before, to evade coming to the attention of the Rosina Hilliard investigation in a traffic stop? This would put him in the area of Caroline's abduction at the A606/A52 roundabout.

In 1974, Sutcliffe owned a lime-green Ford Capri with a black vinyl roof. Caroline was hitchhiking at about

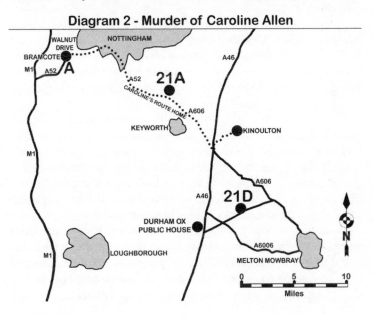

Diagram 2 - Murder of Caroline Allen

No	Location
A	Caroline last seen here
21A	Edwalton roundabout: Probable abduction point
21D	Deposition site at Old Dalby Wood

8.00pm, with sunset being at 7.50pm, and there was low cloud making an overcast sky that evening, making visibility poor. In poor visibility, the black vinyl roof would make a Capri look very similar to a Lotus Europa.

Schoolgirls and hitchhikers fitted with Sutcliffe's victim preferences. Caroline had been beaten about the head, her clothes had been removed and her body concealed. Classic indicators of a Ripper attack.

Sutcliffe married Sonia on Saturday 10 August 1974, honeymooning in Paris. They stopped en route to stay with Maureen and Robin Holland. On their return, Sutcliffe moved in with Sonia at her parents' home at 44 Tanton Crescent, Bradford.

22. 'Jane' AKA 'Cockley Cley Woman'

At 7.15am on Tuesday 27 August 1974, a farm worker found the decapitated body of a woman lying in undergrowth beside a lovers' lane, about 200 yards from the Swaffham to Cockley Cley road.

The body was of a well-built woman aged between twenty-three and thirty-five, who had been between five-feet and five-feet two-inches tall. Her arms and legs were trussed up behind her back with string, presumably for easier transportation and she was covered by a large brown plastic National Cash Register dust sheet. She was wearing only a short pink Marks & Spencer nightdress.

Because the body had lain in the open for about three weeks it was badly decomposed, aggravated further by foxes and other scavengers feeding on the torso. The pathologist was unable to discover the cause of death, but concluded she probably died sometime between the seventh and the fourteenth of August, having been murdered and decapitated elsewhere.

Chris was the Deputy Intelligence Collator at King's Lynn at the time. There were a number of theories as to 'Jane's' identity:

- She may have been a Leeds sex worker who plied her trade at the King's Lynn, Great Yarmouth and Norwich RLDs, or at the USAF bases at Lakenheath, Mildenhall and Sculthorpe (women were picked up from King's Lynn and Thetford and driven onto the base).
- She could have been a sex worker known as 'The Duchess' from the RLD at the Ocean Terminal Dock area of Great Yarmouth, who disappeared around 1974.

It is not known how long the Sutcliffes stayed with Robin and Maureen Holland at Duxford. Chris has had access to crime writer Gordon Burn's notes which indicate they may have stayed more than one night. Maureen told Gordon: 'When they stayed with me in Duxford on the way to their honeymoon, she [Sonia] turned to me and said, "You've got a lovely home. You're a lovely cook."'

There are also references to Sutcliffe having smelly feet: 'A pair of men's shoes appeared outside an upstairs window at Maureen's house in Duxford where Peter and Sonia were staying en route to Paris,' indicating they stayed longer than one day. This fits with the time of death of between the seventh and fourteenth of August.

The body was deposited in a rural area and had been covered. She may have been a sex worker, which fitted with Sutcliffe's victim preferences. Great Yarmouth is just over one-and-a-half hours' drive from Duxford. Sutcliffe used sex workers and may have slipped away to procure one there. If indeed 'Jane' was from Leeds, Sutcliffe may even have known her.

The route from Great Yarmouth to Duxford passes within thirty miles of the deposition site. Maureen's home was about an hour away from the deposition site, which is next to the A1065, giving a fast exit from the area using an A road.

Because 'Jane's' head was missing, it was impossible to rule out ligature strangulation or having the back of the skull crushed with a hammer. It was also impossible to identify if the body had sustained slashing injuries consistent with Sutcliffe's modus operandi.

In the murder of Jean Jordan, Sutcliffe tried to decapitate her body. This is an extract from his confession:

> I forgot to say that before I did this, it was my intention to create a mystery about the body. I felt sure this was the end for me anyway. I had taken a hacksaw out of my car intending to remove her head. I started sawing through her neck; the blade might have been blunt because I was getting nowhere at all, so I gave it up. If I had cut the head off I was going to leave it somewhere else to make a big mystery out of it.

The authors believe Sutcliffe decapitated 'Jane's' body and concealed it to have a wider time of death than just the period he was staying in Duxford, thereby preventing her murder being linked to him because he was at Duxford on the day of her murder.

'Jane' was buried in an unmarked grave at Swaffham Cemetery. Norfolk Constabulary exhumed the body in 2008 and obtained a DNA sample from it. An isotopic analysis was performed to try to establish where she originally came from and lived in the months leading up to her death. A familial DNA search was also performed using the National DNA Database to find possible links between the victim and her family. The knot was examined and the interior was swabbed for DNA, but there was nothing present. Despite these efforts, the body remains unidentified to this day.

23. Child D and Child E
In 1974, Child D and Child E, both aged fifteen, were picked up by Sutcliffe while hitchhiking. Here is the account of Child D:

> My friend and I [we're] both female, got a lift from Peter Sutcliffe in 1974 we only realised years later.
>
> We had been to see a Mott the Hoople concert and spent our fare back to Wakefield so we were hitching.
>
> He picked us up after the gig, in Bradford on Wakefield Road so [it was] sometime after 11pm and he took us all the way to and dropped us off at the Redbeck café, an all-night café on Doncaster Rd in Wakefield.
>
> He had an odd laugh, said his name was Pete and that he used to work nights in a TV factory so didn't sleep well. He gave us money for a cup of tea at the Redbeck but didn't come in. We did a runner out of the back because he was strange.
>
> Our gig was 7th November, we were so close then. Fifteen years old the pair of us with no concept of danger.

Had Sutcliffe been able to entice one of the girls out of the vehicle so he could attack them one after the other, the authors are convinced that both girls would have been murdered. Happily, running off saved them.

24. Child G
Child G was fourteen when Sutcliffe targeted her in Bradford in late October 1974. This is her account of what happened:

> I'd been at my friend's house at Sunderland Road, Bradford. It was a weekday and I had school the following day so I was walking home in the dark at about 9pm. I was obviously a schoolgirl, not a woman.

I walked down Sunderland Road towards Oak Lane and he started following me near the end of the road. I turned left on to Oak Lane and he stayed behind me. His step was slow and stilted. I walked quicker and he stepped up. I slowed down and so did he. By the time I crossed over Roseberry Road I knew he was following me. I was scared by this time. I got to St Mary's Road and crossed over. If you turned right down St Mary's Road it went to the Lumb Lane red-light district.

I was looking for a house with a light on. There were a few terraced houses; the third house had a light on so I shot in there and banged on the door. I explained to the householder I was being followed and he invited me in.

When I knocked on the door, he doubled back and went across Oak Lane and I saw him heading across the road towards St Mary's Road. He was the same build and hair colour as Sutcliffe and wearing a dark suit. This stuck with me because it was very cold, but he didn't have an overcoat.

The man in the house walked with me home near St Joseph's college. He must have realised how scared I was to go to so much trouble to make sure I got home safely.

At that time we didn't know Sutcliffe was living in Heaton and on the night of my encounter I didn't see his car. Maybe he had parked up when he spotted me and I hadn't noticed.

Our parents tried to keep the Yorkshire Ripper from us children as much as they could to protect us from the fear of him. We also thought he was only attacking prostitutes and were told to stay away from Lumb Lane. So I was aware of the Yorkshire Ripper but I didn't know he was in our area. The night I was followed, he never came to my mind, I just knew I was being followed and I felt really scared. It was a few weeks later when a 'Ripper' attack was reported on the news [Gloria Wood, 11 November 1974], that I felt the shivers down my spine for the first time. I still get that same feeling now when I see anything about him.

The authors are satisfied that the man following Child G was Sutcliffe. The modus operandi and description fit perfectly, and the attack on her is part of the Bradford, Belle Vue Sub-Cluster.

During the mid-1970s the Belle Vue Hotel on Manningham Lane in Bradford was a bawdy house with strippers and sex workers. Sutcliffe was a regular customer there and went on regular pub crawls in the Manningham RLD. Victims Maureen Long, Patricia Atkinson and Yvonne Pearson were regulars at the Belle Vue. The authors believe that Sutcliffe pre-selected them as victims there. One of Sutcliffe's friends recalled a conversation with Sutcliffe in a pub in Manningham when he suggested they: 'Go down Lumb Lane for a jump and give a pro a good kicking instead of paying.'

The authors believe there were many occasions in Manningham and Leeds when Sutcliffe would have sex with a prostitute, then beat her – sometimes with accomplices – to evade paying. These were very serious assaults and rapes, which are part of the Belle Vue Sub-Cluster. There is no record of these attacks because they were either not reported, or were not recorded because of the misogynistic attitudes to sex workers of the police at the time.

Sutcliffe was completely familiar with the area. The authors believe he had been hunting for a victim at the Manningham RLD. Because it was a cold, dark weekday, he had not found a suitable victim to attack. So he cruised around locally, saw Child G and parked up. When he got out of the vehicle, he followed Child G straight away, instead of delaying to put a coat on. Fortunately, the area was residential, and a quiet area to launch the attack did not appear before Child G – showing considerable courage and presence of mind – summoned help.

Diagram 3 - Attempted Murder of Child G
& The Belle Vue Hotel Sub-Cluster 1969 - 1978

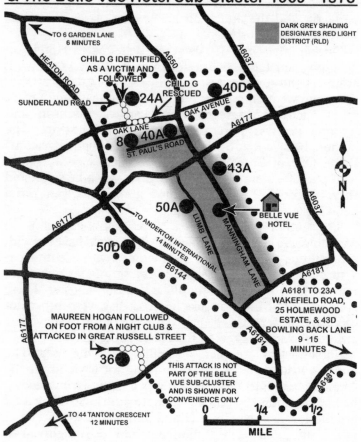

TO 6 GARDEN LANE 6 MINUTES

HEATON ROAD

A650

A6037

DARK GREY SHADING DESIGNATES RED LIGHT DISTRICT (RLD)

CHILD G IDENTIFIED AS A VICTIM AND FOLLOWED

CHILD G RESCUED

24A

40D

SUNDERLAND ROAD

OAK AVENUE

A6177

OAK LANE

8 40A

ST. PAUL'S ROAD

43A

N

A6037

50A

A6177

TO ANDERTON INTERNATIONAL 14 MINUTES

LUMB LANE

MANNINGHAM LANE

BELLE VUE HOTEL

50D

B6144

A6181

A6177

MAUREEN HOGAN FOLLOWED ON FOOT FROM A NIGHT CLUB & ATTACKED IN GREAT RUSSELL STREET

A6181 TO 23A WAKEFIELD ROAD, 25 HOLMEWOOD ESTATE, & 43D BOWLING BACK LANE 9 - 15 MINUTES

36

A6181

A6181

THIS ATTACK IS NOT PART OF THE BELLE VUE SUB-CLUSTER AND IS SHOWN FOR CONVENIENCE ONLY

TO 44 TANTON CRESCENT 12 MINUTES

0   1/4   1/2

MILE

104

No	Name	Date	Location
8	Stone in the sock attack	??/08/69	St Paul's Road
9	Equipped for theft	30/09/69	Manningham area, exact address unknown
23A	Child D, Child E, Abducted	06/11/74	Wakefield Road, Bradford
24	Child G	Mid Oct 1974	Oak Lane
25	Gloria Wood	11/11/74	Holmewood Estate, Bradford
36	Maureen Hogan	29/08/76	Great Russell Street. Maureen Hogan was followed from a nightclub and is not part of the Belle Vue Sub-Cluster. She is shown for completeness.
40A	Patricia Atkinson Abducted	23/04/77	St Paul's Road
40D	Patricia Atkinson Murdered	23/04/77	Oak Avenue
43A	Maureen Long Abducted	10/07/77	Manningham Lane
43D	Maureen Long Attacked	10/07/77	Bowling Back Lane, Bradford
50A	Yvonne Pearson Abducted	22/01/78	Junction of Southfield Square and Lumb Lane
50D	Yvonne Pearson Murdered	22/01/78	Arthington Street

This encounter indicates that Sutcliffe would trawl for victims outside the immediate area of the local RLD and that Sutcliffe attacked schoolgirls. It is indicative of attacks on women and girls in and near RLDs that were either not reported or not connected to the Ripper series. Sutcliffe would have had to pass through Manningham to get to Wakefield Road where he abducted Child D and E and to the Holmewood Estate, where he attacked Gloria Wood. The authors believe that Sutcliffe had been unsuccessful in trawling for a victim in Manningham that evening because it was a weekday, so he searched further afield.

25. Gloria Wood
(Believed to have been attributed to Sutcliffe by ACC Hellawell)

On Monday 11 November 1974, between 7.30pm to 8.00pm, Gloria Wood, a twenty-eight-year-old mature student, was walking home across a school playing field in the Holmewood Estate, Bradford. A man approached her and offered to carry her bags. Then she woke up in hospital.

She had suffered four blows to the back of her head with what was thought to be a claw hammer (probably a ball pein hammer). She suffered severe injuries, including a depressed fracture of the skull with a crescent-shaped wound which would require surgery to remove bone splinters from her brain. The attack had been interrupted by some nearby children who found her and called an ambulance.

Gloria was attacked less than three miles from the street in Manningham where, five years earlier, Sutcliffe had been arrested in possession of a hammer. The WYMP detectives that questioned Gloria in hospital concluded that Gloria's assailant was someone known to her. When she could not identify anyone that would want to kill her, they did not make any further enquiries. They therefore failed to tie this attack to the stone-in-the-sock attack (MPoF).

Gloria described her attacker as being in his early thirties, five-foot eight-inches in height, of medium build with a short curly beard, moustache and dark curly hair and looking smartly dressed wearing a dark suit. A perfect description of Sutcliffe.

The attack took place less than five miles from 44 Tanton Crescent and less than fifteen minutes' drive from Anderton's. It was a classic Sutcliffe attack. Lone female at night, initial attempt to befriend, followed by an attack to the back of the head with a hammer, but fleeing immediately if disturbed. If Sutcliffe left home in good time to clock on, parked the car and went looking for a victim, then fled the scene, got to his car and drove fifteen minutes to work, he would have been able to clock on at Anderton's in good time. He clocked on at 8.30pm that night.

Gloria was in no doubt it was Sutcliffe that attacked her, and she suffered severely as a result. She spent a long time in hospital, lost custody of her children for several years and needed extensive psychological support for many years afterwards. She has never had justice because Sutcliffe was never charged with her attempted murder.

During February 1975, Sutcliffe took redundancy from Anderton International and went on the dole, closing Phase 3 of his life.

Phase 4. February to September 1975: Confident serial killer going up in the world

Sutcliffe used part of the £400 redundancy settlement from Anderton's to pay for HGV driving lessons with the Apex School of Driving at Cullingworth, just off the A629.

The authors believe that Sutcliffe chose the occupation of lorry driver to improve his earnings, provide a better standard of living for Sonia and to give him further opportunities to attack women while out driving, being no longer tied to a workplace for specific hours, under the scrutiny of colleagues.

His lessons were spent driving up and down the A629 and around areas he did not normally visit. Serial killers prefer to operate in areas that they are familiar and comfortable with, and in Sutcliffe's case, where he knew fast routes in and out. Sutcliffe familiarised himself with these areas during his HGV training and later made a number of attacks in them.

On 4 June 1975 Sutcliffe gained a heavy goods vehicle driving licence. He bought a white Ford Corsair with a black roof, registration number KWT721D, whilst retaining the lime-green Ford Capri.

26. Eve Stratford, 30. Lynne Weedon, 44. Elizabeth Parravicini and 57. Lynda Farrow

EVE STRATFORD

Eve Stratford was a Playboy Club 'Bunny Girl' who had appeared in the March 1975 edition of the men's magazine *Mayfair*.

On Tuesday 18 March 1975, Eve arrived at the run-down four-bedroomed flat in Lyndhurst Drive that she shared with her boyfriend at about 4.10pm. It had been raining, so she undressed down to her underwear. A neighbour heard Eve and a man talking at around 4.30pm. At about 5.15pm the same neighbour heard a loud thud like a chair falling over and footsteps leading down the stairs onto the street and then the sound of the phone ringing, which was unanswered.

At 5.25pm her boyfriend found Eve's body face down on the bedroom floor. She was wearing a bra and knickers under a dressing gown. Her hands were tied behind her back with a stocking and dressing-gown belt. The other nylon stocking was tied around one ankle.

Her throat had been cut eight or nine times with a large knife, nearly decapitating her. There were no obvious signs of a struggle. The post-mortem identified that the killer had silenced Eve by clamping his hand over her mouth as he cut her throat. There was evidence that Eve had had intercourse that afternoon, but no evidence of sexual assault. Semen stains were found on one of her stockings.

Eve's boyfriend was quickly eliminated. So the investigation focussed on men in her life and those that she had met as a result of her employment in the Playboy Club. In the days before her death she had received telephone calls from a caller who hung up without speaking. She had also complained of a man hanging around and following her. Detectives concluded that this man had an obsession with her and may have traced her address. They also considered the possibility that an unfortunate statement in the *Mayfair* magazine article: 'I like to be dominated, not whipped or tied up or things like that, just kept in my place,' may have attracted a stalker. The possibility of a stranger-killing appears not to have been considered, or not considered very seriously.

On Saturday 22 March 1975, Sonia's sister Marianne got married in West London. The happy couple then moved to an address in Alperton, Wembley. Sutcliffe and Sonia were wedding guests. The authors suspect that they could have stayed in London that week to help Marianne prepare for the big day and help them move to the new marital home. If so, this puts Sutcliffe in London at the time of Eve's murder, which has several classic Sutcliffe indicators.

Eve was attacked in her home, the same as Fred Craven, Kay O'Connor, Lynda Farrow and Patricia Atkinson, and, like Irene Richardson, Margaret Frame and Lynda Farrow, her throat had been cut. As with Lynda Farrow and Jean Jordan, she had nearly been decapitated. Like Patricia Morris, one stocking had been used to tie Eve's wrists while the other was tied around her ankle. The body was posed. There was an easy escape route from Leyton along the North Circular Road, which is consistent with Sutcliffe's preference for a fast exit from the area, either to Alperton, Bradford or Duxford.

The *Mayfair* magazine with Eve's photo shoot was released in late February 1975 and had a reputed circulation of over 462,841. It may have reached twice that many men. Sutcliffe is known to have read 'nuddy' magazines and may even have seen the edition of *Mayfair* that featured Eve. However, the authors believe it is unlikely this played any part in her murder. They suspect Sutcliffe simply stalked her on foot and followed her home.

LYNNE WEEDON

On Wednesday 3 September 1975, sixteen-year-old Lynne Weedon and some school friends left the Elm Tree pub in New Heston Road, Hounslow, at 10.30pm. They separated at 11.10pm and Lynne took her usual route home down an alleyway known as The Short Hedges.

At about 11.15pm, Lynne was halfway down the alleyway, when she was attacked from behind and the back of her skull was smashed with one massive blow from a blunt instrument. The attacker then undressed Lynne, leaving her naked from the waist downwards and then molested her, leaving semen stains on her body. At this point, the attacker was disturbed by a passer-by walking down the alleyway. So he then either threw his lightly built victim over a five-foot-high fence or dragged her through a hole in the fence into the grounds of an electricity substation, before fleeing, leaving Lynne for dead.

Lynne was found at 7.30am the next day. She died a week later. The post-mortem established that the murder weapon was a lump or masonry hammer. It had fractured her skull with one blow, in the same way as Yvonne Pearson, Carol Wilkinson and Judith Roberts. As with all of Sutcliffe's attacks, the hammer was not recovered.

Lynne's murder was very similar to the attack on Gloria Booth ten miles away in 1971. Both attacks were on young women walking alone at night who had been drinking. They were attacked in alleyways, near a main westbound arterial road out of London and their bodies moved to a secondary crime scene, where the clothes from the lower half of their bodies were removed. Incredibly, the MPS did not connect them (MPoF).

Sutcliffe regularly stayed with Marianne at Alperton and Maureen at Duxford. His visits were return journeys from Bradford or triangular trips for a few days from Bradford to Alperton, then to Duxford, before returning to Bradford. In September 1975, Sutcliffe joined Sonia and her parents visiting relatives in Prague, Czechoslovakia. They all stayed together at Marianne's home in Alperton before travelling to Heathrow the next day. All of these factors indicate that Sutcliffe could have been eight miles away at Alperton on 3 September 1975.

Lynne was a schoolgirl, which fitted with Sutcliffe's victim preferences. Child A has confirmed that both she and Child B were clearly underage. Child C was in school uniform. Lynne's murder was very similar to the attempted murder of fourteen-year-old schoolgirl Tracy Browne one week earlier, who he also threw over a fence when he was disturbed.

Sutcliffe used various hammers, including a walling (lump or masonry) hammer. Lynne was ruthlessly and efficiently attacked from behind. It probably took a few seconds, indicating confidence and practice. The body was undressed from the waist downwards and had been molested sexually. The speed of the attack meant the murderer was not seen and left the area undetected. There was a fast escape route via the A406 North Circular Road to the M1.

ELIZABETH PARRAVICINI

Elizabeth Parravicini was twenty-seven years old and was staying at her parents' home at The Grove, Osterley, with her two children.

On the evening of Thursday 8 September 1977, Elizabeth visited a West End cinema with friends, before catching the last underground train home, arriving at Osterley at 12.45am. She then walked along the main A4 Great West Road and into Osterley Road, where she was attacked from behind, receiving several blows to the back of her head with a blunt instrument, which fractured her skull.

The killer then dragged Elizabeth's body across the road and dumped her body face down in the shrubbery of a residential front garden. Elizabeth's handbag and shoes were left on the footpath at the scene of the initial attack, some 200 yards from her parents' home.

During the night, her father realised that she had not returned. He contacted her friend who confirmed that Elizabeth had caught the last tube train to Osterley. Mr Graham reported her missing at 3.30am. At daylight he went searching for her with another of his daughters. They found Elizabeth's shoes and handbag, then nearby discovered her body.

The officer in charge of the investigation said:

> This was a most brutal attack on a perfectly respectable married woman. We are looking for an extremely savage individual; she was a very striking woman. There are similarities with the murder of Lynne Weedon which are being considered.

Elizabeth was a woman walking alone at night, who was attacked from behind with several blows to the back of her head from a blunt instrument, then moved to a secondary crime scene. The weapon used to murder Elizabeth is consistent with a hammer. All classic Sutcliffe indicators. As with Marguerite Walls, Elizabeth's body was hidden in a front garden. The murder of Lynne Weedon occurred a mile-and-a-half away.

After his wife's recovery in 1976, Sutcliffe often took Sonia to visit her sister Marianne in Alperton, before she started work as a supply teacher. He may also have had overnight stopovers in his lorry, which had a sleeping area in the back of the cab, or he could have been visiting Marianne on his own. So Sutcliffe could have been in West London at the time of the attack.

LYNDA FARROW

On Monday 19 January 1979, Lynda Farrow, a twenty-nine-year-old mother of two, returned home at 155 Whitehall Road, Woodford Green, East London, after a shopping trip at about 2.40pm.

At about 2.50pm two schoolgirls passed 155 Whitehall Road. As they did so, the front door of the property opened slightly and they heard a shriek, before it was slammed shut again. The authors believe Lynda heard the phone ringing and ran in to answer it, leaving the door open, and her murderer entered and slammed the door shut behind him.

Around 3.00pm, Lynda's daughters, aged eight and eleven, arrived home early from school due to a snowstorm. It was snowing heavily. They knocked on the front door and getting no reply, they looked through the letter box and saw Lynda's body lying face down on the floor in a pool of blood. They may have disturbed her killer during his unfinished attack.

Police believe that Lynda, who had been four months pregnant, had struggled with her murderer in the hallway but had been overpowered, before being stabbed repeatedly. Her killer then knelt on her back and tried to sever her head with a deliberate sawing action using a serrated-edge carving knife. They found footprints in the rapidly melting snow which led from the rear door, where the murderer had fled the property, to the front of the property. They were heavily ridged like wellington boots size 7.

The SIO said: 'This man is completely deranged. There is every possibility that he could kill again and has possibly killed before.'

A suspect was seen running up Whitehall Road to where the police believed he had his car parked off the main road. He was described as being in his late thirties, five-foot nine-inches, with deep-set eye sockets, a dark, neat afro-style haircut, curly and flecked grey, with dark sideburns to the bottom of his ears, and his top lip protruding downwards. He had been wearing a check shirt, workman's dark blue donkey jacket, dark trousers and wellington boots which were turned down at the top. A photofit showing a clean-shaven man with heavy sideburns was issued (Illustration 8. Illustration 9 shows the same photofit with a beard superimposed, which should be compared to Marilyn Moore's second photofit Illustration 5 from 1977.).

At around the same time, a white vehicle, described by a witness as possibly a white Mk IV Ford Cortina with a black vinyl roof with a part index number containing P and W in the registration, was seen driving at high speed turning into Whitehall Road and then onto the A104/A121 in the direction of Loughton. Two cars had to swerve to avoid it on the A121.

Sutcliffe was five-foot eight-inches tall, aged thirty-three in 1979 and of slim or medium build. He had a tanned complexion with dark swarthy skin, afro hair with sideburns and fits the description of the man seen running from the crime. Other than being clean shaven, the photofit of the suspect seen fleeing the scene bears a close resemblance to Sutcliffe. Since snow would melt more quickly from the loss of head heat and the face would remain much colder and snow would adhere longer on the face of a man with a beard and moustache whilst running, then a witness would not necessarily realise or identify such features. Had he trimmed his beard off, or could the witness have overlooked this?

Whilst Sutcliffe was delivering and collecting in his lorry, it was a regular occurrence for him to be away from home for three nights a week, returning in the afternoon of the fourth day. One of the areas that Sutcliffe regularly delivered to in London was the LEP Transport Depot just off the A2 at Charlton. Lynda was murdered about twelve miles north of the depot and twelve miles from Marianne's home at Alperton.

There were a set of size-seven boot prints in the snow outside the flat. A BBC TV *Crimewatch* reconstruction in January 1979 stated that Lynda's attacker had worn heavy industrial boots similar in tread to Monkey Boots. Sutcliffe was a size seven. Size-seven boot prints were also found at the deposition sites for Patricia Atkinson and Josephine Whitaker.

The grey hair flecks were probably melting snow falling off the trees in the area. The suspect was described as wearing a check shirt. Sutcliffe wore check clothes which feature in other sightings.

Sutcliffe still had the white Corsair – which is similar to a Cortina in appearance. When Sutcliffe attacked Maureen Long, a witness described it as a Mk II Cortina. He could also have borrowed a Cortina – it was a very common car at this time. Snow had very recently fallen, obscuring the car's number plates. Sutcliffe's Corsair did have a W in the registration; the D could have been mistaken for a P, given that the vehicle was going at speed when the partial registration number was taken by a witness; or Sutcliffe was using false number plates.

Whitehall Road is less than three miles from the North Circular Road, which gives easy access to the M11, then the A1(M) to Bradford. This is consistent with Sutcliffe's choice of a site that allowed a fast exit from the area using a motorway.

As with other Sutcliffe attacks, the victim was attacked in her home, had been stabbed repeatedly, her throat was cut and she had nearly been decapitated. One of the weapons shown as an exhibit at Sutcliffe's trial was a serrated-edge carving knife, identical to the one used to attack Lynda. Proving that Sutcliffe was comfortable with this type of weapon.

In 1979, the MPS linked the murder of Lynda Farrow to the murders of Kay O'Connor and Eve Stratford.

By 1979, the Yorkshire Ripper investigation was in full swing and receiving national publicity. Yet despite the facts that firstly these attacks were on single women walking alone at night, attacked from behind with several blows to the back of the head from a blunt instrument, and secondly that the killer had access to a car, wore size-seven boots and had also tried to decapitate Jean Jordan, the MPS did not connect the above four attacks with the Ripper investigation, probably because the victims were not sex workers (MPoF).

Nor were these attacks connected when Sutcliffe was arrested in 1981 and his occupation as a lorry driver who drove all over England and regularly visited London was revealed (MPoF).

Then in 2006 the MPS reviewed the murders of Eve, Lynne and Lynda. The forensic evidence from Eve and Lynne's murders had been retained, and in 2007 a DNA profile was obtained from semen in both cases. The exhibits from Lynda Farrow's murder were lost (MPoF).

Using DNA analysis, the MPS was able to ascertain that the same unique genetic fingerprints were present in semen found in the Eve Stratford and Lynne Weedon cases. They announced that the murders of Elizabeth Parravicini and Lynda Farrow were also linked, but did not link the murders of Gloria Booth and Kay O'Connor.

Sutcliffe's DNA will have been compared to the DNA samples obtained from the Eve Stratford and Lynne Weedon murders. It presumably did not match. However, this does not rule Sutcliffe out.

Sutcliffe's blood group was Type B Negative, Non-secretor. Non-secretors make up between 15 per cent and 25 per cent of the population and do not leave traces of their blood group in saliva or semen, and do not put, or put very little, of their blood type antigens into these fluids. Consequently, Non-secretors may leave some element of a DNA fingerprint behind, but there is usually not enough DNA information within saliva or semen to provide an identification.

Sonia married Sutcliffe in 1974 when she was aged twenty-four and had several miscarriages, which eventually prevented her from having children. Sutcliffe probably had a low sperm count. There is evidence that the sperm of infertile men contains more DNA damage than that of fertile men. Sperm cannot repair cell damage like other cells in the body and this is a leading cause of male infertility. The damage also affects the DNA structure within the sperm, and if it fertilises an egg, this can potentially lead to miscarriage.

Sutcliffe could also have been a human chimera. This condition can arrive from a variety of sources. Sutcliffe's blood group was Type B Negative, Non-secretor, which means he did not leave traces of his blood group in his saliva or semen.

Saliva samples were taken from Sutcliffe using a buccal swab, not a blood or hair sample. So if he was a human chimera, his saliva samples could have a different DNA to his semen. So the DNA search could have rejected him on the basis of the DNA in his saliva, which was not connected to the DNA contained in his semen.

It is unknown how many men have the condition of human chimera and many of them go through life undetected. Was Sutcliffe one of them?

Forensic techniques were poor in the 1990s and these factors were not well understood. It is possible his sample could have been contaminated during the testing, analysis or search phases.

On 27 March 2015, the *Daily Express* ran an article on the murders of Eve and Lynne which was obviously based on a police briefing:

> With no leads to go on the investigation into Lynne's murder went cold until 2004 when the case was reopened. New forensic technology showed that the *DNA found on Lynne's body matched the DNA found on the stocking that was bound around Eve's foot*. The findings were conclusive: the same man had murdered both women.
> [Authors' emphasis in italics]

This further implicates Sutcliffe in both murders. The semen obtained from Eve's dressing-gown cord and the ankle binding presumably came from the killer's hands from masturbation, or from ejaculating over Eve's body. Lynne had been raped, but the semen was found on her body, indicating that – as with Josephine Whitaker –

she was raped with an instrument while the killer had masturbated and then ejaculated over her. All Sutcliffe indicators.

The linking of these four cases by the MPS shows that the killer was a practised serial killer, regularly attacking victims. He had radically changed his modus operandi for each murder. So he was someone whose previous record of offending had encompassed all the various modi operandi present in these crimes. The only known serial killer in London at this time that fits the various modi operandi involved in all four murders and had a history of varying his modus-operandi throughout his offending is Sutcliffe. It is not credible that the serial killer who committed these murders has not been caught or committed any further offences in London or anywhere else after January 1979.

The authors do not believe that Sutcliffe has ever been considered as a suspect in this series of murders. The only way to irrefutably eliminate him through DNA analysis is from a blood or hair sample.

27. Anna Rogulskyj
(Convicted)

On 5 July 1975, thirty-six-year-old Anna Rogulskyj returned to her home in Keighley after a night's drinking to find that her boyfriend had walked out on her. She then walked ten minutes to his home to remonstrate with him. On the way, she encountered Sutcliffe, who propositioned her for sex. She rebuffed him and walked on.

She arrived at her boyfriend's home at about 2.00am and began banging on the door and windows but was unable to obtain any response. Annoyed, she indicated her displeasure by smashing one of his windows and left to return home. On the way back, Sutcliffe again propositioned her and she again rebuffed him, whereupon he hit her on the back of her head with a hammer and dragged her to a more secluded area close by. He pulled up her blouse then stabbed and slashed her several times in the abdomen. At that point a neighbour in a house overlooking the scene who had been woken by the noise got up and shouted, 'What's going on?' and Sutcliffe fled.

Anna was found at 2.20am by a passer-by. She was rushed to hospital and successfully operated on. She had three fractures to the skull consistent with hammer blows. Her handbag was at the crime scene and nothing was stolen. She described her assailant as around five-foot eight with dark hair and a beard, and produced a photofit.

A neighbour described Anna's attacker as five-foot eight-inches tall wearing a check sports jacket.

Sutcliffe's used his HGV driver training along the A629 to reconnoitre Keighley and other towns for subsequent attacks, giving rise to the Apex Reconnaissance Cluster.

Map 8 - The Apex Reconnaissance Cluster 1975

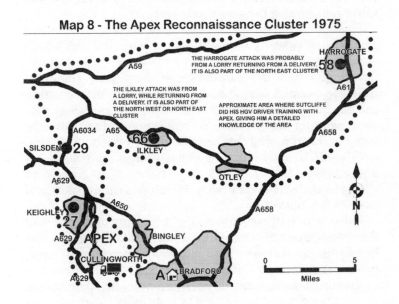

119

No	Name	Date	Cluster(s)	Route Package
A	44 Tanton Crescent			
27	Anna Rogulskyj	05/07/75	Apex	4.1. A629
29	Tracy Browne	27/08/75	Apex	4.1. A629
58	Harrogate Schoolgirl	17/02/79	Apex, North Eastern	
66	Yvonne Mysliwiec	11/10/79	Apex, North Eastern or North Western	

28. Olive Smelt
(Convicted)

On 15 August 1975, office cleaner Olive Smelt, aged forty-six, was drinking with friends at the Royal Oak in Halifax. Also there were Sutcliffe and Trevor Birdsall. Sutcliffe made remarks that the Royal Oak was frequented by prostitutes and that Olive was one. This was untrue and Olive told him so in no uncertain terms.

Friends dropped Olive off close to her home and Sutcliffe, who was passing in his car with Trevor Birdsall on their way home, recognised her as she walked home. Trevor Birdsall gave evidence at Sutcliffe's trial that Sutcliffe stopped the car and, as he got out, 'he seemed to put his hand down the side of the seat'. This was to pick up a hammer and a knife. Sutcliffe then stalked Olive by walking down a road that ran parallel to her route.

Sutcliffe then intercepted Olive, walked up behind her and engaged her in conversation before hitting her over the head with a hammer twice. He then lifted her skirt and slashed her bottom.

Olive was only saved because a passing motorist saw her body, stopped and jumped out. Sutcliffe, seeing the headlights, fled. Like Anna Rogulskyj, her handbag was nearby and nothing was stolen.

Trevor Birdsall testified that when Sutcliffe returned ten to twenty minutes later, he was unusually quiet but said he had been talking to a woman. The next day he read in the local paper of the brutal attack on Olive. He said, 'It crossed my mind there might be a connection,' but in the event did nothing.

Olive was operated on at the Leeds General Infirmary and later examined by Dr Mike Green, who had also examined Anna Rogulskyj. Dr Green opined that they were linked.

The investigation was led by Detective Superintendent Dick Holland, who by now was leading Halifax CID. He ignored the links and treated Olive's husband, Harry, as the prime suspect, because he had access to tools and had been working on home improvements. He was thus in the area and without an alibi (MPoF). Harry was eventually eliminated and the investigation wound down.

29. Caroline 'Tracy' Browne
(Believed to be attributed to Sutcliffe by both Chief Constable Byford and ACC Sampson. Sutcliffe admitted the attack to ACC Hellawell in 1992, but was not prosecuted.)

On Wednesday 27 August 1975, Sutcliffe attacked fourteen-year-old Tracy Browne in Silsden, a village on the A629 between Keighley and Skipton.

Tracy was walking home along a country lane at around 10.30pm when she saw Sutcliffe walking in front of her. Sutcliffe stopped briefly to look at her and then walked on but was clearly taking his time, allowing Tracy to catch up with him. They started talking and continued to walk together. They had further conversation where he gained Tracy's trust; he occasionally dropped back to blow his nose or tie up his shoelace.

At one point Sutcliffe hung back, once again stopping and pretending to retie his shoelaces. Suddenly he struck Tracy on the back of the head five times with a blunt instrument, probably a hammer. Sutcliffe was disturbed by the lights of a passing car, so he threw Tracy over a fence and ran off.

Although seriously injured, Tracy managed to make her way to a caravan about 400 yards from the crime scene. The occupants summoned help and she was rushed to hospital where neurosurgeons removed a splinter of bone from her brain. Tracy survived and was an outstanding witness. She had had a good look at Sutcliffe and gave a very accurate description of him as being in his late twenties or early thirties, having dark afro-style crinkly hair, moustache and beard, staring eyes and a thin face, with an insipid high-pitched voice, wearing a 'V'-neck cardigan over a light blue open-neck shirt, with dark trousers and small-footed brown suede shoes. She confirmed that her attacker had a Bradford accent and told her he lived at Holroyd House, just outside Bingley, indicating that he was a local man.

Tracy's description was confirmed by a witness who came forward and described a dark-haired bearded man who had been noticed in the neighbourhood that night and had been standing near a light-coloured Ford. Sutcliffe had a white Ford Corsair and a lime-green Ford Capri which would look light-coloured under streetlights.

Sutcliffe was familiar with Silsden from his HGV driver training and may have identified Silsden as a likely place for an attack at that time. He may even have spotted Tracy while driving through Silsden in a training lorry.

The SIO into the attack on Tracy was Detective Superintendent Jim Hobson, a veteran of the LCP. Just a few years later he would lead the Ripper investigation. He did not link the attack on Tracy with the Ripper and did not even reissue Tracy's photofit of her attacker, which was the most accurate so far (MPoF).

During 1982 a review carried out by ACC Colin Sampson – who later became WYP Chief Constable – examined Tracy's case for inclusion in the Ripper attacks. Sutcliffe was interviewed about it in Parkhurst Prison but denied being responsible. He finally admitted attacking Tracy in 1992 to the then Chief Constable Keith Hellawell.

30. Lynne Weedon
See 26 Eve Stratford

During the middle of September 1975, while Sutcliffe looked for work, Sonia decided to complete her teacher training and enrolled at the Margaret McMillan College in Bradford. Throughout this period, when he was not attending HGV driver training or signing on for the dole, Sutcliffe was free to roam and continued to visit Marianne in London and Maureen in Duxford.

On 29 September 1975, Sutcliffe started employment as a lorry driver for the Common Road Tyre Company at Oakenshaw, situated at the junction of the M62 Motorway and a spur off the M606 into Bradford, bringing his unemployment and Phase 4 of his life to an end.

Sutcliffe had good reason to be satisfied. At twenty-nine he was happily married to a beautiful woman and had achieved his dream of becoming an HGV driver. This would give him secure employment, and the ability to roam unsupervised, committing murders over a much wider area. He had gone up in the world and improved his earnings significantly.

Then disaster struck.

Phase 5. October 1975 to April 1976: Yorkshire Ripper

Sutcliffe's new job involved short and medium distance hauls all over the North and the Midlands. His sister Anne had moved to Morecambe, to be with her husband's parents. His work often took him past Morecambe on the M6 and he would often divert and visit them.

Sutcliffe appeared happy at work, but on 15 October 1975 he was arrested for stealing tyres from his employer and bailed to appear for trial.

31. Wilma McCann
(Convicted)

Wilma McCann was a single mother of four children who supplemented her income with sex work. She left home at Scott Hall Avenue, Leeds, to go drinking in Chapeltown at about 7.30pm on 29 October 1975, leaving her nine-year-old daughter to babysit. She finished drinking at about 1.00am and started to stagger home during the early hours of 30 October. She was seen trying to force drivers to stop and give her a lift by jumping in front of cars.

According to Sutcliffe's account of the murder, he picked Wilma up and drove her to Prince Philip Playing Fields, close to her home. There, she propositioned him and they agreed to have sex on the grass for £5. She partially undressed and sat on the grass but when he could not get an erection she ridiculed him. Enraged, he took a hammer from his toolbox in the car and hit her twice on the head with it. He then returned to the car, collected a knife and stabbed her fifteen times in her neck, chest and abdomen. This would be wrongly identified as the first crime of the Yorkshire Ripper.

Wilma's body was discovered at about 7.30am. The SIO was DCS Dennis Hoban. It was the first murder in the Gaiety Sub-Cluster.

The autopsy revealed that Wilma was dead when the knife wounds were inflicted. Her killer had pulled her trousers and knickers down and ripped open her blouse. Semen was found on the back of her trousers and knickers, indicating that he had masturbated over the body. Analysis of the semen revealed that the murderer was Blood Group B Negative, Non-secretor.

Because Wilma was known to be a sex worker, Detective Chief Superintendent Hoban focussed on this as the motive and prematurely discounted the possibility that the murderer was also attacking women that were not sex workers. So he failed to link the attacks on Tracy Browne, Olive Smelt and Anna Rogulskyj (MPoF). Nor did he connect Wilma's murder to the murder of Mary Judge in 1968 (MPoF).

The investigation eventually wound down, as information dried up on what was perceived by the police to be a low-priority, difficult-to-solve crime against a vagrant or prostitute, known in police slang at the time as a 'fish and chip' murder.

Here the authors digress to cover another important but neglected aspect of the investigation. Namely, the effect on the police officers that were involved. In 2022, Chris appeared on ITV in a two-part documentary on the unsolved murders Sutcliffe is thought to have committed. A retired policeman, Keith Tordoff, contacted Tim via the NYE with a heartfelt commentary on the case and how it had affected him, printed here:

> I write concerning the two ITV documentaries based on *Yorkshire Ripper: The Secret Murders*.
> I watched part 1 yesterday evening and have just finished watching part 2. I type this with tears in my eyes and feel quite emotional – I didn't feel this way after the first part.
> I attended at the scene where Wilma McCann was discovered by the milkman in 1975, then going into her house and seeing her four young children waiting for her returning home, memories I will never forget. Possibly my emotions this evening are triggered by Richard McCann, who I saw as a very young child in 1975, summarising at the end that so many families have not had justice, a sentiment I fully agree with.
> I worked as an investigator on most of the attacks, including the ones not attributed to Sutcliffe. On the ground, Police Officers working on those attacks not attributed to Sutcliffe by the senior officers, spoke openly that they believed they were the work of the 'Yorkshire Ripper'.
> Many officers I worked with on the enquiries also did not believe the 'tape' or letters were from the attacker, with some at briefings being held by Assistant

Chief Constable George Oldfield openly saying that to him and to the senior officers at his side.

I was the first officer in 1980 at the scene where the body of Jacqueline Hill was discovered on a piece of waste land on Alma Road in Headingley – a memory that unfortunately I can still picture. Jacqueline Hill still upsets me because as well as being first officer to attend, for continuity I stayed with the body in situ and at Leeds mortuary and later that day took her mother and father to identify Jacqueline – getting upset again.

A few years later I met Yvonne [Mysliwiec] (who had changed her name and was the lady who was attacked in Ilkley). Yvonne who lived near me in Bramhope, Leeds, and got to know me and confided in me about the attack knowing I had a police background.

Yes, many of the other attacks were undoubtedly carried out by Sutcliffe and there were miscarriages of justice for the three men who served such long prison sentences. The police 'culture' at the time was sometimes abused by Police Officers 'fitting people up' to please the demanding senior detectives who wanted a 'cough'.

The systems were open to this with handwritten statements of those being interviewed being 'amended' or 'added to'.

Vulnerable suspects were sometimes pressured (including assault) or coerced, as Stephen Downing described in the programme.

The pressure on the officers on the Ripper investigation was intense and it damaged some of them. Many of their marriages failed and some turned to alcohol. I didn't fortunately and came through it.

To miss out from the programme about Andy Laptew was very unfortunate – he was a dedicated, diligent good Police Officer and detective. If his work on the enquiry had been shown it would have shown what good old-fashioned coppering was. A miscarriage of justice for the families and for Andy the way he was dealt with and ignored by senior West Yorkshire Police Officers heading the so-called Yorkshire Ripper enquiry.

Rest in Peace Andy.

Written from my experiences, memories and my heart.

Keith Tordoff MBE

Both authors were very moved by this letter. It shows that many police officers were also victims of the Ripper Investigation, suffering enormous emotional turmoil and/or catastrophic damage in their personal lives, which pursues them to this day.

On 20 November 1975, alcoholic sex worker Joan Harrison, aged twenty-six, was murdered in Preston, Lancashire. The murderer was identified in 2010 through DNA analysis and was completely unconnected to Sutcliffe. But this case was subsequently to play a major part in the investigation.

32. Margaret Lightfoot

At lunchtime on Monday 24 November 1975, Mrs Margaret Lightfoot, a dedicated charity worker for pensioners, took her pet terrier Tessa for its usual walk from the family home on Connaught Avenue, Loughton, Essex, to the nearby Epping Forest. She was last seen going into the forest with Tessa on a lead at 1.00pm. Tessa was found wandering and taken home during the afternoon. Margaret's husband reported her missing when he returned from work.

Immediately dozens of police officers, some with dogs, combed the forest area on the Nursery Road and Earl's Path areas, assisted by about eighty members of the public. Searches continued until the early hours of Tuesday morning and resumed at daylight when a huge force of police officers and dogs arrived. At 8.20am a police dog found Margaret's body in a thicket.

She was naked, her anorak, trousers and underwear were scattered around her body, and her wellington boots were underneath her. Her hand had been cut by a knife. Some of her clothes had been disturbed after she was dragged into the thicket, indicating an initial crime scene and a secondary deposition scene. The post-mortem identified that Margaret had been hit on the head; the cause of death was ligature strangulation.

Epping Forest attracts strange people. Women reported being pestered at various times by perverts who frequented the woods. On the day of the murder, a young man who had been jumping out naked in front of horse riders at lunchtimes had been active.

All known sex offenders were interviewed, but all had watertight alibis. An appeal with a photofit was issued, but to no avail. Despite an extensive investigation, during which more than one hundred potential suspects were interviewed, police were unable to identify Mrs Lightfoot's killer.

On Sunday 21 December, photofits of five main suspects were put on display in Loughton Village Hall for some eighty witnesses who had made statements to look at, in the hope that a man identified as the main suspect could be pinpointed. But the case stalled and went cold.

The authors believe that the man identified as a suspect is probably not the murderer and is more likely to be a local pervert. That is not to say that he is not worth pursuing; this type of low-level sexual offence can lead to a pattern of escalating offending, but is not in itself indicative of an intention to commit a crime of such extreme violence at that time. His identification as the prime suspect may be an example of focussing prematurely on one inadequate suspect because there was nothing else to go on.

Sutcliffe regularly visited Marianne at Alperton. If he was returning to Bradford, his route would be the A406 North Circular to the M1. If he carried on past the M1 and then took the A121, it would take him right past Epping Forest, leaving a fast route back to the M1.

Robin Holland was stationed in Germany from 1975 to 1978, but it is unclear if Robin and his wife were still living in Duxford in November 1975. If Sutcliffe was visiting them from Alperton, his route would take him along the A406 to the M11. He could have gone along the A121 to Epping Forest, committed the murder, and then driven on to join the M11 to Duxford.

The murder of Margaret Lightfoot could have been the first murder Sutcliffe committed from his lorry. However, the authors believe that it is more likely he used a car.

The attack on Margaret is very similar to the attack on Judith Roberts. Her body was face down and had been carefully placed and pushed feet first under a thicket. She was naked from the waist down with the front of her dress and anorak pulled up over her breasts, which still had a bra covering them. Her knickers, tights and shoes were underneath her body.

The attack on Margaret has the other hallmarks of a Sutcliffe attack. The speed and skill with which the attack was conducted, with not one witness noticing anything or hearing screams, would indicate a practised and ruthless assailant, who struck quickly, then calmly left the scene undetected and without arousing suspicion. Use of a ligature and a knife, blows to the head/face, frenzied stripping of clothing to reveal genitalia, dragging the body off a footpath to a secluded secondary crime scene and the scattering of her clothing occurred in several murders Sutcliffe is known to have committed.

On the fortieth anniversary of Margaret Lightfoot's murder, the MPS reviewed the case and were able to recover a detailed type-written report of the case from the officer in charge at the time, together with other items of evidence.

The SIO for the cold case investigation made comments that illustrate the challenges facing a cold case investigation that is seeking to use DNA to progress the case:

We have been lucky because we still have some property from the crime scene. We've asked our forensic scientists to re-examine those items to see if we can use any modern-day techniques – back then we would only have been able to fingerprint items. The investigation focussed on Mrs Lightfoot's wellington boots which were found underneath her body. They may have been pulled off by her killer and could therefore contain traces of his DNA. However, the way the boots were fingerprinted in 1975 may have compromised later tests. [Source BBC]

33. Rosemary Stead
(Believed to be attributed to Sutcliffe by Chief Constable Byford)

Rosemary Stead was an eighteen-year-old shop assistant who was walking home from work at about 6.30pm on 6 January 1976 along a main road in Queensbury next to fields when she was attacked.

Rosemary's assailant hit her from behind with a blunt instrument, possibly a hammer, smashing it into the back of her skull. He was disturbed by motorists and pedestrians, and fled.

Multiple witnesses described the attacker as twenty-five to thirty years old, five-foot nine-inches tall, slim build with dark hair, a moustache and a beard. Their descriptions perfectly matched the descriptions given by Tracy Browne and Anna Rogulskyj and fit Sutcliffe. The victim was walking alone at night along a country road when attacked from behind with a blunt instrument that was probably a hammer. The assailant ran off when disturbed and was fit enough to evade pursuit. Although Rosemary's assailant did not attempt to strike up a conversation, in every other way the attack was very similar to the attack on Tracy Browne, but WYMP did not connect it (MPoF).

34. Emily Jackson
(Convicted)

Outwardly, Emily Jackson, aged forty-two, was a respectable married woman with a family, who helped out with her husband Sydney's roofing business, often driving his blue Commer van and doing the books for him.

In fact, they were in financial distress because the roofing business was failing, so they agreed that Emily would do sex work. They installed a mattress in the back of the van, and he would drive her to The Gaiety pub near the Chapeltown RLD in Leeds, where he would wait for her while she drove around in the van looking for clients. Sometimes her assignations were in the van, sometimes in her client's vehicle.

On the evening of 20 January 1976, Emily dropped Sydney off at The Gaiety. At 7.00pm, Sutcliffe and Emily contracted to have sex, left the van in The Gaiety's car park and went to derelict land at Manor Street. Using the pretext there was something wrong with his car, Sutcliffe got Emily to hold a torch while he looked under the bonnet, then hit her on the back of the head twice with a hammer. He then dragged her to a more secluded place, lifted up her clothes to reveal her breasts, exposed her genitalia and stabbed her breasts, abdomen, neck and back fifty-two times with a Phillips screwdriver. Then he pushed a piece of wood up her vagina. The body of Teresa Thörling was to be similarly posed in 1980.

When Sydney returned to the car park at closing time, Emily was not there and, assuming she was engaged on an assignation, he caught a taxi home.

Emily's body was found at 8.00am the next day. She was the second victim in the Gaiety Sub-Cluster. Detective Superintendent Hoban recognised that Emily and Wilma McCann had been murdered by the same man. He eliminated Sydney as a suspect and issued this telex later that day:

FROM THE ACC NUMBER 2 AREA WEST YORKS METRO POLICE. TO ALL DIVS [DIVISIONS] WEST YORKS, **SURROUNDING FORCES**, POLICE GAZETTE AND POLICE REPORTS.

THE BODY OF EMILY MONICA JACKSON 42 YEARS, HOME ADDRESS 18 BACK GREEEN, CHURWELL, WAS FOUND IN A DERELICT BUILDING IN MANOR STREET, LEEDS 7, AT 8.05 AM TODAY 21ST OF JANUARY 1976.

IT IS KNOWN THAT THE WOMAN HAS RECENTLY BEEN AN ACTIVE PROSTITUTE IN THE CHAPELTOWN AREA OF LEEDS…THE DECEASED SUFFERED SEVERE INJURIES TO THE CHEST, ABDOMEN, AND THROAT, POSSIBLY CAUSED BY AN INSTRUMENT SIMILAR TO A PHILIPS SCREWDRIVER (CROSS PATTERN TYPE).

ASSAILANT MAY BE HEAVILY BLOODSTAINED AND IS BELIEVED TO HAVE BEEN WEARING HEAVY WELLINGTON BOOTS.

THOUGH THERE HAS BEEN NON SEXUAL INTERFERENCE TO THE VAGINA, THE BRA WAS MOVED TO POSITION ABOVE THE DRESS AND THERE ARE SEVERAL INDICATIONS THAT THE PERSON RESPONSIBLE FOR THE CRIME MAY ALSO HAVE BEEN RESPONSIBLE FOR THE DEATH OF THE PROSTITUTE WILMA MCCANN AT LEEDS ON 29/30 TH OF OCTOBER 1975.

MOTIVE APPEARS TO BE HATRED OF PROSTITUTES…A SEARCH OF RECORDS FOR PERSONS CONVICTED OF SERIOUS ATTACKS UPON PROSTITUTES WOULD BE APPRECIATED.

[Authors emphasis in bold]

This telex was fundamentally flawed:
- Wilma, Emily and Mary Judge were all sex workers who had been beaten to death in Leeds, with blows to the head from blunt instruments, which could have been a hammer that was removed from the scene. Yet Hoban did not consider if Mary's murder was linked to this series (MPoF).
- Hoban had assumed – wrongly – that the murderer was motivated by a hatred of sex workers, not by the sadistic pleasure of killing women (MPoF).

132

- The message had gone to the *Police Gazette*, which was available to all forces. However, by prefixing the request for a search of records for attacks on sex workers to only the 'Surrounding Forces' (North Yorkshire (NYP), South Yorkshire (SYP), Lancashire, Greater Manchester Police (GMP) and Derbyshire Constabulary), not 'All Forces', Hoban was indicating that he believed the perpetrator was operating locally in the West Yorkshire and surrounding force areas, not nationally (MPoF).

This ensured that:
- The possibility that the same man had committed attacks on women who were not sex workers was immediately and wrongly excluded. Thereby preventing the attacks being linked to Vicky Williamson, Anna Rogulskyj, Olive Smelt, Tracy Browne and Rosemary Stead (MPoF).
- Forces other than NYP, SYP, Lancashire, GMP and Derbyshire Constabulary were not notified of the investigation, and attacks on sex workers in these areas were not therefore considered. This excluded the attack on Rosina Hilliard in Nottingham and 'Jane' in Norfolk from consideration (MPoF).
- All forces ignored the possibility that the perpetrator could have attacked women who were not sex workers in their force areas (MPoF).

Detective Superintendent Hoban ordered a review of all attacks on women to identify if his man had killed before. The elimination criteria were:
1. That the victim should be a prostitute.
2. That she should have been hit over the head with a hammer.
3. That her clothing should have been disarranged to expose her body.
4. That stab and slash wounds should have been inflicted to the body.

Elimination point 1 resulted in attacks on women who were not sex workers being excluded, which prevented the attacks on Wilma and Emily being connected to other attacks that had occurred.

Detective Superintendent Hoban knew that the public were – like the police – largely unsympathetic to prostitutes, viewing violence as an occupational hazard they chose from their lifestyle. So in his appeals for information, he emphasised that Wilma's four children were now without her. He also issued this warning: 'I believe the man we are looking for is the type who could kill again. He is a sadistic killer and may well be a sexual pervert.'

Linking the McCann and Jackson attacks led to an increase in media interest. On 23 January 1976, the first reference was made in the press to the Yorkshire Ripper.

Detective Superintendent Hoban was subsequently promoted to Deputy Head of WYMP CID. Such was the strength of his reputation that the above unsound assumptions were never questioned. The force obsessively and unquestioningly maintained the position that the Ripper only attacked sex workers until the murder of Josephine Whitaker in April 1979 (MPoF).

The telex arrived on the desk of Lancashire Police's Head of CID, Detective Superintendent Wilf Brooks. He considered carefully if the murder of Joan Harrison had been committed by the same man that murdered Wilma and Emily. Lancashire Police had identified that Joan's killer had a gap in his teeth and was a Blood Group B Negative, Secretor. They conferred with their colleagues in WYMP, and both forces concluded – correctly – that Joan's murder was unconnected.

By the time of Emily Jackson's murder there had been eight attacks on unaccompanied women in three years.

Six attacks had occurred in the new WYMP force area during the previous six months involving the use of a blunt instrument or hammer. Two of them were murders, the others would have been murders had the offender not been disturbed. All involved women walking alone at night, who were attacked from behind with a hammer, with no attempt to rob them. In three cases, the initial attack occurred after an attempt to hold a conversation with them and the victim was moved to a secondary crime scene, where in two cases she was slashed.

Map 9 - The Initial Attacks December 1972 – January 1976

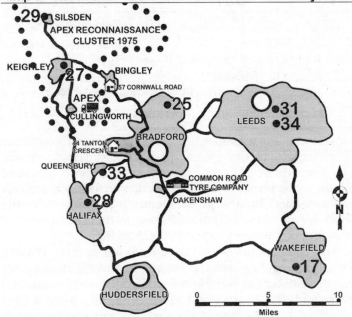

Case No	Date	Name	Cluster	Intelligence Collator	Previous Force
17	Dec 1972	Bernadette Cassidy	N/A	Wakefield	WRC/WYC
On 10 August 1974 Sutcliffe moved from 57 Cornwall Road, Bingley to 44 Tanton Crescent, Bradford					
25	Nov 1974	Gloria Wood	Bradford	Bradford	BCP

135

Case No	Date	Name	Cluster	Intelligence Collator	Previous Force
27	Jul 1975	Anna Rogulskyj	Apex	Keighley	WRC/WYC
28	Aug 1975	Olive Smelt	Halifax	Halifax	WRC/WYC
29	Aug 1975	Tracy Browne	Apex	Keighley	WRC/WYC
From 29 September 1975 until April 1976 Sutcliffe worked for the Common Road Tyre Company at Oakenshaw					
31	Oct 1975	Wilma McCann	Leeds	Leeds	LCP
33	Jan 1976	Rosemary Stead	Bradford	Bradford	BCP
34	Jan 1976	Emily Jackson	Leeds	Leeds	LCP

All the survivors described the offender as being a shortish, medium-build man with dark curly hair, dark eyebrows, short tufted beard and mandarin-type moustache, with a local accent. Photofits had been obtained from some of them.

This information would have been fed into the WYMP Force Intelligence Office at Wakefield and the intelligence collator's offices at Keighley, Bradford, Halifax, Leeds and Wakefield. By the end of August 1975, they should have identified that the four attempted murders were the work of one person and the witness evidence indicated that a short man with black curly hair, a local Bradford accent, a black beard and moustache was responsible.

The description and photofits should then have gone to all stations and surrounding force areas in a Crime Bulletin. The collators should then have conferred and the Bradford Collator should have been able to identify one man in his nominal index who fitted this description: Peter William Sutcliffe. The SIOs should have recognised the strong resemblance. That, coupled with the numerous times Sutcliffe was indexed into the enquiry, should have resulted in his arrest as early as September 1975, before the murder of Wilma McCann.

However, the WYMP intelligence sections that emerged from the amalgamations of smaller forces were not integrated. Investigations were not coordinated between the different area divisions, and the intelligence collators from the previous constituent forces did not liaise with each other. Consequently, there was a complete failure of intelligence at all four stages in the intelligence cycle (Collection, Collation, Analysis and Dissemination). WYMP force intelligence was therefore unable to either link these crimes into a series or give CID the intelligence it needed to arrest Sutcliffe (MPoF).

The attacks on Anna and Olive were only linked to the Ripper attacks following a review by Detective Superintendent John Domaille in June 1978 (MPoF).

On 5 March 1976, Sutcliffe appeared before Dewsbury magistrates and pleaded guilty to stealing five second-hand tyres from the Common Road Tyre Company. He was fined £25. He was sacked one month later in April 1976, ostensibly for poor timekeeping, but actually for the theft. Losing his job was a serious setback; Sutcliffe's earnings decreased significantly, and he returned to being unemployed.

Phase 6. April to October 1976: Hunted, unemployed and undeterred

Sutcliffe settled down to unemployment, searching diligently for a new job as a lorry driver. Other than signing on for unemployment benefit once a fortnight, he was again free to roam and attack at will.

Sutcliffe and Sonia felt the loss of earnings keenly, so Sonia took up part-time work at a local nursing home with her mother, usually on Saturday and Wednesday nights. They often returned home on the Sunday morning to find Sutcliffe in a deep sleep but did not realise this was because he had been out until the early hours searching for victims.

For the detectives working on the investigation, this was a frustrating time. They knew that their man was not going to stop, and yet from the murder of Emily Jackson in January 1976 until the attack on Irene Richardson in February 1977 there were no more attacks. The Ripper was variously thought to be dead, in prison, in a mental institution, to have settled down with a woman, or to have left the country to commit crimes abroad. This latter hypothesis led to WYMP issuing a request to all European forces via Interpol to consider if they had any attacks that could be attributable to the Ripper.

In fact, none of the above hypotheses were correct. Sutcliffe had carried on killing, but WYMP failed to identify this because of incompetence and over-reliance on DCS Hoban's elimination criteria.

35. Marcella Claxton
(Convicted)

On Saturday 8 May 1976, while Sonia and her mother were working at the nursing home, Sutcliffe drove to the Chapeltown RLD in his white Corsair. At 4.00am on the Sunday morning, he spotted Marcella Claxton staggering home under the influence of drink. She was three months pregnant.

Sutcliffe pulled up next to her and propositioned her for sex. Marcella wasn't a sex worker and rejected him, but he offered her a lift, which she accepted. Instead of driving her home, he drove her to Soldier's Field in Roundhay Park and propositioned her for sex there for £5. She said she needed to urinate and went behind some bushes.

Sutcliffe then dealt her eight or nine blows to the head with his ball pein hammer. Stunned and covered in blood from her wounds, she saw that Sutcliffe was masturbating and had a good look at his face. He went back to the Corsair and got some tissues to wipe up the semen, threw them on the ground and gave Marcella a £5 note, telling her not to go to the police.

Marcella was a very tough woman. Despite her injuries and inebriated state, she crawled to a telephone box, using her knickers to stem the bleeding, and called an ambulance. As she waited, she saw Sutcliffe driving around, passing the call box several times before getting out and going to the bushes that were the scene of the attack, before driving off. He was obviously searching for her to finish her off.

Marcella described her attacker as a smartly dressed white man with dark hair, a beard and moustache. A photofit was made, which was similar to the one made by Tracy Browne. The detectives that interviewed her immediately dismissed her as 'just this side of a gorilla', insisted that her attacker was black, disregarded her evidence and eliminated her as a Ripper victim (MPoF). Marcella's was yet another case that was not linked until Sutcliffe confessed to it in 1981.

To prevent further murders, WYMP arrested hundreds of sex workers to force them off the streets. It also started covert surveillance of the Chapeltown RLD to identify kerb crawlers. Anyone spotted three times was interviewed by detectives. In June 1977 the Manningham RLD in Bradford was also put under surveillance.

Marcella miscarried and suffered years of nightmares of the Ripper returning to finish her off.

Shortly after Marcella left hospital, she was drinking with friends in The Gaiety when Sutcliffe came into the pub. He looked around then left, either because he recognised Marcella, or because there were no suitable victims present. When Marcella and her friends rushed outside, he had vanished.

This is a significant sighting. The authors believe that sometimes Sutcliffe pre-identified his intended victim. He was obviously searching The Gaiety for a victim. It featured strippers, and sex workers frequented it. It was a regular haunt for Sutcliffe. Irene Richardson frequented The Gaiety, and he picked up several of his victims in the vicinity, which became the epicentre of a Sub-Cluster of attacks.

Map 10 - The Gaiety Sub-Cluster 1975 - 1977

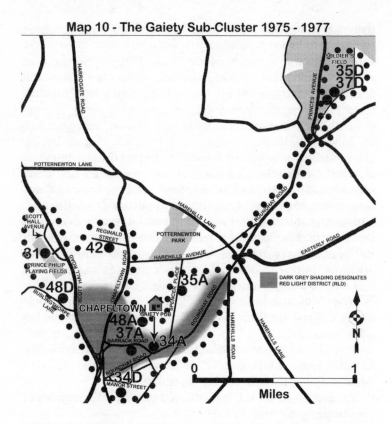

No	Name	Date
31	Wilma McCann	30/10/75
34	Emily Jackson	20/01/76
35	Marcella Claxton	08/05/76
37	Irene Richardson	05/02/77
42	Jayne MacDonald	25/06/77
48	Marilyn Moore	14/12/77

For months after the attack, Marcella hated men. Even five years after, she was still plagued by depression and dizzy spells and unable to hold a job down. The birth of her son five years later in 1981 coincided with Sutcliffe's arrest, but neither event eased her pain and she wished that she, too, had died that night.

Sutcliffe could not be charged with the murder of Marcella's unborn child because it had not reached twenty-eight weeks' gestation.

36. Maureen Hogan
(Believed to be attributed to Sutcliffe by Chief Constable Byford)

On Sunday 29 August 1976 a twenty-nine-year-old housewife, Maureen Hogan, was attacked in Bradford after a night out. She had left the Pentagon Club at 1.30am and been hit on the back of her head then stabbed repeatedly in the abdomen. She was left for dead in a shop doorway and was found at about 5.40am.

The wounds were very similar to those inflicted on Wilma McCann and Emily Jackson. Maureen was so badly injured that she could not give a description of her attacker.

In 2017 Maureen contacted Chris and told him that the SIO was Detective Superintendent Dick Holland, who wrote the case off as domestic related. She was accordingly eliminated from the Ripper investigation (MPoF). Understandably following her ordeal, Maureen is very angry about this and feels she has never had justice or closure.

The attack bears all the hallmarks of an attack by Sutcliffe: lone woman walking on her own at night attacked from behind with a blow to the back of the skull with a blunt instrument, followed by multiple stab wounds to the abdomen. The attack took place in Great Russell Street, eight minutes' drive from 44 Tanton Crescent. When Sutcliffe was arrested, Maureen Hogan recognised him as being in the Pentagon Club when she was there. The authors believe Sutcliffe pre-selected her in the club, followed her from there and attacked her as she was walking home.

In September 1976, Sutcliffe's unemployment and this phase of his life finished when he started working as an HGV driver for T&WH Clark, a small engineering transport firm situated in the Canal Road Industrial Estate in Bradford, close to 44 Tanton Crescent.

Phase 7. October 1976 to John Humble (June 1979): Respectable married man and experienced serial killer

Sutcliffe was very happy in his work, often staying overnight in truck stops, leaving him free of family and work supervision. His work took him all over England and Scotland. So by 1976, Sutcliffe had an employment that increased his opportunities to murder and his geographical area of operation.

Sutcliffe swiftly achieved a reputation as Clarks' best driver. He had a collection of 'A–Z' street maps and was always willing to advise his mates on the best routes, making him respected and valued within the firm. Clarks was suddenly forced to sack all its drivers for stealing from the loads. Sutcliffe was the only exception. He drove Clarks' Ford Transcontinental, a £250,000 monster, and he was chosen to appear in a promotional brochure, showing him with hair and beard neatly trimmed behind the wheel of the Transcontinental. A giant enlargement of the photograph was given pride of place in the entrance to the firm's offices.

Sutcliffe had obviously learned from his earlier theft conviction that it was not worth risking his increased earnings from lorry driving by committing petty acts of theft from his employer. He had assumed the image of a hard-working lorry driver who, after a period of instability and petty offending, had settled down to be an apparently model citizen and happily married man. This helped assuage any cursory enquiries by the police and served him well when he was interviewed by detectives.

Access to the lorry gave him new opportunities to murder women. Sutcliffe picked up hitchhikers in his lorry and may have had sex workers in the cab while staying over at truck stops. He was forensically aware and always left the cab free of blood splatter. Victims could be enticed out of the cab on the pretext of having sex or urinating, then when they got out, he could murder them, or murder them in the cab using a ligature. He spent hours cleaning and polishing both the inside and outside of the cab whilst waiting to load and unload, obviously to remove any forensic evidence. Some of his colleagues at Clarks noticed that Sutcliffe occasionally turned up at work with false number plates on his car.

During 1977 and 1978, Sonia frequently went to stay with Marianne at Alperton. Sutcliffe would take her and collect her, which would allow him to roam and be in London when not lorry driving.

37. Irene Richardson
(Convicted)

On 5 February 1977, Sutcliffe spent the evening searching for a victim in his white Ford Corsair. Not far from The Gaiety, he spotted twenty-eight-year-old Irene Richardson and picked her up. According to his confession:

She told me to drive to the park. At this time you [WYMP] knew where I was picking them up [authors' note: This is highly significant; it indicates Sutcliffe knew the RLDs were under surveillance]. She told me where to drive and we came to this big field which was on my left. I drove off the road onto the field and stopped near some toilets. She wanted to use the toilets, so she got out and went over to them. She came back and said they were locked. Before she went to the toilet, she took off her coat and placed it on the ground. When she came back, she said she would

143

have a wee on the ground. She took her boots off and placed them on the ground, then she crouched down to have a pee. By this time I was out of the car and I had my hammer in my hand.

As she was crouching down, I hit her on the head from behind, at least twice, maybe three times. She fell down. I then lifted up her clothes and slashed her in the lower abdomen and also slashed her throat. I left her lying face down and I covered her up with her coat. I put her knee boots on top of her before I covered her up. I then got into my car and drove off the field.

He took the time to rearrange her clothes and boots and cover her legs with her coat. Sutcliffe's actions were calm, deliberate, calculated and controlled. Typical of the confident serial killer he had become.

Irene's body was discovered at 7.30am the next day. She was lying face down, her hands under her stomach, and her head turned to the left with her long hair matted with blood and hiding the stab wounds in her neck and throat. Her coat had been draped over her bottom and legs, with only her feet showing. Her calf-length brown boots had been placed over her thighs. Her bra was still in position, but her skirt had been pulled up. Her tights had been pulled off her right leg and pulled down. Besides the neck and throat wounds, she had three stab wounds in the stomach that had caused her intestines to spill out.

Near the body, the police discovered that the killer had left tyre tracks. The police were able to determine the front tyres were two India Autoway tyres, the rear offside was a Pneumant and the rear nearside an Esso 110, all cross-ply. The rear track width was between four-foot one-and-a-half inches and four-foot two-and-a-half inches, which fitted twenty-six makes of cars, including the Ford Corsair.

Based on this, a tyre-tracking investigation started. Uniform Branch officers were told to stop and examine relevant vehicles and to record the registration number and details of the car. An index card was then completed to show that the vehicle had been examined and eliminated. Lorry drivers were also questioned. One trucker wrote:

> One of our drivers had a more serious encounter with them when he got pulled for speeding on the A1. The lad they stopped for speeding fit [sic] all the criteria they were using at the time, he had black curly hair, a beard and a Geordie accent. He got a night in the cells. It really shook him up.

Online access to the vehicle records at the Driver and Vehicle Licensing Authority (DVLA) records was not available, so the 53,000 vehicles that fitted the track width were listed on a huge printout that was spread out along the floor of the Millgarth Incident Room and checked against the card index to eliminate vehicles that had been seen by Uniform Branch. The remaining vehicles were then followed up with a visit to the owner by detectives.

38. Barbara Young and 47.1 and 47.2 Doncaster sex worker (name withheld)
(Barbara Young's murder is believed to have been attributed to Sutcliffe by ACC Colin Sampson and 47.1 may have been attributed to Sutcliffe by Chief Constable Byford)

These three attacks comprise the Doncaster Cluster, which is shown on Map 2B. They were all lorry based and there is no evidence of attacks in Doncaster mounted from a car.

BARBARA YOUNG

On Tuesday 22 March 1977, Barbara Young, a twenty-nine-year-old mother of two and a sex worker, was found by a female friend with severe head injuries in Broxholme Lane, Doncaster at around 8.45pm.

Barbara's friend said that she had gone with a client to an alleyway in an area between the lorry parks and the transport hotels, and this is where he had attacked her. A post-mortem revealed that her skull was fractured, causing death from a massive haemorrhage.

The attack on Barbara was ruled out as a Ripper attack because her handbag was stolen, indicating robbery as a motive. The attack was from the front not the back, she had been punched, there were no stab wounds and there had been no attacks in South Yorkshire before. Sutcliffe subsequently denied committing this murder.

As a lorry driver, Sutcliffe knew and frequented the lorry parks and transport hotels. One correspondent contacted Chris with this information:

> My father-in-law was a truck driver and regularly saw Peter Sutcliffe at truck stops on numerous occasions from 1976 until his arrest, and knew him to speak to. He regularly parked up at the City Arms in Peterborough.

Sutcliffe may have stayed over in a lorry park in Doncaster because he had used up his tachograph hours, and wanted to attack a sex worker there. Barbara's injuries are completely consistent with an attack with a hammer.

DONCASTER SEX WORKER (NAME WITHHELD BY SYP)

47.1: In late November or early December 1977, a sex worker was attacked in a Doncaster multistorey car park. Her description of her assailant was of a man aged about thirty-five, tall, slim build with brushed back dark hair, beard and moustache. She produced a photofit, which was published in the local press but didn't come to the attention of the Ripper enquiry team, so it was never assessed as a Ripper attack.

The description of her attacker fits Sutcliffe. The photofit was shown to other sex workers and they failed to identify him, indicating that he was from out of town, not a regular local punter.

47.2: The same woman saw the same man some months later driving away from a Doncaster lorry park in a lorry, which confirms he was a lorry driver that frequented lorry parks. The victim believed that the man was searching for other victims in the park.

Taken with the attack on Barbara Young this indicates that sex workers worked Doncaster's truck stops and that Sutcliffe was looking for victims in lorry parks while driving for Clarks.

39. Debra 'Debbie' Schlesinger
(Believed to have been attributed to Sutcliffe by ACC Hellawell)
WYP confirmed that it had enough evidence to charge Sutcliffe with this murder, but he was never prosecuted.)
On Thursday 21 April 1977, Debra Schlesinger, aged eighteen years, was stabbed through the heart as she walked down the path of her home in Leeds after a night out with friends.

She fled and was chased by her assailant until she reached the doorway to her home where, at Cragside Walk, she collapsed and died. Witnesses saw a dark-bearded man near the scene.

Sutcliffe delivered regularly to Kirkstall Forge, which was one hundred yards from Debbie's home, and had delivered there on the day she was murdered. Debbie got off the bus at the forge on her way back from work. Sutcliffe sometimes pre-selected victims and – as with Tracy Browne – may have first noticed Debbie from his lorry while delivering. Debbie's murder was eliminated from the Ripper series because she was not a sex worker and a knife was used, not a hammer.

ACC Hellawell put Debbie's murder to Sutcliffe and he denied it. During 2002 it was reported in the *Sunday Telegraph* that WYP had enough evidence to charge Sutcliffe with the murder of Debra Schlesinger and the attempted murder of Mo Lea.

40. Patricia 'Tina' Atkinson
(Convicted)

Patricia Atkinson was a thirty-two-year-old divorced mother of three who lived on her own and was a sex worker. She operated from a flat at Oak Avenue, Bradford.

On Saturday 23 April 1977 at about 11.00pm, Tina got into Sutcliffe's car and he drove them back to her flat. Once inside, Sutcliffe hung up his coat and Tina sat down. He struck her on the back of the head with four massive blows from a ball pein hammer. She fell onto the floor, so he lifted her up, carried her to the bedroom and threw her down on the bed. He then removed her coat, ripped open her black leather jacket and blue blouse, pulled up her bra to reveal her breasts and pulled down her pale blue jeans and knickers to her ankles.

He stabbed at Tina's exposed stomach with a chisel then turned her over and stabbed her in the back then quickly turned her over again to continue stabbing at her stomach, altogether seven times. Before he left her, he partly pulled her jeans back up and threw the bed linen over the top of her body. He left a size-seven boot print on the bottom bed sheet, which matched the prints left at Emily Jackson's crime scene.

Sutcliffe drove to 44 Tanton Crescent, taking care not to attract attention from the police. On arrival he went through his standard counter-forensic routine of checking his clothes. He discovered blood on his jeans, so he rinsed them in the kitchen sink and hung them up to dry, then wiped blood off his boots. Satisfied, he got into bed, taking care not to wake Sonia, so she would not know what time he arrived home and went to sleep.

41. Stephanie Spencer and Michael Hodgson
(Miscarriage of Justice)

The body of twenty-five-year-old Stephanie Spencer was found hidden in bushes alongside Haughton Road, Darlington, next to a mixed car and lorry park at about 11.00am on Sunday 29 May 1977.

Next to her body was a rock with her blood and hair on it, which weighed about eight pounds. She was partially clothed; her knickers were on a bush beside the body.

The autopsy established that:
- Stephanie died of a fractured skull, having been hit with a blunt instrument.
- Death had occurred between 48 and 72 hours before the autopsy; that is between 4.00pm on the Thursday and 4.00pm on the Friday.
- She had had sex with a man who was Blood Group O up to twenty-four hours before her death.
- Her murderer had punched or hit her with his hand.

House-to-house enquiries established that:
- Stephanie lived with her husband at the marital home at 50 East Mount Road, but they were leading separate lives.
- Stephanie drank heavily and enjoyed casual sex.
- On Thursday nights, Stephanie regularly met with friends at the Flamingo nightclub on Victoria Road, Darlington. She left the club at about 1.00am on Friday 27 May, to walk home along Borough Road, into Haughton Road and then to her home at East Mount Road.
- A witness saw Stephanie arguing with a man outside the club, saying, 'No, no, no.' She described him as 'swarthy with a droopy moustache...about twenty-eight, broadly built with black hair...curly greasy hair and heavy black eyebrows'. He resembled the man in a police photofit shown in the local press.
- A witness saw Stephanie arguing with a man in Borough Road and the police issued a photofit of this man (Illustration 4).

Detectives contacted haulage companies to identify lorry drivers that had passed through Darlington or who were sleeping in the lorry park. They also visited Flamingos and appealed for witnesses who had been there on the night Stephanie was murdered.

MICHAEL HODGSON

Michael Hodgson, a thirty-four-year-old unemployed labourer who was lodging in Dundee Street, and his landlady, Mrs Olive Raper (with whom he was having an affair), had both been in Flamingos on 27 May. However, instead of coming forward, they left in a taxi, which was stopped by the police. Mrs Raper gave their names as Mr and Mrs Raper and Michael did not correct her. This raised their suspicions; he was questioned, then charged and remanded in custody on 30 June 1977.

During the trial in February 1978:

- Evidence was given that initially Michael said he had been in the club but had walked home with Mrs Raper. He then admitted that this was untrue and that he and Mrs Raper had quarrelled because she had danced with another man. So he left. He walked home and got into conversation with Stephanie en route, then left her at the junction of Dundee Street and Haughton Road. Finally, he admitted that he had met Stephanie walking up Borough Road. They were on opposite sides of the road and she crossed over. They walked together and talked, and he propositioned her for sex by the bushes where her body was later found. She agreed, but he could not get an erection, and Stephanie ridiculed him. He said, 'Something snapped, she just provoked me.' He also stated that he had gone to the edge of the bushes to urinate but had not gone into the bushes.

- The prosecution alleged that Michael and Stephanie had gone into the bushes to have consensual sex. When he could not obtain an erection, she had taunted Michael. Enraged, he attacked her with the rock, and his statement 'something snapped, she just provoked me' was a confession to murdering Stephanie.

- Defence Counsel Mr James Chadwin QC pointed out that when they interrogated Michael, the detectives asserted that he was the man with Blood Group O who had had intercourse with Stephanie and this man was the murderer.

Michael denied having had intercourse with Stephanie and a blood test confirmed he was not Blood Group O. At trial, the prosecution reversed its position, claiming that Stephanie led a promiscuous life, so it was quite possible that the man she had intercourse with was not the killer, leaving Michael as the prime suspect. Mr Chadwin asserted that the original police hypothesis was correct and the unknown lover was probably the man that killed Stephanie.

Michael maintained his innocence but was convicted of murder by a majority verdict of ten to two and sentenced to life imprisonment. This was reduced on appeal to manslaughter in May 1979 because Stephanie's taunts amounted to provocation. His sentence was reduced to six years. He served three years and continues to maintain his innocence to this day.

The authors are concerned that, as with the murders of Roberts, Sewell and Wilkinson, this was a miscarriage of justice. Leaving aside the possibility that Sutcliffe is the murderer, Michael's conviction is unsafe because:

- The prosecution completely misread the crime scene. In his statement, Sergeant Benison made reference to blood being found on ivy leaves between the deceased's body and the footpath. The implication of this is that the attack took place on the footpath and the body was dragged to a secondary crime scene over the ivy leaves, leaving a bloodstain. Stephanie was then left unconscious and dying at the deposition site in the bushes. The condition of Stephanie's clothing is completely inconsistent with consensual sex, but entirely consistent with her being violently stripped to facilitate posing of her body.
- The acts of hitting Stephanie with one blow and then dragging her body to the deposition site would have left her assailant covered in blood. However, no bloodstains, hair or fibre evidence was found on Michael's clothes or in his room and there was no forensic evidence linking Michael to the crime.

- The pathologist gave cause of death as a fractured skull and shock. He observed that both lungs were congested, but did not state that this is consistent with asphyxiation, indicating strangulation.

- Michael was a person of previous good character. It is unlikely he had any previous experience of being interrogated and it is unclear if he had access to a solicitor. At trial, he admitted lying to the police but said this was because he was covering up his affair with Olive Raper and because he was frightened of the police. It is clear that he was relentlessly broken down during the interrogation and this left him open to manipulation. The authors have the impression of a man who – like Stephen Downing and Anthony Steel – collapsed under the weight of aggressive questioning. This must leave some doubt about the reliability of his statements after the interrogation.

- Michael's remarks that 'something snapped, she just provoked me' are not a confession to murder. It is entirely consistent with him feeling angry at having had an argument with Mrs Raper over her having gone off with another man. Then being humiliated again by being ridiculed by another woman for failing to achieve an erection.

- Michael may not have been taken back to the crime scene. If this is so, it is uncertain if the bushes he was referring to are the same bushes where Stephanie's body was found.

- Three witnesses reported seeing Stephanie alive on the Friday evening, after the time the police said she was dead. One witness who knew Stephanie said he saw her buying cigarettes and ice cream at 8.00pm on Friday. Another said he saw Stephanie at 9.00pm on the Friday, distressed and crying. A third witness said she saw Stephanie at about 7.30pm on the Friday. The jury rejected these claims on the basis that they were contrary to the time of death identified by the pathologist. The authors concur with this conclusion, but would add that the pathologist's report is only a medical opinion and no one is infallible. It is just possible that she was still alive after the estimated time of death.

- A fourth witness said that on the Friday and Saturday afternoon she had been playing with her sons, building a den in the bushes where Stephanie's body was found and it could not have been there at that time unless it was well concealed. Again, the jury rejected this and the authors concur with their view. The body was concealed in a thicket and fly larvae had been laid on the Saturday. But it is just possible it could have been put there after having been left in another place, possibly in one of the lorries in the car and lorry park.
- The man with Blood Group O who had sex with Stephanie on the evening of her death was never identified.
- The second suspect – the man seen talking with Stephanie outside the nightclub – was never traced.
- The third suspect – the man seen arguing with Stephanie who featured in the photofit – was never traced.
- The trial judge, Mr Justice Boreham, misdirected the jury by emphasising that it must have taken the 'fiendish strength' of an angry man to wield an eight-pound rock with enough strength to inflict this injury. Michael was a labourer and probably quite strong. He had already admitted to being angry over his humiliation, so Mr Justice Boreham's remarks essentially singled him out as the murderer. In fact, there is no basis to Mr Justice Boreham's assertions, and as a judge, he was not competent to make them. An experiment by Tim, who is five-foot eleven-inches tall and lightly built, demonstrated that while calm, he could wield a four-kilo weight with sufficient force to inflict a fatal blow to the back of a skull. The impact of the blow would be improved by using a two-handed grip, adopting a strong 'combat' stance with the left foot and weight forward. Stephanie was five-foot six-inches tall. Any superiority in height between the assailant and the victim would also increase the lethality of the blow since the weapon would gain momentum as it travelled further along its path.
- Mr Justice Boreham further misdirected the jury by stating that the fact that all the evidence was circumstantial as irrelevant. He said that: 'For

153

eyewitnesses can be mistaken and they may even be untruthful, although proven fact and circumstance do not lie.' This caused the jury to give greater credence to an entirely circumstantial case than it should have done and to ignore the lack of any forensic evidence.

Michael had lied to the police, was an unemployed labourer having an affair with a married woman, and had tried to be intimate with the victim. This created a poor impression with the jury. This, coupled with Mr Justice Boreham's prejudicial remarks and Michael's statement that 'something snapped, she just provoked me' ensured his conviction. Even though there was more than enough ambiguity in the prosecution case to cause a reasonable doubt and to ensure his acquittal.

Turning to the question of who murdered Stephanie, there are five suspects. Three of them were never identified; Suspect Four – Michael – was convicted. However, because Stephanie's murder was recorded as solved before Sutcliffe was arrested, Suspect Five – Sutcliffe – has never been considered in any antecedent investigation. Concerning the three unidentified suspects:

- The authors believe that Stephanie was promiscuous and had casual sex with a man of Blood Group O before her death. The authors agree with the prosecution's opinion that there is no evidence linking him to the crime and Suspect One can be eliminated.
- The other two suspects seen talking with Stephanie outside Flamingos and then on Borough Road both bear a striking resemblance to Sutcliffe, but not to Michael. The authors believe that both sightings were of Sutcliffe, who is Suspect Two and Three.

Concerning Suspect Five – Sutcliffe – Stephanie's murder has all the classic indicators of one of his attacks:

- Serial killers operate in areas they are familiar with and comfortable operating in. Sutcliffe's work routinely took him to Sunderland, Darlington and Newton Aycliffe.

- The deposition site was next to a lorry park that Sutcliffe had probably used. His car or lorry may have been parked there.
- On the night of Stephanie's murder, Sutcliffe was staying in bed-and-breakfast accommodation at 98 Victoria Road, Darlington. This is one minute's walk from Flamingos and ten minutes' walk from the lorry park.
- After Sutcliffe's arrest in 1981, a doorman at Flamingos recognised him from his photograph. He confirmed that Sutcliffe had visited the club regularly and was in the club on the night Stephanie was murdered.
- Stephanie was not a sex worker but she was promiscuous, and this fitted with Sutcliffe's victim preferences. He may have used Flamingos to pre-select victims, as he did with the Belle Vue and The Gaiety.
- A man fitting Sutcliffe's description was seen talking with Stephanie outside the nightclub. It could have been Sutcliffe propositioning Stephanie to have sex with him or offering her a lift home.
- A man fitting Sutcliffe's description was seen arguing with Stephanie on Borough Road.
- Sutcliffe looks like the photofit of the suspect issued by the police shown as Illustration 4, which should be compared to the 1977/78 photograph of him (Illustration 6).
- Stephanie was killed by a blow to the head with a blunt instrument.
- As in the attacks on Jean Jordan, Yvonne Pearson and Marguerite Walls, Stephanie was punched.
- Stephanie may have been strangled, possibly with a garrotte.
- Stephanie was then moved, while alive but insensible, to a secondary crime scene in a secluded spot in the bushes.
- The lower portion of Stephanie's body was undressed to expose her genitalia and her clothes were strewn around.
- The victim's coat was thrown over her, as in the attacks on Wilma McCann, Emily Jackson, Irene Richardson, Vera Millward, Josephine Whitaker, Jackie Ansell-Lamb, Barbara Mayo and Marie Burke.
- The body was concealed.

Stephanie's murder contains all the classic indicators of an attack by Sutcliffe. The authors are therefore satisfied that Sutcliffe is a very strong suspect for the murder of Stephanie Spencer and a far stronger suspect than Michael Hodgson.

Sutcliffe enjoyed driving and travelled widely. Darlington is about one-and-a-half hours' drive from Bradford. At this time, Sutcliffe was varying his area of operation to evade police surveillance, by operating in areas he was not believed to offend in. Sutcliffe delivered to Coles Cranes, in Darlington, less than forty-eight hours after Stephanie's body was found. He may have been in Darlington in the course of a delivery for Clarks Transport with his lorry parked in the lorry park. Or he may have gone to Darlington on a 'run out' in his car. The authors believe he chose Darlington to commit his next murder, intending to select his victim at Flamingos. Hence the choice of accommodation nearby.

He identified Stephanie as his target and tried to engage her in conversation. The authors believe Sutcliffe is the suspect seen talking with Stephanie outside the Flamingo nightclub and then arguing with her in Borough Road. Stephanie rejected him, so he walked on quickly to the lorry park, intending to intercept and attack her there – as with the attack on Olive Smelt.

At this point, Michael started walking with Stephanie along Borough Road. He was more successful in persuading her to have sex with him. However, when he failed to get an erection, he walked off, angry and humiliated, leaving Stephanie alive by the bushes. Sutcliffe then emerged and attacked Stephanie. Because he had been to the disco, he did not have a hammer or knife with him. So he armed himself with a rock from the pathway, came up behind her and bashed in the back of her skull with one blow. He then dragged her and the rock to the thicket, ripped at her clothes and tights, scattered her clothes and posed the body. He did not mutilate Stephanie's body because he did not have a knife or screwdriver. Sutcliffe then walked back to 98 Victoria Road and let himself in with his late key.

His Honour Mr Justice Boreham presided over the trial which wrongfully convicted Anthony Steel of the murder of Carol Wilkinson, which the authors believe was also committed by Sutcliffe. He later presided over Sutcliffe's trial in May 1981, while James Chadwin QC defended him.

According to media reports, Mr Chadwin believed that the Stephanie Spencer case should be reopened. The authors concur with his view.

Diagram 4 - Murder of Stephanie Spencer

No	Name
V	Stephanie's home
W	Bed-and-breakfast where Sutcliffe stayed
Z	Michael's home
41	Crime scene

Map 11 – The North East Cluster 1975 - 1980

No	Name	Date	Cluster(s)	Route Package
I	Bradford: Clarks Transport (attacks using a lorry), 44 Tanton Crescent and 6 Garden Lane (attacks using a car).			
41	Stephanie Spencer	29/05/77	North East	5.1. Bradford-Darlington/ Newton Aycliffe
49D	Child A and Child B Deposition site	1977/78	Abduction Central Deposition North East	6.1. London/ South East-Bradford/ Sunderland Docks
58	Harrogate schoolgirl	17/02/79	Apex, North East	N/A
61A	'Hope' Abduction	Aug 1979	North East	5.2. Bradford-Scarborough

No	Name	Date	Cluster(s)	Route Package
61D	'Hope' Deposition	Aug 1979	North East	5.3. Scarborough-Darlington 5.4. Scarborough-Sunderland Docks
66	Yvonne Mysliwiec	11/10/79	North East, North West	5.1. Bradford-Darlington/ Newton Aycliffe, 5.2. Bradford-Scarborough, 5.5. Bradford-Sunderland Docks, 7.1. Bradford to Peterhead Western Route, 7.2. Bradford to Peterhead Eastern Route, 8.1 Bradford to Motherwell
72	Woman A and Woman B	June 1980	North East	5.2. Bradford-Scarborough

In June 1977, Chief Constable Gregory appointed ACC Oldfield to lead the Ripper investigation, a role for which he would become known nationally and which would destroy him.

Sonia Sutcliffe was approaching the end of her training and was confident that she would get a job before the summer so they would be able to buy their own home. On Saturday 25 June 1977, they viewed 6 Garden Lane, Heaton, Bradford.

42. Jayne MacDonald (Convicted)

Following the house viewing, Sutcliffe dropped Sonia off at the nursing home for her night shift. He then went on a pub crawl in his white Ford Corsair with his neighbours Ronnie and David Barker in Bradford. It was well past midnight when Sutcliffe dropped the brothers home, but instead of going home himself, he drove to Chapeltown.

Jayne MacDonald, aged sixteen years, had been out dancing. She had missed the last bus home and started walking home just before midnight with a young man she had met that evening. He promised to organise her a lift with his sister when they got to his home, but the sister wasn't there so they went their separate ways. As she walked home, she passed an adventure playground, where Sutcliffe struck her on the back of her head with his hammer and dragged her lifeless body twenty yards into the playground. Then he hit her twice more, stabbed her in the back and then repeatedly in the chest.

Two children found Jayne's body on the Sunday morning inside the playground. She was lying face down; her skirt was disarranged and her white halter-neck top was pulled up to expose her breasts.

Jayne's father died of a broken heart two years later.

Newspaper headlines the following day stated that 'an innocent young woman has been slaughtered'. This concern was missing when sex workers were murdered, reflecting the underlying attitude of the police and the public that sex workers were not innocent, and violence was an inevitable consequence of their chosen lifestyle.

WYMP recognised that Jayne had been murdered by the same man who had murdered Wilma McCann, Emily Jackson, Irene Richardson and Patricia Atkinson. But because they had not linked the attacks on Tracy Browne, Anna Rogulskyj, Bernadette Cassidy, Olive Smelt and Marcella Claxton, vital evidence of a description of a man with a local accent, with dark hair, beard and moustache, and the vehicles he used, was overlooked.

Jayne was not a sex workers and was killed in an area unconnected to the vice trade. Nevertheless, WYMP could not abandon its obsession that their man only attacked sex workers, and issued a statement saying that Jayne had been mistaken for a prostitute (MPoF).

43. First attack on Maureen Long
(Convicted)

On Saturday 9 July 1977, Maureen Long from Farsley near Leeds went for a night out in Bradford.

Maureen was promiscuous and drank heavily, making her an easy target. At the end of the evening Maureen was drunk and walking to a taxi rank when she accepted a lift home from Sutcliffe. They talked in the car and she propositioned him for sex, directing him to Bowling Back Lane, which was a place she used for that purpose. When they arrived, she got out of the car and squatted down to urinate. Sutcliffe struck her with a massive blow to the back of her head. As she lay on the ground, he pulled down her underwear and stabbed her in the chest, abdomen and back.

A nightwatchman was checking nearby premises at 3.27am when his dog started barking. Disturbed, Sutcliffe fled, leaving Maureen for dead. Women from a nearby travellers' camp heard Maureen's cries the following morning. She should have died from her terrible injuries, but was tough and survived after major neurological surgery. When she was interviewed by detectives, she was unable to describe her attacker or his vehicle.

The watchman described the car as a white Ford Cortina Mark II with a black roof, although it was actually Sutcliffe's white Corsair.

A fingertip search of the scene found a partial bloody palm print on a piece of ceramic sink. This was one of the few times Sutcliffe left forensic evidence behind.

In July 1977, WYMP took the decision to close down the tyre-track enquiry because it could no longer resource it. Sutcliffe's white Corsair was one of the 20,000 vehicles still unchecked. This removed a major piece of hard evidence from the investigation (MPoF) which, if pursued, would have led to Sutcliffe's arrest in November 1977.

The nightwatchman's account of a white Cortina was reported in the press. Sutcliffe would have known that the police would be aware of the similarity of a Corsair to a Cortina and that this may have made it more likely that he would be stopped and questioned. This may explain why he sold the white Corsair to Ronnie Barker on 3 September 1977. It broke down a week later, so Sutcliffe bought it back. Sutcliffe should have notified the DVLA that he had re-purchased the white Corsair, but did not. Leaving him in possession of a vehicle registered to Ronnie Barker from September 1977 onwards. This would allow him to use this vehicle to cruise RLDs without being recorded as a regular punter by police observations.

Sonia began her first teaching position in September 1977. On 26 September 1977, the Sutcliffes moved into 6 Garden Lane. Things were looking up for the pair, who were perceived as being a happily married, successful and upwardly mobile middle-class couple.

44. Elizabeth Parravicini
See 26 Eve Stratford

45. Jean Jordan
(Convicted)
On Friday 30 September 1977, Sutcliffe collected his pay packet, which contained brand new £5 notes. The next day he drove to Manchester, which had three RLDs: Cheetham Hill in the north of the city, Whalley Range and Moss Side in the south. At 9.30pm he gave £5 to Jean Jordan in return for sex at the Moss Side RLD. Jean put the note in a pocket in her handbag. They then drove to some allotments she had suggested.

Once out of the car, Sutcliffe hit her head a total of thirteen times with a hammer left by the previous owner in the garage of 6 Garden Lane. He smashed Jean's skull like an egg. Other cars, conveying sex workers and their clients, started arriving, so Sutcliffe pulled Jean's body to bushes near the perimeter fence. Realising the chances of discovery were high, he waited calmly for the vehicles to leave, got into the Corsair, and drove home.

En route he remembered that he had not retrieved the brand new £5 note from Jean's handbag. When detectives found the body, they would know that £5 was the standard fee for sex and conclude that the note had come from one of Jean's clients; probably the one who had murdered her. They would then use the serial number to trace it back to the notes issued to him by Clarks Transport.

Sutcliffe returned home and quickly spent the remaining £5 notes, so he had none in the same numbered sequence in his possession. By 9 October there had still been no mention in the papers of the discovery of Jean's body, but Sutcliffe was still worried that the £5 note would be traced back to him. That night, the Sutcliffes had a housewarming party. He drove his parents home around midnight, whilst Sonia went to bed. After dropping them off, Sutcliffe returned to the allotments where Jean's body still lay concealed.

Sutcliffe searched frantically for Jean's handbag without success. Enraged, he dragged Jean's body out of concealment and tore the clothes off her body until it was naked. He searched her clothes, and when he could not find the note, he vented his frustration, fear and anger on Jean's corpse. He stabbed her breasts, chest, stomach and vagina eighteen times, using a knife and a large shard of glass taken from a nearby greenhouse.

They were fierce, deep slashing swipes that caused her stomach to blow open, which made him vomit. But he continued and attempted to decapitate Jean's body with a hacksaw he had brought from the garage and the piece of glass, chosen because they had not featured in Ripper attacks before. His intention was to ensure this killing would not be associated with a Ripper attack and lead

GMP to Yorkshire. He couldn't decapitate Jean's body with these tools, so he gave up and returned home.

The next day, Jean's body was discovered by Bruce Jones, who had an allotment where Jean had been murdered. Bruce was later to become a successful actor, best known for his role as Les Battersby in Coronation Street. He discovered the horrific sight of her decomposing, disembowelled and partially decapitated body and called the police.

Although Bruce had behaved responsibly and had called the police with the best of intentions, he was immediately treated as a suspect, put in a police van and taken to a police station. GMP did not inform his wife where he was for twelve hours and interrogated him pitilessly before clearing him and releasing him.

Bruce was so badly affected by the sight of Jean's body and the treatment he received from GMP that he did not work for a year, his marriage collapsed and he lost his children. The experience contributed to the depression and nightmares he suffered for years afterwards. Many witnesses to Sutcliffe's crimes or the aftermath of them, as well as the 494 men who became suspects over the course of the enquiry, received similar treatment and may have been similarly affected. They are also victims of Sutcliffe.

On 15 October, Jean's handbag was found 189 feet from where her body was discovered. The new £5 note, no. AW51 121565, was found in the pocket. The GMP detectives realised that the handbag had been searched and concluded correctly that Jean's murderer had tried to retrieve the £5 note to prevent it from being traced to him. This led to what became the first £5-note enquiry to trace the note back to Jean's murderer.

The note had been sent to the Shipley branch of the Midland Bank, which had distributed it to local firms to make up the weekly pay packets for about 5,943 employees. The underlying analysis of the distribution was not as sophisticated as it should have been (MPoF). Nevertheless, all the men who'd received these notes were traced and interviewed by a joint force of GMP and WYMP detectives.

INTERVIEW 1: 2 NOVEMBER 1977

Sutcliffe was interviewed at home by two detectives. They asked him if he had any of the £5 notes from his wage packet left and he told them he did not.

They asked Sutcliffe where he had been on the first and ninth of October. He told them he had been at home on both days and had been at the housewarming party on the ninth. This was corroborated by Sonia. Neither of them volunteered the information that he had driven his parents back to Bingley at midnight and returned home after Sonia was asleep. So Sutcliffe's movements on both nights were only alibied by his wife. This should have caused more enquiries but none were made (MPoF).

Neither officer enquired where Sutcliffe had been on the dates of the other Ripper attacks (MPoF).

Prior to the interview, the detectives should have run a trace on Sutcliffe with the DVLA to identify his vehicle ownership. This would have revealed that a red Corsair was registered to him and he had just sold a white Corsair. They should have enquired about the white Corsair and examined it, but did not (MPoF).

They reported that Sutcliffe had an alibi for 9 October and did not own a vehicle, and he was eliminated (MPoF).

The tyre investigation had been closed down in July 1977. Had it still been in operation, they would have had to complete an index card on the white Corsair. This would have forced them to question Sutcliffe on the car's whereabouts and examine it, which in turn would have shown the matching tyres and led immediately to Sutcliffe's arrest.

Both the first £5-note investigation and the tyre-tracking investigation had been spectacularly successful and had led detectives to the killer. However, Sutcliffe escaped because both detectives were not sufficiently diligent in testing his alibi and they did not check Sutcliffe's vehicles. These failings rendered the massive effort put into both lines of enquiry useless (MPoF). The first £5-note enquiry was closed in January 1978.

46. Carol Wilkinson Part 1

On Monday 10 October 1977 – the same day that Sutcliffe had mutilated Jean Jordan's body – twenty-year-old Carol Wilkinson was attacked between 9.00am and 9.30am. She had been walking to work from her home at 131 Ranelagh Avenue, Bradford, along a secluded lane through a field at the back of her workplace in Gain Lane.

Carol died from multiple skull fractures and severe brain damage two days later without regaining consciousness. Pathologist Professor David Gee concluded that the injuries could not be inflicted with a ball pein hammer and the murder weapon was a fifty-six-pound coping stone. Carol was eliminated as a Ripper victim because she was not a sex worker, a hammer was not used, the attack occurred in the morning, not at night, and the body was not mutilated.

A stone of that weight cannot be lifted high enough to bring sufficient force to bear on the back of the head of a five-foot-tall woman. The authors believe Carol had fallen onto the coping stone after the fatal blow had been struck, leaving blood and hair on it, leading to Professor Gee's erroneous conclusion. Carol had the same skull fractures as Yvonne Pearson and Judith Roberts. Sutcliffe admitted in his confession that he had attacked Yvonne using a heavy walling hammer, not his lighter ball pein hammer.

INTERVIEW 2: 8 NOVEMBER 1977

Detectives interviewed Sutcliffe because his white Ford Corsair had been spotted thirty-six times in three different RLDs. His response was that driving to and from home and work took him through those areas. This was a credible response for the sightings in Manningham but did not explain the sightings in Chapeltown or Huddersfield. This should have resulted in further enquiries, particularly given his facial resemblance to the photofits, gap in the teeth and his occupation as a lorry driver. Nevertheless, he was cleared (MPoF).

47. Doncaster Sex Worker
See 38 Barbara Young

48. Marilyn Moore
(Convicted)

On the evening of Wednesday 14 December 1977 at around 8.00pm, Marilyn Moore, a twenty-five-year-old Leeds sex worker, was walking to her 'beat' in Frankland Place, Leeds. She saw Sutcliffe's red Corsair, which she had seen kerb crawling previously. Sutcliffe and Marilyn agreed a price and she got into the car. Sutcliffe drove to Buslingthorpe Lane to have sex on the back seat. When Marilyn got out, she found the rear door was locked. This was a standard ploy Sutcliffe used to get his victim out of the car, but to prevent her re-entering, so his victim was outside the car when he attacked and the vehicle interior was never fouled with blood.

Sutcliffe came up behind Marilyn on the pretext of opening the door and struck the top of her head a massive blow with a hammer. She screamed loudly, and as she fell to the ground, he hit her with another seven blows before she lost consciousness. Marilyn's screams had started a dog barking. So Sutcliffe followed his standard procedure of leaving at the first risk of discovery and fled without finishing Marilyn off. She remembered him walking back to the car and driving off at speed, the rear wheels skidding.

Marilyn began to stumble towards a telephone kiosk but a couple saw her and called an ambulance. She was rushed to Leeds General Infirmary. She gave a description of a white man, aged about thirty years, stocky build, around five-foot six-inches tall, dark wavy hair and a 'Jason King' moustache (Jason King, played by moustachioed Peter Wyngarde, was the eponymous protagonist of a popular TV series), wearing a yellow shirt, a navy blue/black zip-up anorak and blue jeans, and that he had a soft local accent. Marilyn compiled two photofits. The second one, issued in early 1978, was an excellent likeness of Sutcliffe and is shown as Illustration 5. It should be compared to the 1977/78 photograph of Sutcliffe (Illustration 7) and Illustration 9.

She also identified the car as maroon, about the size of a Morris Oxford, and that it had four doors and two rear-view mirrors. Although the car was red, in every other way this was very accurate information. However, because of the extent of Marilyn's injuries, the police concluded her evidence was unreliable and disregarded it (MPoF).

When Marilyn Moore's photofit of her attacker was published, Tracy Browne recognised it instantly as the man who had attacked her two years earlier. Her mother took her to Keighley Police Station and explained that Tracy had been attacked by the same man. The PC at the front desk dismissed them, saying, 'We're all having fun and games today, aren't we?' Had Tracy been listened to, the attacks on Olive Smelt and Anna Rogulskyj would have been identified as part of the series and the police would have had a survivor that could corroborate that the Marilyn Moore photofit was completely accurate (MPoF).

Tracy was subsequently interviewed by ACC Oldfield, who played the Humble hoax tape (see below) to her. When she stated forthrightly that the man who attacked her had a local accent and was not the man on the tape with a Geordie accent, she was again wrongly eliminated as a Ripper victim (MPoF).

The impressions of the tyre tracks left at the scene showed the same rear track width of between four-foot one-and-a-half inches and four-foot two-and-a-half inches, and that the front tyres were two India Autoway tyres: the same type as were found at the Irene Richardson crime scene. But the rear offside had changed from a Pneumant to an India Autoway and the rear nearside had changed from an Esso 110 to an Avon Super. The investigation team concluded that the Ripper was using the same car, but had changed the rear tyres.

In fact, Sutcliffe had changed cars from a white Corsair to a red Corsair and taken the best two India Autoway tyres from the white Corsair and put them on the front of the red Corsair. This would indicate that the white Corsair was immobile. Sutcliffe stated that it was never returned to roadworthy condition and he used it for spare parts for the red Corsair PHE 355 G he bought in September 1977, then sold it for scrap. Had Sutcliffe sold the car for scrap, the scrap merchant would have notified the DVLA of the purchase and the scrapping, so the road tax could be transferred and cancelled. This did not happen. There is no evidence that the white Corsair was ever scrapped, and to this day, no one knows what happened to it. Chief Constable Byford commented:

> Although the records show that Sutcliffe sold his white Corsair KWT721D on 3 September 1977 it is now known that he retained possession of it for some time after that date.

Sutcliffe enjoyed working on cars and normally had two or three at any one time. If the white Corsair was indeed stripped down for spare parts, it should have been immobile and parked on the drive, outside the house or in the garage. Yet neither detective saw it when they interviewed Sutcliffe on 2 November 1977. Sutcliffe was a very capable mechanic who could have returned it to working order and parked it somewhere else, possibly in a rented lock-up garage. Which would explain why the detectives did not see it.

The authors believe that having transferred two tyres from the white Corsair onto the red Corsair in December 1977, he subsequently put two tyres on the white Corsair, probably obtained from a scrapyard. He then used it as transport when he murdered Carol Wilkinson on 10 October 1977, and Lynda Farrow in London on 19 January 1979, thirteen months after the tyre change. Unfortunately, it was misidentified as a Cortina.

49. Child A and Child B

Child A lived in Fulham, London, and was aged thirteen or fourteen in 1977 or 1978 when she and her friend, Child B, also fourteen, ran away from home.

They went to the roundabout at Hammersmith at midday to hitchhike out of London. Child A has confirmed that Sutcliffe stopped in his lorry, chatted to them for a short while and they accepted a lift to Sunderland.

Child A is certain the driver was Sutcliffe, stating that:

> When Sutcliffe was arrested, I saw the photograph of Peter Sutcliffe and said, 'That's the man. He looks like him.' It was the big black eyes that stood out to me, the black hair and the thick bushy sideburns.

Other details, including her descriptions of the lorry, Sutcliffe and his accent, have verified that her recollection is accurate. Illustration 7 shows Sutcliffe in the cab of the lorry he used to abduct Child A. He has sideburns, exactly as Child A described. He was probably driving through London after a delivery to the South Coast or to South London.

Child A sat next to the door; Child B sat in the middle next to Sutcliffe. They instantly sensed that they were in grave danger. Child A admitted she was terrified. Sutcliffe drove non-stop towards Sunderland, stopping once to get out of the cab to urinate. He then returned and started driving while 'looking again at us both very eerily'. When they were in Sunderland she asked Sutcliffe to drop them off. He left them in an open area near parked cars in the early hours of the morning.

They found a car that happened to be left open and slept there until the morning. They then tried to claim unemployment benefit. Fortunately, the staff at the unemployment office called the police. Northumbria Police took them to Sunderland Police Station and questioned them about what they had been doing in Sunderland and if they had been involved in crime there. Northumbria Police contacted their parents, who collected both girls.

1. Peter Sutcliffe, around 1964, in Bingley Cemetery.

2. Sutcliffe's arrest photograph, 1969.

3. Photofit of Bernadette Cassidy's attacker, 1972 (Case 17).

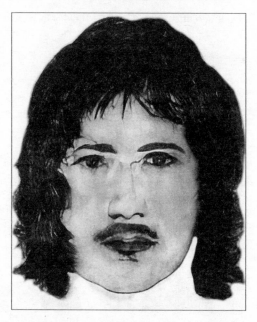

4. Photofit of Stephanie Spencer's attacker, 1977 (Case 41).

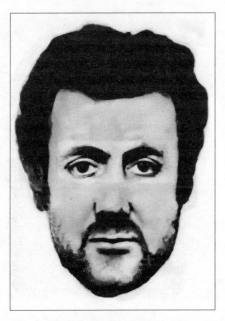

5. Marilyn Moore's second photofit of her attacker, 1977 (Case 48).

6. Sutcliffe in about 1978.

7. Sutcliffe in his Clark's Transport lorry in 1977 or 1978.

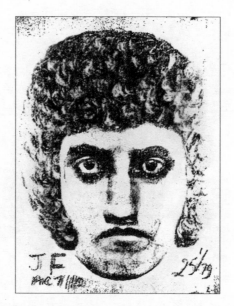

8. Photofit of the clean-shaven suspect seen running from the murder of Lynda Farrow, 1979 (Case 57).

9. Photofit of Lynda Farrow's attacker (Case 57), with a beard superimposed.

10. Photofit of Josephine Whitaker's attacker, 1979 (Case 60).

11. Sutcliffe's arrest photograph, 1981.

'stributions: 1. L.E.Lamont
                2. D.H.Gerty
                3. R.Harvey
                4. A.K.Sloan
             ✗. S.S.Kind
                6. Spare

What Factors suggest that x is a Local Man?

1. He uses a car, probably an old type, with worn crossply tyres.
    Hardly the car for a long distance driver.

2. The centre of gravity of the incidents, weighted and unweighted,
    tends to be near Bradford.

3. Time of offence correlates well with day length but the late
    "fliers" tend to be in Leeds and Bradford.

4. Very good local knowledge.

5. The good description given by the victim Moore does not mention a
    marked accent, so x probably has a local accent.

6. A five-pound note was issued in Manningham or Shipley (Jordan case
    in Manchester).

Hypothesis 1   x lives in or near Bradford, possibly in the Manningham
                    or Shipley area.

Hypothesis 2   x selects target towns which are different from the
                    previous two incidents.

Hypothesis 3   x goes out and if unsuccessful in finding a victim in
                    the target town, he looks for one on the way home. It
                    follows that...

Hypothesis 4   The next incident is unlikely to be in Leeds and, on the
                    principle of maximum variety, it is likely to be in
                    Huddersfield or Manchester or, in default, Bradford.

Hypothesis 5   Consideration should be given, should a woman be found
                    in any of these locations suffering from head wounds, to
                    maximum police coverage in Bradford, particularly in the
                    Manningham/Shipley area. Obviously, for maximum
                    likelihood of success, a Manchester incident would give
                    most opportunity for the deployment of police effort.

Note: The purpose in producing this document at this stage is to attempt
to record how the situation looks to me on a broad basis and before it
becomes fogged in my mind by detail. In no way should it be taken to
pre-empt any joint report by the group, formal or informal.

                                                    S.S.Kind
                                                    Wednesday
                                                    10th December 1980

12. The Consultative Committee report which identified that the Ripper lived
in Manningham or Shipley.

13. Typical media criticism of the failure of the Yorkshire Ripper investigation.

Ripper's unknown victims

By John Twomey

He may have killed more than 13, says secret report

YORKSHIRE Ripper Peter Sutcliffe may have murdered more women than the 13 he confessed to killing, a secret report revealed.

Sutcliffe - 60 today - almost certainly attacked other lone women but has kept silent about the full extent of his crimes for a quarter of a century.

The "unexplained lull" in his activities from 1969 to 1975 was identified in a confidential inquiry headed by Sir Lawrence Byford into the bungled police investigation.

Sir Lawrence's 1981 report - minus censored sections - was published by the Home Office yesterday after 25 years under wraps. Apart from expressing fears about the full horror of Sutcliffe's crimes, Sir Lawrence said: "We feel it is highly improbable that the crimes in respect of which Sutcliffe has been charged and convicted are the only ones attributable to him.

"This feeling is reinforced by examining the details of a number of assaults on women since 1969 which, in some ways, clearly fall into the established pattern of Sutcliffe's overall modus-operandi."

Sir Lawrence details a list of mistakes by detectives who missed several chances to cut short the Ripper's reign of terror He highlights a "vital error" which gave Sutcliffe the opportunity to commit a further seven murders

Cracked

The tyres would have linked him to third murder victim Irene Richardson nine months earlier.

This gave Sutcliffe the opportunity to commit a further seven murders before his arrest in January 1981, the report said.

Sir Lawrence, a former Inspector of Constabulary, praised hard-working constables and sergeants who eventually cracked the case despite blunders by their superiors. Lorry driver Sutcliffe admitted 13 murders of women - some of them pros-

titutes - in northern towns between October 1975, and November 1980.

He also confessed to attempting to murder seven others and was given 20 life sentences at the Old Bailey in May 1981.

Sir Lawrence said in his report to the then Home Secretary William Whitelaw: "It is my firm conclusion that between 1969 and 1980 Sutcliffe was probably responsible for many attacks on unaccompanied women, which he has not yet admitted, not only in the West Yorkshire and Manchester areas but also in other parts of the country."

Time and time again, failures by police to link vital clues to Sutcliffe allowed him to roam free.

One glaring example of incompetence was the treatment of major witness Trevor Birdsall, a friend of Sutcliffe's since 1966.

Mr Birdsall sent an anonymous letter to police in November 1980, naming Sutcliffe as the Ripper. An officer marked it "Priority No1" and

SUTCLIFFE: Twenty life sentences

it was discovered that Sutcliffe was the subject of three separate index cards in the incident room records.

But "for some inexplicable reason", papers on Mr Birdsall were left to gather dust in a filing tray for a month before Sutcliffe was arrested.

A £5 note found in the handbag of sixth victim Jean Jordan was traced to wages paid to one of 241 people - one of them Sutcliffe. The names were cross-checked to suspects in incident room files. But Sutcliffe -

who featured prominently in the files - was not picked out and the connection was missed.

The single biggest mistake was when officers were taken in by the tape and letters sent to Assistant Chief Constable George Oldfield by "Wearside Jack", who convinced Oldfield that he was the Ripper.

Yorkshireman Sutcliffe was ruled out because he did not speak with a North-east accent, though surviving victims said their attacker was neither a Geordie or Wearsider.

Sutcliffe went on to claim the lives of his last three victims - Barbara Leach, Marguerite Walls and Jacqueline Hill He later said of Humble's hoax: "While that was going on, I felt safe."

He was finally unmasked as the Ripper after he was arrested in January 1981 in Sheffield, for suspected theft. He was with a prostitute who would have undoubtedly become another victim.

A hammer and two knives - the Ripper's trademark weapons - were later found and Sutcliffe confessed.

"Wearside Jack" - unemployed alcoholic John Humble, now 50 - was eventually identified by DNA from the saliva on an envelope.

He was jailed for eight years last June after admitting perverting the course of justice.

14. *Daily Express*, 2 June 2006: 'Ripper's unknown victims'.

Judges reject appeal plea

Ripper's help sought on death riddles

By ROGER CROSS

A NUMBER of police forces want to interview Peter Sutcliffe, the Yorkshire Ripper, about unsolved murders and attacks, some dating back more than ten years.

The queue is expected to form following yesterday's rejection at the Court of Appeal of Sutcliffe's application to appeal against his conviction at the Old Bailey last year.

If unofficial police inquiries already made are followed up then more than 20 attacks would be involved.

They cover crimes in Scotland, Derbyshire, Lancashire and South Yorkshire, as well as West Yorkshire.

The Court of Appeal held yesterday that the judge at the trial of Sutcliffe, 36, was right to refuse his pleas of guilty to manslaughter.

The Lord Chief Justice Lane, said that although doctors agreed that Sutcliffe — who claimed he had a divine mission to kill prostitutes — was suffering from paranoid schizophrenia, there was a suggestion that he was trying to hoodwink the doctors.

Mr. Justice Boreham was right to insist on a murder trial.

"It is of the greatest importance that trials are by juries and not by doctors," said Lord Lane.

There was nothing unsafe or unsatisfactory about the murder verdicts, he ruled.

Lord Lane said that it was urged generally on Sutcliffe's behalf that the verdicts were "against the weight of the evidence."

He said that was merely a reliable or usually successful ground of appeal, and it was not so in this case.

Sutcliffe, of Garden Lane, Heaton, Bradford, was jailed for life on May 22 last year after his conviction on 13 murder counts. He had admitted seven charges of attempted murder.

Sutcliffe's solicitor, Mr. Kerry MaGill, from the Bradford firm of Lumb and Kennington, said after yesterday's hearing that they were considering taking the case to the House of Lords, but "it would be inappropriate to comment further at this stage."

Unsolved murders Sutcliffe's name has been linked with as a possible suspect include two in the Glasgow area and that of hitch-hiker Barbara Mayo in Derbyshire 12 years ago.

But at the head of the queue will be the West Yorkshire Police, the force the bearded Bradford lorry driver marked indelibly during the ill-fated and often acrimonious murder hunt.

There are two attacks in particular that some West Yorkshire officers feel strikingly resemble the work of Sutcliffe, now held at Parkhurst Jail on the Isle of Wight.

There is the brutal attack on a 16-year-old schoolgirl, Caroline Brown, at Silsden, near Keighley, in August, 1975.

A photo-fit picture released by the police at the time strongly resembled Sutcliffe. Caroline's attacker had a moustache and beard, a frizzy hairstyle, staring eyes and a thin face.

Police said that the attacker suffered from hayfever, as does Sutcliffe.

Another attack in West Yorkshire under scrutiny was on 21-year-old reporter, Miss Yvonne Mysliwiec who

was battered over the head with a hammer-like instrument at Ilkley in October, 1979. She caught a glimpse of a bearded man before passing out.

South Yorkshire Police, the force which caught Sutcliffe, would like to interview him about two unsolved murders.

Mrs. Anne Marie Harold, 22, who was seven months pregnant, was battered and garrotted to death after shopping at Mexborough in September, 1980.

Her body was found hidden in a ditch outside the town 17 days later and detectives now recognise there are startling similarities with some of the Yorkshire Ripper attacks.

South Yorkshire detectives would also like to speak to Sutcliffe about the murder of a Doncaster prostitute, Mrs Barbara Ann Young.

But perhaps the most puzzling murder linked with Sutcliffe's name has been that of 26-year-old Barbara Mayo, a schoolteacher from Hammersmith, West London.

She was thumbing a lift to Yorkshire on the M1 to recover her boyfriend's car — it had broken down at Catterick — when she was last seen alive.

Her body was found at Ault Hucknall, Derbyshire, a mile from Exit 29, in October, 1970. She had been strangled and beaten about the head.

Later that year police said they wanted to interview each of the 100,000 owners of Morris 1000 Travellers after witnesses said Barbara had been picked up in one.

Sutcliffe used to drive a Morris Minor when he went to London regularly to visit his future wife at college there.

Sutcliffe is entitled to refuse to be interviewed about the unsolved crimes.

Mr. MaGill said: "We will resist that bridge if and when we come to it. I can't say how my client would react to such a request."

Even if Sutcliffe was to confess to other murders or attacks no charges would follow. An admission would simply allow those involved to announce that a certain file had been "closed."

15. *Yorkshire Evening Post*, 26 May 1982: 'Ripper's help sought on death riddles'.

Sampson's 'more crime' theory

Police chief points finger at Ripper

THE Chief Constable of West Yorkshire told a public meeting he thinks the Yorkshire Ripper may be guilty of more crimes than the 20 for which he was jailed.

Mr Colin Sampson made his comments at a public forum on police affairs. They were later explained by his Press office as having been made "off the cuff".

Though it has often been speculated that the Ripper, Peter Sutcliffe, was responsible for a number of unsolved attacks, it is the first time Mr Sampson or anyone of such senior rank has put forward such a view publicly.

Mr Sampson hinted to the police community forum, held in Holmfirth, near Huddersfield, that he was prepared to play a waiting game to find out whether Sutcliffe carried endless further crimes.

Sutcliffe was convicted of 13 murders and seven attempted murders at the Old Bailey in 1981.

Some senior police officers have said that he was possibly also responsible for other attacks on women — both in Yorkshire and in other parts of Britain.

Mr Sampson told the forum that he was one of those people who happened to believe that there could be more victims.

In a reference to the Moors Murder inquiries, he said he was prepared to do what "police across the Pennines" had done — namely wait.

In 1982, while Sutcliffe was imprisoned in Parkhurst Prison, on the Isle of Wight, he was questioned about other attacks on women.

The interviews were conducted by Mr Keith Hellawell, then a Chief Superintendent with West Yorkshire Police, and Det Insp John Boyle, whose interrogation of Sutcliffe at the time of his arrest brought the killer's initial confession.

Though Sutcliffe was said to have been "friendly and composed", the interviews are believed to have been inconclusive.

He was questioned particularly about an attack in 1975 on a 14-year-old schoolgirl, Caroline Brown, at Silsden, near Keighley, and the savage bludgeoning in 1979 of Miss Yvonne Mysliwiec, a journalist, at Ilkley.

It is believed he was also questioned by Derbyshire detectives about the murder in 1970 of a 24-year-old teacher, Barbara Mayo, who was last seen alive when she accepted a lift in a Morris Traveller similar to one Sutcliffe drove.

16. *Yorkshire Evening Post*, 15 October 1987: 'Police chief points finger at Ripper'.

Picking up two obviously underage girls in his employer's lorry and then taking them to the other end of the country was taking a huge risk. Sutcliffe clearly did not do this out of kindness. If he had been stopped by the police, he would have been charged with abducting two minors – a very serious charge. He obviously intended to do them harm. Nothing else justified taking this risk.

The authors believe he did not attack them in the cab because that would foul it with forensic evidence. When he pulled over to urinate, he was hoping that one of the girls would also leave the cab to relieve herself and he could attack her outside the cab, then drag the other girl out and kill her. Neither girl needed to relieve themselves and this is probably what saved them.

Both girls were interviewed by detectives, who would have observed that they were obviously underage, had been abducted by a lorry driver and then driven to the other end of the country. This should have caused them concern. They should have tried to identify the lorry driver by obtaining a description and photofit of him and circulating it to all forces. This should have led to enquiries about a flatbed lorry that had made a delivery from the London area to Sunderland and stayed overnight in a lorry park on the day the girls were dropped off. Given the likeness to the other Ripper victims' descriptions and that lorry driver was a suspect occupation, this would have come to the attention of the Ripper investigation, possibly leading to his arrest.

Instead, Northumbria Police confirmed the girls had not committed any crimes in their force area and did nothing more (MPoF). This failure to exchange information with other forces was prevalent in the police service at the time.

Child A's evidence confirms that Sutcliffe picked up hitchhikers, that he used his lorry to commit crime and that he attacked schoolgirls.

Map 12A - The South East Cluster 1970 – 1980 (1)

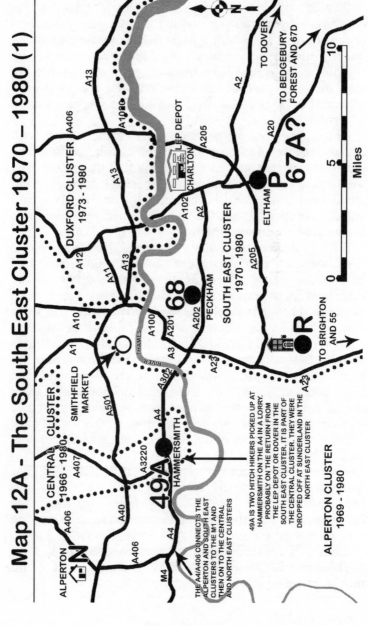

ALPERTON

CENTRAL CLUSTER
1966 - 1980

SMITHFIELD MARKET

DUXFORD CLUSTER
1973 - 1980

LEP DEPOT
CHARLTON

SOUTH EAST CLUSTER
1970 - 1980

PECKHAM
68

HAMMERSMITH
49A

RIVER THAMES

ELTHAM
67A?

TO DOVER

TO BEDGEBURY
FOREST AND 67D

TO BRIGHTON
AND 55

ALPERTON CLUSTER
1969 - 1980

49A IS TWO HITCH HIKERS PICKED UP AT
HAMMERSMITH ON THE A4 IN A LORRY.
PROBABLY ON THE RETURN FROM
THE LEP DEPOT OR DOVER IN THE
SOUTH EAST CLUSTER. IT IS PART OF
THE CENTRAL CLUSTER. THEY WERE
DROPPED OFF AT SUNDERLAND IN THE
NORTH EAST CLUSTER

THE A4/A406 CONNECTS THE
ALPERTON AND SOUTH EAST
CLUSTERS TO THE M1 AND
THEN ON TO THE CENTRAL
AND NORTH EAST CLUSTERS

Miles

0   5   10

N

180

Map 12B - The South East Cluster 1970 - 1980 (2)

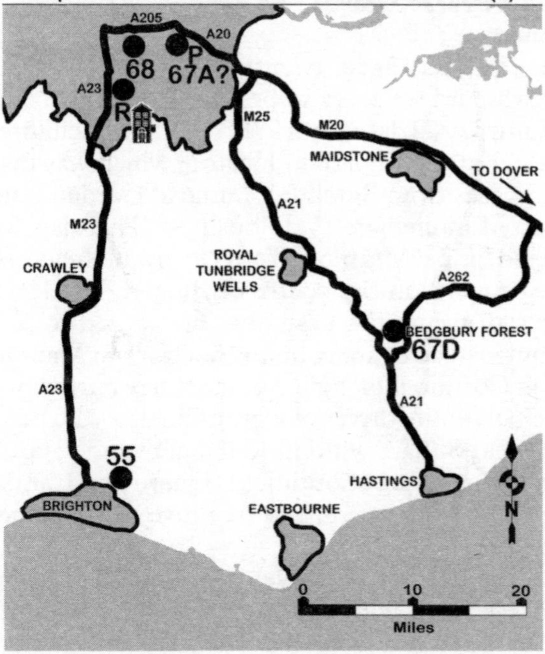

No	Name	Date	Cluster	Route Package
N	Marianne's home at Alperton			
P	Dutch House pub where Harry Pennells said he left 'Margaret'			
R	Conquering Hero pub			
49A	Child A and Child B	1977/1978	Central	6.1. London/South East to Bradford/ Sunderland Docks
55	Margaret Frame	12/10/78	South East	
67D	'Margaret' Deposition site	21/10/79	South East	6.1. London/South East to Bradford/ Sunderland Docks
68	Sally Shepherd	30/11/79	South East	6.2. Bradford-LEP Depot

50. Yvonne Pearson Part 1
(Convicted)

Yvonne Pearson, aged twenty-two years, was a single mother who did sex work to provide for her two children.

On Saturday 21 January 1978, she left her children with a babysitter at their home in Heaton, which was just a few hundred yards from Sutcliffe's home at Garden Lane, and went into Manningham to do business. That day, Sutcliffe had helped his parents move from Cornwall Road to a more suitable property in the centre of Bingley. He declined to stay for a drink on the basis that he wanted to return to Sonia, but instead of going home, he drove to Manningham in the red Corsair, looking for a victim. He narrowly missed a collision with the driver of a grey Cortina who pulled out of Southfield Square without looking. Yvonne approached him at the junction of Southfield Square and Lumb Lane, they agreed a price of £5, and he drove her to some waste ground.

When she got out of his vehicle, Sutcliffe hit the back of Yvonne's head with a lump or walling hammer that had been hidden under the seat. At this point a car pulled up next to his, so Sutcliffe dragged Yvonne under an old sofa. She was still alive and gurgling, so he stuffed handfuls of horsehair into her mouth and clamped his hand over her nose to suffocate her. He released his grip, but she was still gurgling, so he clamped his hand tight until she died.

The other vehicle left and Sutcliffe enjoyed a necrophiliac frenzy of abuse of Yvonne's body. He pulled down her trousers and knickers, lifted up her blouse and bra, kicked her head and body and then jumped up and down on her chest, splintering her ribcage. He probably also masturbated over Yvonne's body, but no trace of semen was found by the autopsy, probably because two months had passed before the body was discovered.

The authors believe that Sutcliffe suspected that if the body was discovered the next day, the driver of the vehicle that had parked next to him, or the driver of the grey Cortina, may have been able to identify his vehicle. So he hid the body with soil, rubble and turf, then pulled the sofa over it to delay discovery.

Yvonne was reported missing the next day. She had been convicted for soliciting twice and was due in court again, meaning that she was likely to receive a prison sentence. She was known to operate in London and Leeds, so the police concluded that she may have absconded rather than face prison. This was clearly untenable, because it would involve Yvonne abandoning her children, to whom she was devoted. Nevertheless, the media was alerted and her case was covered at length locally.

Yvonne's severely mutilated body was not discovered until 26 March 1978.

51. Elena 'Helen' Rytka
(Convicted)
Elena and Rita Rytka were eighteen-year-old twins who did sex work in Huddersfield.

On Tuesday 31 January 1978 they were working in Huddersfield's RLD, and at 9.25pm Helen got into Sutcliffe's car. They drove to Garrards Timber Yard near the railway – a haunt for sex workers and their clients. When she got out and went to the rear door he struck at her with a hammer, which missed and hit the car door instead. Before she had a chance to scream, he hit her again and she crumpled to the ground. Sutcliffe then realised that two taxi drivers were standing talking nearby. Taking Helen by the hair, he dragged her to the back of the wood yard. Helen vainly tried to protect herself as Sutcliffe hit her with the hammer again.

Fearing the taxi drivers would see them, he lay on top of Helen and covered her mouth with his hand. Unusually, he managed to achieve an erection so he raped her. When the taxi drivers left, Sutcliffe got up and searched for the hammer to finish Helen off. Helen seized her chance and ran from him, but Sutcliffe caught her and hit her several more times on the back of her head. He then dragged her to the front of the car and finished her off by stabbing her through the heart and lungs with a kitchen knife. He then concealed her body and left.

When he got home he cleaned the knife and returned it to a kitchen drawer, wiped Helen's blood off his clothes and shoes and went to bed.

Rita was afraid of the police and did not report Helen missing until 2 February 1978. A police dog found her body the following day. It had been hidden behind a stack of timber concealed in an inaccessible spot under a sheet of corrugated asbestos (as in the case of Judith Roberts) and some pieces of wood. Her clothes were scattered over a wide area – one shoe was found twenty yards away up an embankment. She was naked apart from her socks, bra and black polo-neck jumper, which were found in the characteristic position above her breasts.

Helen was identified immediately as a Ripper victim and this led to a furore of comment in the media. ACC Oldfield tried to use this media interest to generate information and made an appeal on Jimmy Young's radio programme, the most listened-to radio show in the country. His reasoning was that someone was shielding the Ripper, and his appeal was for that person to come forward. This was an innovative idea which for some offenders no doubt would have delivered vital information. However, Sutcliffe acted alone, did not confide in anyone and appeared to be a hardworking, respectable married man. No one suspected him or was shielding him. So this media effort failed, only serving to produce more superfluous information from the public, which all had to be indexed and followed up on. This only increased the workload on the incident room, which was already overwhelmed.

Between the murders of Helen Rytka and the discovery of the body of Yvonne Pearson, the Ripper Investigation received two letters purporting to be from the Ripper.

The first letter was posted on 8 March 1978 to ACC Oldfield and was received on the tenth. The text is below. (Authors' emphasis in bold):

Dear Sir

I am sorry I cannot give my name for obvious reasons. I am the Ripper. I've been dubbed a maniac by the Press but not by you, you call me clever and I am. You and your mates havent a clue that photo in the paper gave me fits and that bit about killing myself, no chance. I've got things to do. **My purpose to rid the streets of them sluts. My one regret is that young lassie McDonald, did not know cause changed routine that night. Up to number 8 now you say 7 but remember Preston '75.** get about you know. You were right I travel a bit. You probably look for me in Sunderland, don't bother, I am not daft, just posted letter there on one of my trips. Not a bad place compared with Chapeltown and Manningham and other places. **Warn whores to keep off streets cause I feel it coming on again.**

Sorry about young lassie.

Yours respectfully

Jack the Ripper

Might write again later I not sure last one really deserved it. **Whores getting younger each time. Old slut next time** I hope. Huddersfield never again, too small close call last one.

The second letter was sent to the *Daily Mirror* on 13 March 1978, and staff immediately contacted the police and agreed not to publish it. The exact text is below:

Dear Sir,

I have already written Chief Constable, Oldfield "a man I respect" concerning the recent Ripper murders. I told him and I am telling you to **warn**

them whores I'll strike again and soon when heat cools off. About the Mcdonald lassie, I did nt know that she was decent and I am sorry I changed my routine that night.

Up to murder 8 now You say seven but remember Preston 75. Easy picken them up dont even have to try, you think theyre learn but they dont Most are young lassies, **next time try older one I hope.** Police haven't a clue yet and I don't leave any I am very clever and don't think of looking for any fingerprints cause there arent any and dont look for me up in Sunderland cause I not stupid just passed through the place not bad place compared with Chapeltown and manningham **can't walk the streets for them whore, Dont forget warn them I feel it coming on again if I get the chance. Sorry about lassie I didn't know.**

Yours respectfully

Jack the Ripper

Might write again after another ones' gone. **Maybe Liverpool or even Manchester again, to hot here in Yorkshire, Bye.**

I have given advance warning so its yours and their's fault.

It is not unusual in a major investigation to get false confessions or crank letters. Both letters had the same distinctive sloped writing, were postmarked Sunderland and had no fingerprints. The highlighted passages above all indicate that the writer was obsessed with murdering sex workers and that the murder of Jayne MacDonald had been a mistake. Which fitted the narrative that ACC Oldfield was following.

The phrase 'Up to number 8 now you say 7 but remember Preston '75' was a reference to the murder of Joan Harrison in Preston in 1975, which had already been eliminated from the series. ACC Oldfield assessed that based on the lack of specific information and the poor grammar it was a crank letter. He notified Detective Superintendent Wilf Brooks in Lancashire and asked Sunderland CID to check the handwriting against all known cranks, had the handwriting analysed by a police graphologist, then filed both letters.

52. 'Miss R' AKA Leeds Shop Assistant
(Believed to be attributed to Sutcliffe by Chief Constable Byford)

On Thursday 2 March 1978, 'Miss R', an eighteen-year-old shop assistant who was walking along Kingston Road, Leeds, was struck on the head from behind and rendered unconscious. The authors believe her attacker was then scared off by someone or something and fled.

'Miss R' could not give any description of her attacker. The attack was motiveless and obviously intended to cause death or serious injury. Her attacker was able to approach her from behind unseen, strike one major blow with a blunt instrument – probably a hammer – and render her incapable of any further resistance. All standard Ripper tradecraft. Yet this attempted murder was not linked to the Ripper series (MPoF).

After the murder of Marilyn Moore in December 1977, Sutcliffe stopped attacking in The Gaiety area. Likewise, after murdering Yvonne the following month, he stopped attacking in the Belle Vue area. The area around Leeds University had many young, unattached students living in digs and university accommodation. Consequently, there were women walking around unaccompanied late at night. His subsequent attacks in Leeds were all in the university area, and this attack was the first of what was to become the Leeds University Sub-Cluster, which (uniquely) was linear and has never before been identified. This change in geographical area of operations was obviously intended to defeat the police investigation.

There were six attacks in the Leeds University Sub-Cluster in the period March 1978 to November 1980.

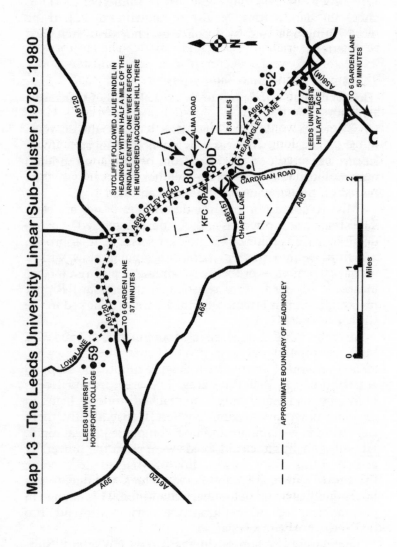

Map 13 - The Leeds University Linear Sub-Cluster 1978 - 1980

SUTCLIFFE FOLLOWED JULIE BINDEL IN HEADINGLEY WITHIN HALF A MILE OF THE ARNDALE CENTRE, ONE WEEK BEFORE HE MURDERED JACQUELINE HILL THERE

5.6 MILES

ALMA ROAD

A660 HEADINGLEY LANE

LEEDS UNIVERSITY HILLARY PLACE

A58(M)

TO 6 GARDEN LANE 50 MINUTES

80A

80D

76

52

77

KFC OP

A660 OTLEY ROAD

B6157

CARDIGAN ROAD

CHAPEL LANE

A65

A120

A6120

TO 6 GARDEN LANE 37 MINUTES

LOW LANE

LEEDS UNIVERSITY HORSFORTH COLLEGE 59

A65

A6120

— — — APPROXIMATE BOUNDARY OF HEADINGLEY

Miles

0   1   2

Five of the victims were students who were on university premises or travelling there. This should have prompted a review of incidents in the area, to identify if there had been other attacks.

Similar analysis by A&SP in March 1979 identified that the attacks of serial rapist Ronald Evans, who had terrorised Bristol for two years, occurred in a linear cluster along Whiteladies Road. Surveillance of Whiteladies Road led to his arrest in March 1979. However, WYMP did not perform this analysis, so the attacks were not linked (MPoF). Had it occurred, it would have identified that the attacks were taking place along the 5.6-mile route A660/Headingley Lane/Otley Road/A6120/Low Lane. Surveillance of this route would have identified Sutcliffe's car as he entered and exited it after an attack, leading to his arrest.

No	Name	Date	Location
KFC OP	Kentucky Fried Chicken		Observation point used to select Upadhya Bandara and Jacqueline Hill as victims
52	'Miss R'	02/03/78	Kingston Road
59	Ann Rooney	02/03/79	Horsforth College
76	Upadhya Bandara	24/09/80	Chapel Lane
77	Mo Lea	25/10/80	Hillary Place
N/A	Julie Bindel	10/11/80 Approx	Headingley area
80A	Jacqueline Hill	17/11/80	Alma Rd
80D	Jacqueline Hill	17/11/80	Arndale Centre

50. Yvonne Pearson (Convicted) Part 2, 46. Carol Wilkinson and Anthony Steel (Miscarriage of Justice) Part 2

YVONNE PEARSON PART 2
On 26 March 1978, Yvonne Pearson's body was found on wasteland off Lumb Lane in Bradford. Sutcliffe had

murdered Yvonne in January 1978 and concealed the body under a sofa.

A copy of the *Daily Mirror* dated 21 February 1978 was found under her body. The police concluded that Yvonne had been killed some time before 21 February and that the killer had returned after the murder to place the newspaper under her body.

Sutcliffe read the *Bradford Telegraph and Argus* and would have read its reports that Yvonne was missing and thought to be in hiding. The authors believe he returned after 21 February and put the *Daily Mirror* under her body to deceive the investigation into believing that Yvonne had – as the papers suggested – gone to ground for a month to avoid the court appearance, then returned to Bradford and been murdered after 21 February. This would ensure that if any of the witnesses who saw him or his car on 21 January came forward, they would be disregarded by the police. On this occasion, this ploy was unsuccessful. However, the authors believe Sutcliffe employed the same technique in the murder of 'Hope', using the sell-by date on a food product's labelling. On that occasion he did succeed in deceiving NYP as to the date of 'Hope's' death.

CAROL WILKINSON AND ANTHONY STEEL PART 2

Other than the fact that Carol Wilkinson had been murdered in daylight in the morning, her attack mirrored Yvonne's murder. So both Professor Gee and the Coroner concluded that the same man had murdered both Carol and Yvonne, but this man was not the Ripper because he did not use a ball pein hammer and there were no stab or slash wounds.

Professor Gee examined the bodies of many of Sutcliffe's victims. He was Professor Emeritus at Leeds University and was arguably the leading forensic pathologist in the UK at that time, and this was a rare error on his part. In common with many of the professionals involved in the investigation, he suffered nightmares about Sutcliffe's victims for the rest of his life.

However, DCS Hobson ignored the linking and convicted the wrong man.

Anthony Steel was a twenty-two-year-old unemployed gardener with an IQ of 65, within the range of what was called in those days 'retarded'. He came to the attention of the police eighteen months after the murder because, his mother-in-law alleged, he was the murderer when a keyring he had given his wife had belonged to Carol.

Anthony was arrested and aggressively interviewed for two days without a solicitor or an appropriate adult. The interviews were not tape recorded and predictably, he was intimidated into signing a false confession.

When he was finally given access to a solicitor, Anthony retracted the confession. Incredibly, His Honour Mr Justice Boreham allowed it to be given in evidence against him. Four youths gave evidence that Carol had a keyring similar to one that Anthony had given to his wife. On this flimsiest of evidence, Anthony was convicted of Carol's murder in December 1979.

Anthony was released on licence in 1998 and his conviction was quashed on appeal in 2003. He died of a heart attack aged fifty-two in September 2007, having served twenty years in prison for a crime he did not commit. Quoted in *The Yorkshire Post*, his comments on the aggressive way he was interrogated are illuminating:

> I was young and I'd never had experience of being in custody or anything like that. That pressure builds up on you so much and there's only so much you can take, so to ease that pressure you do something to get them off your back and that's what I did. They kept intimidating me, telling me what I did that day, and I think I ended up believing what they were telling me. They were saying, 'We know you've done it. We've got the proof; we've got the evidence.'

This was standard CID practice in those days and probably reflects the experience of Stephen Downing and Andrew Evans.

Re-examining Carol's murder, it is clear that her killer had local knowledge of the area and her route to work. Sutcliffe's home was just over three miles from the crime scene and his place of work about two-and-a-half miles from it.

Prior to Carol's murder, there was a chain of events linking Sutcliffe to Ranelagh Avenue:

- Sutcliffe was friends with Carol's opposite neighbour. The neighbour's stepdaughter Kay Lintern recalled that the year before Carol's murder, Sutcliffe had fixed her stepdad's freezer.
- Kay noticed that from then on, Sutcliffe was seen regularly in the street and he sometimes followed her when she walked to school.
- Sutcliffe was found hanging around outside nineteen-year-old Lynne Hodson's home on Ranelagh Avenue and was seen off by her brother.
- Kay and other witnesses confirmed that Sutcliffe was seen hanging around the estate, particularly on Langdale Road, which was on the route Carol took to work, and that he had been reported to the police.
- Carol's father was alleged to have chased Sutcliffe off the estate on a number of occasions for pestering Carol.

On the day Carol was murdered, Kay was ill and could not go to school. She looked out of the landing window and saw Sutcliffe in a white car and concluded he was waiting there to follow her to school again. Knowing that she was staying home, she thought nothing more of it. She then saw her neighbour Carol leave home to walk to work.

Incredibly, despite his reputation and having been reported to the police for troublemaking and stalking, Sutcliffe was never considered as a suspect in Carol's murder (MPoF).

The authors' reconstruction is that on the morning of Carol's murder, Sutcliffe returned home from mutilating Jean Jordan's corpse. The effect of mutilating a corpse gave Sutcliffe an overpowering necrophiliac sexual arousal, without the satisfaction of masturbating over the body to relieve it. Sutcliffe may also have been in imminent fear of arrest and this may have increased these feelings, giving him an overwhelming and irresistible need to kill, and he went to Ranelagh Avenue to satisfy it, knowing that Carol, Lynne and Kay lived there.

It is possible he targeted Kay because he knew her route to school. He waited outside her house, keeping it under surveillance, but when she had not left home by 9.00am, he realised that she was not going to school. When he saw Carol leaving for work, he selected her as his new victim.

Sutcliffe had detailed knowledge of the area and would have known Carol's route to work via a shortcut through the field at the back of the bakery. He drove off in the white car seen by Kay – probably the white Corsair, or a car borrowed from a friend or family member – to a point where he could intercept Carol. The authors believe Sutcliffe followed Carol, engaging her in conversation before attacking her with his walling hammer.

Carol's murder has all the classic indicators of a Sutcliffe attack. She was walking alone and was attacked with a blow to the back of the skull with a blunt instrument. Her blouse and bra had been pulled up; her trousers and knickers had been pulled down to expose her genitalia. The authors suspect he was disturbed, possibly by the man who discovered Carol's body, so he fled and did not have time to move the body to a more secluded spot, mutilate it and then masturbate over it. This and Sutcliffe's emotional state that morning, coupled with being seen outside her house on the day she was murdered, means there can be little doubt that Carol was murdered by Sutcliffe.

DCS Hobson did not reopen Carol's case during the antecedent investigation he led following Sutcliffe's arrest. Had he done so, it would have shown he had railroaded an innocent man into a false confession and caused a serious miscarriage of justice. Carol's murder has never been impartially considered by any antecedent investigation into Sutcliffe.

Diagram 5 - Murder of Carol Wilkinson

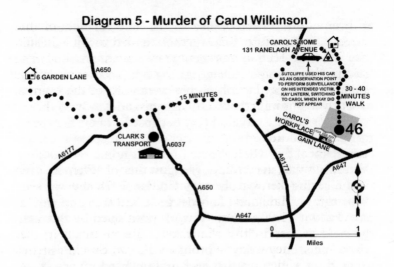

In April 1978, DCS John Domaille was appointed to support the Ripper investigation. His appointment perhaps recognised that ACC Oldfield was being overwhelmed by the size and strain of the enquiry. Domaille was a very capable detective and he set about an impartial analysis of the nine known murders and the others that had been eliminated or ignored. He concluded (wrongly) that Joan Harrison was a Ripper victim (MPoF) and the attacks on Tracy Browne and Marcella Claxton were not Ripper attacks (MPoF). However, he correctly identified the attacks on Anna Rogulskyj, Olive Smelt, Maureen Long and Marilyn Moore as Ripper attacks.

A Special Bulletin containing details of all the Ripper cases identified so far was issued to all forces and should have resulted in a review of all unsolved cases to identify if they could have been perpetrated by the Ripper. No cases were brought to the attention of WYMP, although there were several that had all the indicators of a Ripper attack in other force areas (MPoF). This was a pivotal point of failure in the investigation, because the additional information yielded by these cases could have identified Sutcliffe.

From July 1978 onwards, the surveillance of the Leeds and Bradford RLDs was extended to Manchester, Sheffield and Hull. Index numbers were fed into the Police National Computer (PNC) at Hendon. If the same vehicle was identified as having been seen in two of these areas, the driver was interviewed by detectives.

53. Vera Millward
(Convicted)

Vera Millward, aged forty, was a mother of seven children and a sex worker. On Tuesday 16 May 1978 she was seen soliciting at Manchester's Moss Side RLD.

At about 11.00pm Vera was propositioned by Sutcliffe, who drove her to the Manchester Royal Infirmary car park. When they were both out of the car, Sutcliffe struck Vera three times on the back of the head, exposed her breasts and genitalia, then slashed her across the stomach, disembowelling her. Sutcliffe then stabbed her repeatedly in and out of one wound in her back then stabbed her right eyelid, dragged her body twelve feet across the car park to a more secluded spot and dumped her on a pile of rubbish by a chain-link fence in the corner of the car park. He laid Vera's body face down with her arms folded underneath her and her legs straight, put her shoes neatly on her body, got into the red Corsair and drove home.

Vera's body was found the following morning. Her injuries were so severe that initially she was misidentified by vice squad officers as another local sex worker. Her fingerprints were used to obtain an accurate identification. Casts were taken of all four tyre tracks found at the crime scene, which matched the impressions obtained at both the Irene Richardson and Marilyn Moore crime scenes, conclusively proving they were Ripper attacks. The North West Forensic Science Laboratory identified eleven vehicles that could have left the tracks, one of which was a Ford Corsair.

On 14 May 1978, Sutcliffe bought a 1970 model, metallic grey Sunbeam Rapier, registration number NKU

888 H. On 23 March 1980 he also bought a red Mini (car) from a Bristol businessman, registration number 372 SRR, which he gave to his sister, but retained access to.

54. Carol Reeves

On 16 June 1978, the body of Carol Reeves was found in Hyeres, France. Investigative journalist David Yallop has alleged that she was murdered by Sutcliffe. Carol's murder is considered in the section on the foreign attacks.

On 7 August 1978, Sutcliffe sold his red Ford Corsair PHE 355 G. He had bought two cars and sold one in three months. This seems fortuitous for him, given the content of his next police interview six days later. The authors believe this was part of a strategy of changing cars regularly to defeat surveillance and remove forensic evidence.

INTERVIEW 3: 13 AUGUST 1978

Sutcliffe was interviewed because his red Corsair had been seen in the Leeds and Bradford RLDs. Sutcliffe denied having visited Leeds and Bradford during the evenings in the relevant period, despite the fact that his car had been recorded there. He told the interviewing officer he was using only the Sunbeam Rapier at the time. He had only bought the Sunbeam Rapier on 14 May, so this was clearly not credible and should have led to further enquiries. But the officers did not enquire further (MPoF).

During September 1978, an audit checked a sample of 10 per cent of completed enquiries and found that actions had been signed off as completed which had not been performed. Two detectives resigned and a further thirteen were subjected to internal disciplinary action for falsely stating they had completed actions, in order to justify fraudulent overtime claims. The above unsatisfactory responses to glaring deficiencies revealed at interview may not therefore have been unusual. One cannot help wondering how many other WYMP detectives had made false statements on crucial actions and if this helped Sutcliffe to evade detection for as long as he did.

Sutcliffe would regularly be on the road for three or four days at a time whilst he was delivering for Clarks Transport, returning during the afternoon of the fourth day. This would allow him to use his lorry to commit attacks on women all over the UK.

INTERVIEW 4: 23 NOVEMBER 1978

Sutcliffe was interviewed again and the new owners of the red Ford Corsair were visited. This established that all four tyres had been changed after the vehicle changed hands. This, coupled with the disappearance of the white Corsair, meant that the tyre evidence had been destroyed and this most promising line of enquiry was extinct.

55. Margaret Frame
(Believed to have been attributed to Sutcliffe by ACC Hellawell)

On 12 October 1978, thirty-six-year-old Margaret Frame vanished on her way home from work at Falmer High School in Brighton. Her husband, Peter, raised the alarm the next day.

Ten days later, Margaret's body was found in Stanmer Park, Brighton. She had been struck on the head from behind, stabbed in the back, then stripped. Her throat had been cut from ear to ear, but no knife was found. A determined attempt had been made to decapitate her. All her rings were taken. The killer returned to the crime scene sometime later and dragged her body 500 yards to a more secluded spot before mutilating it further and burying it in a shallow grave.

Sutcliffe's work as a lorry driver took him all over the country so it is quite possible that he was making a delivery to the Brighton area at the time.

Sutcliffe loved to take his nephews and nieces to the seaside. Brighton would be a favourite destination from West London and he may have visited Brighton socially. Sonia's sister Marianne eventually moved to Chichester in West Sussex. It has not been possible to establish if she had any connections to the south coast during 1978.

The murder has many of the essential components of a Sutcliffe attack. Unaccompanied female victim, attacked from behind with a blunt instrument then stabbed with a knife in a public place in the hours of darkness. As with the murders of Kay O'Connor, Rosina Hilliard, Eve Stratford and Lynda Farrow, the victim's throat had been cut. The victim was then dragged some distance to a more secluded secondary crime scene, where her body was further mutilated. As with the murder of Jean Jordan the previous year, the murderer tried to decapitate the victim and then concealed the body.

There were no confirmed Ripper attacks in the ten months between the murder of Vera Millward on 17 May 1978 and the attempted murder of Ann Rooney on 2 March 1979. Sutcliffe was a prolific attacker and there is no obvious reason why he should suddenly pause his attacks. He was by this time varying his geographical area of operations and his modus-operandi. So it is entirely feasible that he committed a murder in another part of the country while making a delivery with his lorry.

The authors believe that, as with the murder of Yvonne Pearson, he concealed the body in a grave to delay discovery and, as with the case of Jean Jordan, he tried to decapitate the body to conceal that it was a Ripper murder. He had stolen rings from corpses when he was a gravedigger. He may have taken the rings to show a false motive of theft and so as to prevent Margaret's murder being connected to the Ripper.

56. Carole Montgomery AKA Bradford Addressograph Operator
(Believed to be attributed to Sutcliffe by Chief Constable Byford)

On Tuesday 28 November 1978, Carole Montgomery, an eighteen-year-old addressograph operator, was walking home in Bradford in the middle of the evening. She was followed by a man who grabbed her by the hair. Showing herself to be a very gutsy young lady indeed, in the ensuing struggle she managed to throw a brick at her assailant and he ran off. She provided a photofit of the man and described him as being aged thirty years, slim build, with dark straggly hair, a mandarin moustache and goatee beard.

Whilst there was no weapon involved, the attack was on a single woman walking alone at night. When faced with his intended victim's screams and fierce resistance, her attacker followed Sutcliffe's standard operating procedure of fleeing. Her description of her assailant is a perfect likeness of Sutcliffe.

Both the attack and photofit were disregarded by the Ripper investigation (MPoF).

At some point in 1979, Sutcliffe confided in his brother-in-law Robin Holland that he had contracted a sexually transmitted disease and was trying to get as many overnight trips driving his lorry as possible so that he did not have to go near Sonia. He presumably contracted this from a sex worker and it is not known if she survived the encounter. This meant that he was away from home much more often in 1979 and travelling widely for work.

57. Lynda Farrow
See 26 Eve Stratford

The white Corsair does not feature after the murder of Lynda Farrow in January 1979. Its fate is unknown. Sutcliffe must have disposed of it himself, which would mean foregoing the cash for its scrap value. This would only be logical if it was contaminated with bloodstains from an unknown victim, therefore requiring immediate destruction. The alternative would be allowing the vehicle to be hanging around in a scrapyard being used for spare parts for eighteen months before it was crushed – leaving it available to be examined for evidence should he be arrested.

58. Harrogate Schoolgirl, name withheld by NYP
(Believed to be attributed to Sutcliffe by Chief Constable Byford)

A sixteen-year-old student was attacked from behind in Harrogate in the early hours of Saturday 17 February 1979, suffering severe head injuries from a blunt instrument. NYP initially concluded that she had injured herself falling on the icy pavement. An x-ray of her skull showed three semi-circular injuries that were typical of a ball pein hammer blow and not from a fall.

Sutcliffe was familiar with Harrogate from his HGV driver training. As with the attack on the Leeds shop assistant, the attacker was able to approach the victim from behind, strike one major blow with a blunt instrument – almost certainly a ball pein hammer – and render her incapable of any further resistance. She survived but could not give a description of the attacker, whom she had not seen.

The authors believe that Sutcliffe was in his lorry returning along the A658 from a delivery in Sunderland or Darlington and deviated into Harrogate to commit another attack.

NYP was aware that the Ripper could be a lorry driver operating in its force area. One lorry driver wrote:

Around 1979 or '80 I was taking a removal up to Middlesbrough in a Ford D series D1311 Vanplan. On the way back from Middlesbrough we stopped for the night in Ripon, North Yorkshire. Early hours of the morning we were woken by the local Police. They made us get up get out of the vehicle with loads of questions and searched the vehicle, obviously at that time looking for Peter Sutcliffe. Something I will never forget. Thinking back now I think they were looking for a truck driver at that time.

Sutcliffe appears to have varied his modus-operandi. Instead of lulling his victims into a false sense of security with conversation, he was stalking them then stealthily approaching from behind and attacking with a hammer. The authors believe that this, coupled with the move from West Yorkshire to North Yorkshire, confirms that he was trying to deceive the investigation into overlooking his attacks. He was completely successful in this and the attack was not linked to the Ripper series (MPoF).

Sutcliffe was questioned about the attack in 1982 and denied it.

59. Ann Rooney
(Believed to be attributed to Sutcliffe by Chief Constable Byford. Sutcliffe subsequently admitted the attack to ACC Hellawell in 1992.)

In the evening of Friday 2 March 1979, Ann Rooney, a twenty-two-year-old student, was attacked from behind in the grounds of Horsforth College, Leeds. She was struck on the head three times, leaving distinctive semicircular wounds which had been caused by a round hammer. She sustained no other injuries and it appears that Sutcliffe had been disturbed and fled.

Ann described her attacker as being in his late twenties, five-foot ten-inches in height, broad build, with dark curly hair, a droopy moustache and a small beard. Other than describing Sutcliffe's build as broad, probably because Sutcliffe was wearing a large coat on a cold night, Ann's description was accurate and tallied with the other descriptions.

Ann stated she had seen the man sitting in a dark-coloured Sunbeam Rapier immediately before the attack. This was obviously Sutcliffe's dark grey Sunbeam Rapier, which had been flagged numerous times going through RLDs in Leeds, Bradford and Manchester.

The investigation discounted Ann as a Ripper victim because she was not a sex worker, could not be mistaken for one, and the diameter of the hammer used to attack her did not match the diameter of hammer used on his previous victims, as specified in the elimination criteria the investigation was using:

- Blows to the head with a hammer of diameter 1.2 to 1.1 inches (plus or minus 5 per cent).
- Attack on the body with some other stabbing/mutilating instrument.
- Displacement of the brassiere to give access to breasts.
- Lowering of knickers/tights to pubic hair level (in many instances, vulva remains covered by crotch of garment, precluding penetration).
- Movement of the body after the initial attack before the infliction of further injuries – frequently to the trunk.
- Reluctance of the assailant to stab through clothing.
- Assailant's return to the body to inflict further injuries or secrete it.

Sutcliffe had used a ball pein hammer, a claw hammer and a lump hammer. After Sutcliffe's arrest, it transpired that he discarded hammers and other tools he had used in attacks, then replaced them. This was to destroy forensic evidence and deceive the investigation into believing that the attack had been perpetrated by someone else. On this occasion, this tactic served him well. Sutcliffe was the only man attacking women in Yorkshire by smashing the back of their head with a hammer. However, the above elimination criteria were too precise, applied rigidly and assumed that the Ripper would use the same weapon in each attack. Resulting in many Ripper attacks being eliminated (MPoF).

The attack on Ann was identical to the attack on the schoolgirl in Harrogate less than two weeks before and to the attack on the shop assistant the previous year. The description and modus-operandi obviously indicated a Ripper attack. But these three cases were not linked to the Ripper series (MPoF).

The attack also indicated another change in Sutcliffe's geographical area of operation to the area around Leeds University. However, this change was also not identified (MPoF).

Ann's description of the vehicle was followed up and a search of all the Sunbeam Rapiers identified by the surveillance operation loitering in RLDs identified 850 suspect vehicles. One of them was Sutcliffe's, which had been sighted forty-six times in RLDs. Sutcliffe was one of only three Sunbeam Rapier owners who had been flagged in all three high-profile Ripper areas. This, together with his rapidly growing nominal index with all of the other intelligence and being the owner of a white Corsair also previously flagged, should have raised him to high profile and led to his arrest. However, the enquiry was not followed up (MPoF).

In 1992 Sutcliffe confessed to having attacked Ann. She had had to wait thirteen years before obtaining some form of closure.

60. Josephine Whitaker
(Convicted)

On Wednesday 4 April 1979, building society clerk Josephine Whitaker, aged nineteen, left her grandparents' house in Halifax at about 11.00pm to walk home. It was almost midnight when she reached Savile Park Moor, an open park surrounded by well-lit roads. As she walked across the damp grass in the park, Sutcliffe stopped her to ask the time. She looked towards the town clock in the distance and he took a hammer out of his jacket and smashed it down on her head. As she lay on the grass, he hit her again and then dragged her thirty feet into the darkness away from the road. He pulled her clothing off and stabbed her breasts, stomach, thighs and vagina twenty-five times.

Significantly, he committed this murder having travelled some 260 miles in his lorry that day.

Josephine was found the next morning. At around the same time, Josephine's younger brother was going to the newsagents for his early morning paper round. He saw police officers huddled around something lying near the roadside and recognised his sister's shoe.

The same size-seven wellington boot prints were found as at the Patricia Atkinson and Emily Jackson crime scenes. The right impression was worn more than the left, possibly from pressing the accelerator pedal repeatedly, suggesting a lorry driver. The pathologist's report revealed that Josephine had a bite mark on her breast from a man with a gap in his teeth. There were also traces of milling oil and metal particles found in the victim's wounds, which suggested an engineering connection. This was possibly from Sutcliffe sharpening knives, chisels, etc., or working on engines.

A man who had tried to pick up a woman in the town centre at around 9.00pm had been seen near the scene of the murder sitting in a dark-coloured Ford Escort. Sutcliffe had access to his mother-in-law's dark-coloured Ford Escort at this time. A photofit was issued and is shown as Illustration 10.

WYMP finally realised that the Ripper was not only attacking sex workers and issued a warning that no woman walking alone at night in the North of England was safe.

On 23 March 1979, John Humble posted a third hoax letter to ACC Oldfield. Analysis of the saliva on the envelope revealed that the sender was a Blood Group B Negative, Secretor:

Dear Officer,

Sorry I havn't written, about a year to be exact but I havn't been up North for quite a while. **I was'nt kidding last time I wrote saying the whore would be older this time and maybe I'd strike in Manchester for a change.** You should have took heed. **That bit about her being in hospital, funny the lady mentioned something about being in the same hospital before I stopped her whoring ways.**

The lady wont worry about hospitals now will she I bet you are wondering how come I hav'nt been to work for ages, well I would have been if it hadnt been for your curserred coppers I had the lady just where I wanted her and was about to strike when one of your cursen police cars stopped right outside the land, he must have been a dumn copper cause he didn't say anything, he didnt know how close he was to catching me.

Tell you the truth I thought I was collared, the lady said dont worry about coppers, little did she know that bloody copper saved her neck. That was last month, so I don't know know when I will get back on the job but I know it won t be Chapeltown too bloody hot there maybe Bradfords Manningham. Might write again if up North.

Jack the Ripper

PS Did you get letter I sent to Daily Mirror in Manchester.

[Bold used for emphasis]

On 4 June 1979 Sutcliffe bought a brown 3.5 Rover, registration number FHY400K.

Then on 17 June 1979, Humble posted a tape to ACC Oldfield. A transcript is below:

I'm Jack. I see you are still having no luck catching me. I have the greatest respect for you, George, but Lord, you are no nearer to catching me now than four years ago when I started. I reckon your boys are letting you down, George. Ya can't be much good, can ya?

The only time they came near catching me was a few months back in Chapeltown when I was disturbed. Even then it was a uniform copper, not a detective.

I warned you in March that I'd strike again, sorry it wasn't Bradford, I did promise you that but I couldn't get there. I'm not sure when I will strike again but it will definitely be some time this year, maybe September or October, even soon if I get the chance. I'm not sure where. Maybe Manchester; I like there, there's plenty of them knocking about.

They never learn, do they, George? I bet you've warned them, but they never listen. At the rate I'm going I should be in the book of records, *I think it's 11 up to now, isn't it?* Well, I'll keep on going for quite a while yet. I can't see myself being nicked just yet. Even if you do get near, I'll probably top myself first.

Well, it's been nice chatting to you, George. Yours, Jack the Ripper.

No good looking for fingerprints, you should know by now it's clean as a whistle. See you soon. 'Bye. Hope you like the catchy tune at the end. Ha-ha!

[Bold used for emphasis]

Voice experts accurately identified that [1] the accent originated in the Castletown area of Sunderland and [2] the speaker had a gap between his teeth. A decision was taken that the tape and letters should be treated as accurate and released to the public.

This flawed decision was based on seven factors:

- The murder of Joan Harrison had many similarities to the other Ripper attacks.
- The Humble hoax letters were not in the public domain when Sutcliffes travelled to Manchester to commit his next murder. His selection of a forty-year-old sex worker coincided with the two passages 'next time try older one I hope' and 'Maybe Liverpool or even Manchester again' contained in the second letter. This appeared to confirm that the writer was the man who had gone on to attack an older victim in Manchester. In fact, this was a coincidence.
- The references to a conversation with Vera in which she said that she had been a patient in the Manchester Royal Infirmary and to the murder of Joan Harrison led police to believe the writer had specific knowledge of these crimes that could only be known to the killer. In fact, this information had been released by the *Daily Mirror*, but WYMP did not check this (MPoF).
- Blood Group B Negative belonged to only 6 per cent of the population and matched the blood group of Joan

Harrison's killer. Forensic analysis of the saliva on the gum on the envelopes indicated that it came from a man with the Blood Group B Negative, Secretor. The Ripper was known to be B Negative, Non-secretor, but the man that murdered Joan was known to be a B Negative, Secretor. This should have identified immediately that the writer was not the Ripper, but this was ignored (MPoF).

- The murder of Josephine Whitaker was taken as confirmation of the prediction that the writer would strike again contained in the second letter. The fact that the attack occurred in Halifax, not Bradford, was ignored (MPoF).
- The bite mark on Josephine Whitaker's body was similar to a bite mark on Joan Harrison.
- The sender had a gap in his teeth.

The investigation noticed the inconsistency between the second letter 'Up to number 8 now you say 7 but remember Preston '75', indicating the writer was unaware of Yvonne Pearson's murder (no. 8), whose body was still concealed when he wrote the letter, and the third letter, which included it. The discovery of Yvonne's body should have discredited the first two letters and identified them as a hoax. Unfortunately, ACC Oldfield would not accept that this invalidated the conclusion that the letters and tape were from the Ripper (MPoF).

ACC Oldfield called all the detectives working on the investigation to a meeting at Halifax's Old Court House to listen to the tape. He stated he was satisfied it was from the killer and asked them if they had questioned anyone with a similar accent. Needless to say, none of the detectives recognised the accent, because no one from the Castletown area had ever been interviewed. So on 20 June 1979, he called a press conference and played Humble's hoax tape to the assembled journalists and stated it was from the Ripper. This resulted in an enormous number of calls to the Millgarth Incident Room, which by now had been overwhelmed (MPoF).

Northumbria Police descended on Castletown and interviewed local men. All had the same accent but all had an alibi for some or all of the attacks and/or their handwriting did not match. Humble was not interviewed, probably because he was known to be an alcoholic and not to travel, and therefore was incapable of perpetrating the attacks. Additional enquiries were undertaken to identify men from the North East that were living in West Yorkshire or travelling into it regularly. All of this further distracted the investigation (MPoF).

A handwriting expert was installed in the Millgarth Incident Room to eliminate suspects on the basis of their handwriting. On 13 September 1979, a Special Notice was issued authorising suspects to be eliminated from the enquiries if they did not have a Geordie accent, although suspects were eliminated on these criteria immediately after the press conference on 20 June (MPoF).

On 25 September, the Special Notice was changed to prohibit elimination based on handwriting and accent alone, but this was not effectively promulgated and the practice of eliminating on the basis of handwriting and accent continued (MPoF).

INTERVIEW 5: 29 JULY 1979

DCs Greenwood and Laptew interviewed Sutcliffe because his Sunbeam Rapier had been seen in the RLDs of Leeds, Bradford and Manchester; it is unclear if this was only the Moss Side RLD or if he had been seen in the Cheetham Hill and Whalley Range RLDs. Greenwood and Laptew were suspicious because Sutcliffe had not provided a convincing explanation for why his car had been seen in these RLDs. His car and garage were searched and nothing incriminating was found. They took a handwriting sample and duly reported their concerns. Laptew's report was ignored and Sutcliffe was eliminated because his handwriting did not match the hoax letters and he was not a Geordie (MPoF).

Initially, WYMP had only provided Northumbria Police with a handwriting sample. Northumbria Police then requested access to the full text of the letters and DI David

Zackrisson conducted an assessment of the letters to try and identify if they were genuine. He identified that the letters were based on the 'Jack the Ripper' letters from the famous case in London in the previous century and contained no information that had not been reported in the media. Most tellingly, the failure of the writer to claim the murder of Yvonne Pearson in the first and second letters confirmed that the sender was unaware of the murder, and therefore that the letters and tape were a hoax. DI Zackrisson's conclusions were accepted by Northumbria Police, who duly notified WYMP that the letters and tape were a hoax. WYMP ignored this information (MPoF). This may have been because WYMP did not want to admit it had failed to conduct this analysis before releasing the tape and attributing it to the Ripper.

There were other indications. The FBI advised that the tape was a hoax, as did the prominent American profiling expert Robert Ressler.

From then on, Lancashire Constabulary, Northumbria Police and GMP did not use handwriting or accent to eliminate suspects, but WYMP continued to. Of the five forces involved in the investigation, four disagreed with the line taken by WYMP but did not publicly or privately oppose it (MPoF).

The pressure of these relentless enquiries rattled Humble. He phoned Sunderland Police Station after the murder of Barbara Leach and confirmed to PC Keith Mount that the tape was a hoax before hanging up. PC Mount was able to record the final part of the conversation. Northumbria Police officers listened to the conversation, realised it was the same man that had sent the tape, and notified WYMP it was a hoax. WYMP ignored this information (MPoF).

None of the surviving victims recognised the voice on the tape as their attacker, but WYMP ignored this, obsessively clinging to the belief that the man who sent the tape and letters was the Ripper (MPoF).

On 2 October 1979, WYMP initiated a huge publicity campaign, 'Project R', which had a telephone line to allow people to hear the tape, and billboards and adverts with samples of the writing on the letters. The resulting publicity did not produce any useful information but generated an enormous number of calls to the incident room, which was by now completely overwhelmed under the weight of work (MPoF). At some points there was a nine-month backlog of actions and reports waiting to be filed (MPoF).

In November 1980, following concern being expressed by the external advisory team over the weight attached to the tape and letters, WYMP conducted a similar review to that conducted by DI Zackrisson. Its report was issued after Sutcliffe's arrest and concluded that: 'There are sufficient factors to justify previous actions taken'. Or, put another way, WYMP was refusing to admit that the focus on the letters and tape was a catastrophic error.

Phase 8. June 1979 to January 1981: Impunity

The hoax letters and tapes diverted the investigation onto lines of enquiry that were never going to produce an arrest. They ensured that Sutcliffe would always be eliminated because he did not have a Geordie accent or handwriting that resembled Humble's and the collapse of the Millgarth Incident Room under the weight of spurious information from the public about Humble's voice and writing. Sutcliffe put it perfectly when he said: 'While that was going on I felt safe. I'm not a Geordie.'

In mid-summer 1979, ACC Oldfield suffered a heart attack – no doubt brought on by overwork and stress – and went on sick leave. He was replaced as ACC Crime by DCS Hobson, with Oldfield's protégé and close friend from the WRC, Detective Superintendent Dick Holland, running the investigation day-to-day. There was no officer in full-time command of the investigation (MPoF).

61. 'Hope' AKA 'The nude in the nettles'

On Friday 28 August 1981, NYP discovered the decomposing body of a woman at Sutton Bank, North Yorkshire, just off the A170, which runs between Scarborough and Thirsk. The following information was released by NYP as part of a 2011 cold case review:

An anonymous male caller telephoned North Yorkshire Police providing the exact location for police officers to search. On Friday 28th August 1981 Police officers attended the described location, a lay-by on the unclassified road leading from Sutton Bank [A170] to the villages of Scawton and Rievaulx. The location is a quiet road used by local people and occasional caravaners heading to a nearby site. The rural area consists mainly of arable and pasture farmland with occasional conifer plantations. It was to the side of this road and between two small plantations that officers found the skeletal remains of an unknown female laid in undergrowth.

A forensic examination of the naked body revealed no jewellery or personal effects laid nearby that may assist in establishing who she was. A Home Office pathologist estimated she may have laid at that place situ for up to two years due to plant growth and state of the body. The post-mortem did not establish a cause of death.

What could be established was that body was that of a female, five-foot two-inches in height, aged between thirty-five and forty and may have been a mother. The deceased appeared to have short dark-coloured hair. There was evidence of an old fracture to the right ankle but nothing conclusive to provide an identification.

At the time a three-dimensional wax reconstruction of her head, which was first such reconstruction, indicated the investigators were keen to use new technology. It was a positive action as the circulations of this image generated significant interest and possible identities but these failed to provide the identification required.

As stated above, based on plant growth and the state of the body, it may have laid in situ for up to two years, putting the date of death at August 1979. This was confirmed by a jockey, who stated that while exercising a horse he had smelt the stench of a decaying body there at that time. The sell-by date of a food product top label found underneath the body was used to date the approximate time of death.

The autopsy was performed by Professor Mike Green, who was coincidentally a member of the Ripper investigation team. He established that 'Hope':

- Was five-foot two-inches in height, aged between thirty-five and forty.
- Had a slender build, wore a size four shoe and wore her natural dark brown hair in a page-boy style.
- Had given birth to two or three children.
- Was a heavy smoker who did not look after herself.
- Had lost all of her upper teeth, had an upper dental plate fitted and only had six lower teeth.

Professor Green could not establish a cause of death. In correspondence with Tim he confirmed that if 'Hope' had been stabbed and the knife struck bone it would have left a mark. All of the bones were examined carefully and no such injuries were seen, but he stated: 'One cannot exclude a knife passing between the ribs, or a stab to the belly.'

Likewise, use of a ligature could not be excluded.

Various structures were missing because of the activities of wild animals such as foxes. Ligature strangulation may occasionally break the little bones of the voice box and hyoid. These were missing. There was no trace of any material in the region of the neck.

I think it is most likely that she was killed and stripped elsewhere and the body simply dumped at the roadside. The body was not posed, it looked as though it had just been laid on its back a few feet from the roadside in the undergrowth.

The investigation failed and was closed in early 1983. A cold case review in 2011 also maintained the mystery caller as the prime suspect and did not question using the food product top to date the body. Sutcliffe was not considered as a suspect in either investigation.

Both investigations were fundamentally flawed:

- Declaring the caller as the prime suspect no doubt dissuaded him from coming forward, which ensured any evidence he may have had was lost. It also ensured all other suspects were ignored.
- A member of the original investigation team has confirmed that Sutcliffe was not considered as a suspect because when the body was discovered, he was believed to operate in West and South Yorkshire and Greater Manchester. The Byford review of the Yorkshire Ripper investigation was published four months after the discovery of the body. It concluded that Sutcliffe's geographic area of offending extended beyond the WYP, SYP and GMP force areas. This should have been considered by both investigations, but was not (MPoF).
- The length of time the body had lain out in the open and interference by animals removed a lot of the forensic evidence. The crime scene did not therefore bear the usual Ripper hallmarks, which made it difficult to draw parallels with Sutcliffe's various modi operandi and he was therefore not considered as a suspect.
- The investigation failed to consider the possibility that the murderer had left a dated item underneath the body to deceive the investigation over the date of death (MPoF).
- From the start, the investigation concluded that 'Hope' was a female abscondee from Askham Grange Open Prison. This ensured that no local enquiries were made

by police about missing sex workers locally (MPoF). She was subsequently eliminated when she wrote to NYP confirming she was alive and living in the Irish Republic.

The body was exhumed in 2012 and DNA extracted from it, but this did not lead to an identification. The next big advance in the case occurred when the NYE ran a series of appeals for information, which produced four new witnesses.

WITNESS 1
Long-term Scarborough resident and former Scarborough Councillor Alderman Norman Murphy, who stated:

I owned the shop Murphyvacs, 190/192 Victoria Road, Scarborough. My business was repairing, selling and refurbishing vacuum cleaners. Attached to the side wall of my shop is a Victorian shelter which is large enough to accommodate about 8 people. This shelter became a refuge for several alcoholics and drug addicts and they would habitually congregate in the shelter to drink and be out of the bad weather.

When I opened my shop in October 1975 the café opposite was owned by a guy called David Siddle. The café had no name as far as I can remember. Taxi drivers used the café and were in and out all the time. Not far from the café was the driving test centre for Scarborough and the instructors used the café all the time when their pupils were taking their tests.

The period I am referring to must have been from 1978 till Sutcliffe was caught.

I would go to the café each morning for a cup of tea. It was very convenient as I could watch the shop from the seat in the window. From time to time a dark-haired man with a neatly trimmed beard and moustache and a strong Yorkshire accent would come to the café and have something to eat and chat to the café owner, Iris Scott. I am sure he was not a local. I think it may have been Sutcliffe. He told Iris that he was a wagon driver and as at that time there were loads of small engineering firms in the area, and other commercial businesses his arrival at the café was perfectly logical as he could park up and walk to the café.

When the Ripper was caught and his picture was all over the media, Iris was convinced that the same dark-haired man who had eaten at the café was the Ripper.

With regard to the woman whose artist's impression featured in the NYE article, the connection is this: As I recall, she was one of the people who used to drink in the shelter. I remember her as she was small and would have been about 40 at the time.

She usually wore a kind of quilted body warmer, winter or summer. It was dark blue, I think. Underneath she would usually wear a blouse or jumper. She usually wore dark-coloured miniskirts or if not mini, quite short. She was small, stocky – but not fat. Dark brown frizzy hair, very similar to the drawing. She smoked.

I believe she might have been selling herself when she was in Scarborough, hence the very short miniskirts years too young for her. Accent, was Yorkshire or Lancashire. I don't think she was local to Scarborough.

Also the drinking gang were always fighting and one day when she came in she had been beaten up and had some of her teeth knocked out.

I would say it was inevitable that they were all known to the police. They were habitual drinkers, probably drug-users as well, although I can't say I ever saw them take drugs. The shelter next to my shop was a regular haunt for them and well known to the police, who had to drive right by it to get to our police station.

Suddenly this group all disappeared. It was a bit strange and might be coincidental. I, of course, thought nothing of it at the time.

I don't remember any police investigation into the 'Nude in the Nettles' murder or this woman. I would still not have thought anything of it but for the article in the NYE jogging my memory.

There were a lot of engineering firms around my end of town in those days. In Roscoe Street alone there was Andrews of Scarborough (motorcycle dealers), Deardens builders merchants, North Sea Winches (they did work relating to marine engineering but also did a lot of welding work), D Wray and Sons was a bakery but they had their vehicle workshop in Roscoe St, Scarborough, Ignition Co Ltd (automobile electrical engineers) then there was Pickups (a really big engineering firm – this firm still exists and is now situated on our trading estate). Pickups had deliveries every day and as Roscoe St is not very wide the deliveries were resented by the residents in the area. However, the old goods yard was quite busy in those days; it is now our Sainsbury's. As an aside many of the people who worked at these firms used Iris's café so if they had Sutcliffe deliver to them they would have almost certainly either taken him, or directed him to the café.

No idea where Sutcliffe's lorry might have been parked, but in those days it was a lot easier to park up my end of town. Also there were several places he could have been delivering to so he might have used their premises I suppose he could have been being loaded so might have gone for a cuppa while he was loaded up.

WITNESS 2
Iris Scott, who is now sadly deceased. Her evidence at the time, as related by Norman, was that Sutcliffe had been a regular patron of her café.

WITNESS 3
A friend of Iris Scott who confirmed that Iris was definite she had seen Sutcliffe in her café on multiple occasions:

Yes, top end, next to Boro taxis. I remember Iris saying she was convinced Peter Sutcliffe had been in her café.

WITNESS 4

A retired policeman, who has confirmed that the bus stop and its inhabitants were known to Scarborough police and it was used for prostitution.

The autopsy confirmed Norman's observations that the victim smoked, had missing teeth and did not look after herself. The age is also correct. The victim's hair survived and is the most accurate part of the reconstruction. Hence the reason why Norman particularly recognised it when the NYE publicised the photofit. The original police investigation concluded 'Hope' was a sex worker. Sutcliffe's description, accent and occupation all fitted.

The original caller declined to give his details for 'reasons of national security'. The authors have identified six servicemen engaged on sensitive missions locally who could have been the mystery caller. They would not have disclosed any information for reasons of military secrecy.

Sutcliffe's work brought him to Scarborough to deliver and collect from the engineering businesses there. The direct route from Bradford to Scarborough uses the A64, but it is possible Sutcliffe also used the A170 through Sutton Bank to make subsequent deliveries after Scarborough to Darlington and Sunderland Docks via Thirsk.

The authors believe Sutcliffe saw 'Hope' at the bus stop and recognised she was a sex worker, enticed her into his lorry to have sex in the cab or to drive to a more secluded location. Once in the cab, he strangled 'Hope' with a ligature then stripped her body. He knew if the body was found the next day, Clarks' records would place him in Scarborough on the day of the murder. So he transported 'Hope's' body along the A170 and concealed it at Sutton Bank – a rural location similar to the one he had left Tracy Browne for dead at in 1975.

Sutcliffe was strong and proficient at moving a body. It would only take him a few minutes to park, move the body from the cab, dump it and go. The body was dumped in a secluded location, shielded from the road by tall plants and the lorry, so it is possible he slashed the corpse while it was in cover at the deposition site without nicking any of the bones. He may also have masturbated over it. As with Jean Jordan, 'Hope' was left nude. No weapon was found.

On his next trip to Scarborough, Sutcliffe returned and left the food product top as a decoy to give a false date of death. Thereby dating the murder to a period that Sutcliffe had not been in Scarborough, negating the evidence in the transport records and establishing a false alibi.

62. Wendy Jenkins
(Believed to be attributed to Sutcliffe by ACC Hellawell)
Wendy Jenkins was a thirty-two-year-old Bristol sex worker whose body was found at around 8.30am on Tuesday 28 August 1979 at a building site where she took clients. Her body was found lying next to the sand heap and a few shovelfuls had been thrown over her body and brushed over, so it partially concealed her from view.

Wendy had head injuries from several blows from a blunt instrument. She had been stabbed, but was not mutilated and was found fully clothed. Her handbag, shoes, a coat and nylons were found in an alley nearby. Wendy had been attacked in the alley where these items were found, then dragged to the second location. A witness, who is believed to be the last person to have seen Wendy alive, saw her talking to a tidily dressed coloured man in his thirties, who was about five-foot eight with shortish hair, at the junction of City Road and Drummond Road, Bristol, at about 3.30am on Monday 27 August.

Wendy's murder was immediately suspected to be a Ripper attack and WYMP detectives conferred with Avon and Somerset Police (A&SP). On 30 August the A&SP SIO said:

> We have to maintain an open mind and a connection cannot be ruled out. However there are certain features common to all the Yorkshire offences which don't appear in the Bristol offence.

These common features are the interference and mutilation of the body by knife and/or screwdriver. This overlooked the possibility that Sutcliffe had been disturbed and fled, which would have prevented him from mutilating the body and penetrating it multiple times with a weapon whilst masturbating over it.

Having stated that A&SP could not rule out the Yorkshire Ripper as a suspect, that is exactly what it did (MPoF).

A&SP concluded that Wendy's murderer was a local man, although there is no evidence to support this. This may also have been because at the time, the criteria for identifying a Ripper attack were too restrictive. In particular, the key criterion was that the attack had to be made with a hammer. The existence of stab wounds may have eliminated the Ripper as a suspect, although he had stabbed Debbie Schlesinger to death on 21 April 1977.

Sutcliffe fits the description of the man Wendy was last seen with. He was a smart dresser, his height was between five-foot seven and five-foot nine and he was aged thirty-three in 1979. He was at various times described as an Arab, Asian or half-caste due to the swarthy colour of his skin.

Wendy was a sex worker, which fitted Sutcliffe's victim preferences. Dragging the victim from the initial attack scene to a secondary scene followed by partial concealment featured in many confirmed Ripper attacks.

At the time, Sutcliffe was aware that the RLDs closer to home were under observation and was avoiding them. Bristol has a RLD and is less than four hours' driving time from Bradford. It was also far enough away from Yorkshire for an attack not to be connected to him. Sutcliffe enjoyed driving and travelled long distances. He used the motorways to attack in different cities and liked to have a clear exit route to a motorway. The abduction point at the junction of City Road and Drummond Road is about seven minutes' drive from the beginning of the M32, which heads north east eventually to the M1 and Bradford.

A&SP appealed for information on an orange or red-coloured Hillman Minx or Hunter Estate. At this time,

Sutcliffe was driving his Rover and a 1970 model, metallic grey Sunbeam Rapier.

Here Chris draws on his experience as a police officer:

> Municipal authorities worldwide eventually began to adopt sodium lamps, and these burn with an orange glow. As a beat officer and panda car driver, I noticed that under the sodium streetlights of the era, most vehicles showed out with an orangey hue, thus making the correct colour of the vehicle difficult to identify. It is entirely possible that a grey Sunbeam Rapier could be mistaken in a few seconds' glance for an orange Hillman Minx or Hunter.

Monday 27 August was a Bank Holiday. Was Sutcliffe roaming that long weekend, with the intention of committing a murder far from Bradford and returning early on the Tuesday morning to be ready for work at 9.00am?

We know that Sutcliffe visited the Bristol area because on 23 March 1980 he bought a red Mini motor car from a West Country businessman.

63. Alison Morris
(Attributed to Sutcliffe by DC Mick Saunders)
64. Barbara Leach
(Convicted)

Between the afternoon of Saturday 1 September 1979 and 1.00pm on Sunday 2 September 1979, two murders occurred some 230 miles apart. The first was that of twenty-five-year-old university lecturer Alison Morris in Essex and the second was that of Barbara Leach in Bradford.

ALISON MORRIS
On Saturday 1 September, Alison went out for an early evening walk down a lane through woods some 250 yards from her home in the village of Ramsey, Essex. At around

6.30pm a man came up behind her and stabbed her repeatedly in the chest with a single-bladed knife.

When she failed to return home an hour later, Alison's father went out to look for her and found her body 250 yards away.

There was no sexual assault or robbery. The SIO on the case stated:

> We can't do other than conclude that the attack was made by a mentally deranged person or by a person for some sort of sexual gratification. It is more than likely that he may attack again.

This deduction is, in the authors' view, accurate and applies perfectly to Sutcliffe. As do other aspects of this crime.

Ramsey is just off the direct A120 route to and from Harwich three miles away, which Sutcliffe delivered to, so he was familiar with the area.

At one stage a man who was about five-foot ten-inches tall with a small beard and wearing a long light trench coat was being sought. Sutcliffe had a beard, and was five-foot nine-inches tall, but this height discrepancy could be an error by the witness. The modus-operandi also fits with Sutcliffe.

Retired police officer Mick Saunders was stationed at Harwich at the time of Alison's murder. Later, he worked on the investigation as a detective in the Essex Police Cold Case Unit. He has revealed that Sutcliffe was a suspect in Alison's murder and that in 1983/4 he requested permission to interview Sutcliffe. His request was denied because Sutcliffe was a patient at Broadmoor. Mick wanted to continue investigating Sutcliffe in connection with Alison's death but was prevented from doing so by resourcing issues. Mr Saunders explains:

> Ramsey isn't the place you think a killer would be lurking around in the woods looking to kill, it is the sort of place I would let my children walk around

alone. But he was known to frequent Essex and had been to Parkeston Quay [Port of Harwich]. A witness said she had spoken with a man who looked like Sutcliffe in Thorpe. I still believe it was Peter Sutcliffe.

BARBARA LEACH

At 1.00am on Sunday 2 September 1979, Sutcliffe murdered twenty-year-old student Barbara Leach.

Barbara was walking up Great Horton Road in Bradford, having left a local pub at 12.45am where she had been drinking with friends. Having identified his victim, Sutcliffe drove past her, parked, got out of his car and let Barbara walk past him. He then turned and hit the back of her head with a hammer, rendering her dead or unconscious instantly. The attack probably took about four seconds.

Sutcliffe dragged Barbara's body to a nearby backyard, where he pushed her bra and blouse up, undid her jeans and pulled them partially down to expose her genitalia. He then mutilated Barbara's body with multiple stab wounds using a screwdriver, posed her body, then concealed it in the bin area, under a carpet with the edges held down with stones. He failed to notice that one of her shoes was showing through the carpet, which led to the discovery of Barbara's body the next day.

Sutcliffe chose to strike in the university area. This change in location again indicates that he was aware that the RLDs were under surveillance and he was avoiding them.

Barbara's murder was instantly recognised as a Ripper attack. Consequently, the possibility of the Ripper having murdered Alison was ruled out, because she was murdered with a knife 230 miles away. Detectives reasoned that he could not have committed Alison's murder and travelled to Bradford in time to murder Alison some six-and-a-half hours later (MPoF).

There are two scenarios for the attack on Alison. The first possibility is that Sutcliffe was out roaming for the weekend in his Rover and drove through the rural villages of Essex looking for a victim. The second option is that Sutcliffe was in his lorry, making a weekend delivery to Harwich for Clarks Transport. On the way back from Harwich, he took a detour to look for a victim in one of the local villages. A couple who ran a garden furniture shop in Thorpe-le-Soken, some eight miles south of Ramsey, recalled that at about the same time as the murder, a large dark blue delivery lorry with a Yorkshire address stopped outside their yard and the driver asked directions for Harwich. It is possible this could have happened on the same day. They described him as slightly built, with dark hair, a small goatee beard, and creepy, staring eyes. They both recognised Sutcliffe as the driver who had asked for directions from his arrest photographs. Did Sutcliffe get lost in the narrow roads between villages and need directions back to the A120? Did he then drive north across the A120 to Ramsey to murder Alison?

Sutcliffe could have committed this attack whichever vehicle he was using. Ramsey is close to the B1352, which leads to the A120, M11 and A1(M) for a quick getaway to Bradford. Assuming he attacked Alison at 6.30pm and left the crime scene at 6.40pm, this left six hours and five minutes for him to travel to Great Horton Road, Bradford, so as to arrive at 12.45am. The journey time in the Rover is just over four hours. If he was in the lorry, it would have taken about four-and-a-half to five hours to travel to Clarks' premises in Bradford, park up, and get into his car. The journey to Great Horton Road from there is about ten minutes.

The attack on Tina Atkinson occurred two days after the attack on Debbie Schlesinger. A very short time interval. The authors believe he attacked Carol Wilkinson at about 9.30am the same day he mutilated the body of Jean Jordan. On the night that he murdered Josephine Whitaker, he had travelled some 260 miles that day, so the length of time spent travelling would not have prevented him from committing another murder. It is entirely credible that Sutcliffe could have killed Alison Morris then driven to Bradford and killed Barbara Leach six-and-a-half hours later.

DI Zackrisson has suggested that Sutcliffe chose Bradford for his attack on Barbara to mislead the investigation into focussing on the unknown Geordie in the hoax letters and tape, by fulfilling the threats made by Humble of a Bradford attack in September or October. The authors concur.

After the attack on Barbara Leach on 2 September 1979, there appeared to be a gap until Sutcliffe's next known attack on Marguerite Walls on 20 August 1980. Yet there is no reason for any pause. This length of time indicates that during this twelve-month period, there were more attacks which were not linked to the Yorkshire Ripper.

In April 1979, Sutcliffe made a delivery to the General Motors plant in Motherwell, about fifteen miles from Glasgow. He parked his lorry at the plant or in a lorry park overnight to comply with the tachograph requirements, then went out for the evening, possibly looking for a victim. He met thirty-five-year-old divorcee Theresa Douglas in the nearby Crown Bar at Holytown and they entered into a relationship. He stayed with Theresa regularly and told her he was 'Peter Logan', a widower from Yorkshire, also writing romantic letters to her using his parents' home for return mail.

This gives rise to a major concern. While in Broadmoor, Sutcliffe conducted long-distance relationships with dozens of women, which demonstrates that he was able to keep track of multiple long-distance relationships. He boasted to his brother Carl that he was having an affair with a married woman in Bradford whose husband worked nights. It is possible he may have had similar relationships, giving him a reason to visit and stay, then use his girlfriends' homes as a base to slip away and commit attacks in other parts of the country, which have not been linked to him.

Sutcliffe used his sister-in-law Marianne's house in Alperton as a base and visited regularly. An extract from the *Daily Express* from 23 May 1981 confirmed Sutcliffe kept a photograph of Marianne in her underwear in his wallet. Sutcliffe did not have a camera and the question arises: how did he obtain this photograph? Was it given to him by Marianne as part of a deeper relationship?

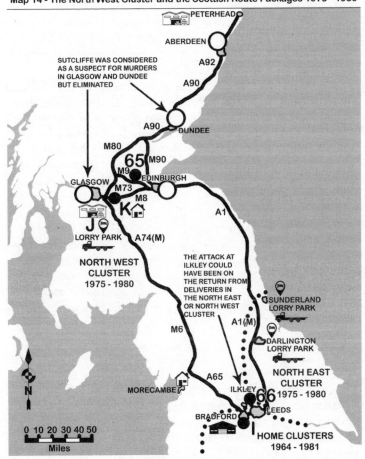

SUTCLIFFE WAS CONSIDERED
AS A SUSPECT FOR MURDERS
IN GLASGOW AND DUNDEE
BUT ELIMINATED

PETERHEAD

ABERDEEN

A92

A90

A90

DUNDEE

M80

65 M90

M9 EDINBURGH

GLASGOW

M73

K

M8

J

LORRY PARK   A74(M)

NORTH WEST
CLUSTER
1975 - 1980

A1

THE ATTACK AT
ILKLEY COULD
HAVE BEEN ON
THE RETURN FROM
DELIVERIES IN
THE NORTH EAST
OR NORTH WEST
CLUSTER

SUNDERLAND
LORRY PARK

A1(M)

DARLINGTON
LORRY PARK

M6

NORTH EAST
CLUSTER
1975 - 1980

A65

ILKLEY

66

MORECAMBE

LEEDS

BRADFORD

HOME CLUSTERS
1964 - 1981

N

0 10 20 30 40 50
Miles

225

No	Name	Date	Cluster(s)	Route Package
I	Clarks Transport			
J	Motherwell: Where Sutcliffe delivered to General Motors			
K	Holytown: Where Sutcliffe stayed with Theresa Douglas			
65	Dawn Webster	14/09/79	North Western	7.1. Bradford to Peterhead Western Route, 7.2. Bradford to Peterhead Eastern Route
66	Yvonne Mysliwiec	11/10/79	North Eastern, North Western	5.1. Bradford-Darlington/ Newton Aycliffe, 5.2. Bradford-Scarborough, 5.5. Bradford-Sunderland Docks, 7.1. Bradford to Peterhead Western Route, 7.2. Bradford to Peterhead Eastern Route, 8.1 Bradford to Motherwell

There were two principal routes from Bradford to Scotland available to Sutcliffe. The Western route A650, A629, A65, A66, M6, A74(M), M74 to Motherwell, about fifteen miles from Glasgow, and four miles from Holytown. Then M74, M73, M80, A9, M90, A90 to Sterling, Perth, Dundee, Aberdeen and Peterhead. Or the Eastern Route A658, A1(M), A168, A19, A1058, A1, A720 to Edinburgh. Then M8, M90, A90 to Perth, Dundee, Aberdeen and Peterhead.

It is inconceivable that Sutcliffe would stop attacking women just because he was outside West Yorkshire. Sutcliffe was arrested in Sheffield in 1981 because he had moved away from his West Yorkshire hunting grounds to escape police surveillance and operate in a different force area, to avoid the attack being linked to him. He may have preferred to commit attacks in Scotland, or on the way there or back. The attack on Yvonne Mysliwiec at Ilkley may have been one of these. Sutcliffe is known to have picked up hitchhikers and therefore had the opportunity to attack them while travelling along the above routes.

The tachograph requirement to take rest would have forced him to stop and sleep overnight in the cab of his lorry in a lorry park. So if he could not stay with his girlfriend(s), he may have been sleeping in a lay-by, lorry park or bed and breakfast. This gave him the opportunity to attack the sex workers that worked the truck parks or the RLDs of Aberdeen, Edinburgh, Dundee and Glasgow which were accessible from them. The interaction between the police and sex workers at the time was antagonistic, so it is highly unlikely that if Sutcliffe did attack a sex worker and she escaped, the attack would have been reported to the police or connected to him.

65. Dawn Webster
(Believed to be attributed to Sutcliffe by ACC Hellawell)
On Friday 14 September 1979, eighteen-year-old hospital worker Dawn Webster from Stenhousemuir went to a party at the ICI Club in the Earls Road Industrial Estate, Grangemouth, and disappeared.

Fifteen days later, Dawn's partially stripped body was found by police using tracker dogs down an embankment beside the M9, at a roundabout where it intersects the A904 and A905 routes from Grangemouth to Stenhousemuir, about a mile from the ICI Club.

The authors have not been able to obtain the pathologists' report and have had to rely on press reports for information, which appear to be contradictory. In

227

summary, the information available is that two pathologists carried out the autopsy. Neither could be certain of the cause of death, or could find any evidence of sexual activity or violence. The cause of death was recorded as a heart attack following a blow or pressure to certain parts of her body. They commented that the circumstances in which the body was discovered suggested foul play.

The autopsy did not discover any heart defect or identify any innocent cause for the blow or pressure to her body that would cause a heart attack. It is clearly not credible that a young, healthy woman would partially undress herself by a motorway then suddenly have a heart attack and roll down an embankment for no reason. So the authors believe Dawn was murdered.

A Fatal Accident Inquiry (the Scottish equivalent of an inquest) established that the last person to see Dawn alive was a former police officer who gave her a lift after the party. He became a suspect, but insisted that she was alive when he left her.

It was suggested at the time that the body had been pushed out of a moving vehicle. However, there were no injuries from hitting the tarmac. Furthermore, the driver would not have been able to push a body with enough force to eject it far enough to clear the vehicle, the hard shoulder and the verge, so that it rolled down the embankment. In his career as a Uniform Branch Constable, Chris attended many RTAs and this is his view:

In my experience, it would be impossible for Miss Webster to have been hit by a vehicle while walking along the motorway hitchhiking, because the impact of a vehicle would have left bruising, crushed bones and graze marks. Nor would this have resulted in her clothes coming off. So an accidental death can be eliminated.

Overall, the authors have the impression of a superficial autopsy, followed by a bungled police investigation which focussed prematurely on an innocent prime suspect (MPoF).

Dawn was obviously hitchhiking back to her home along the A904 and was picked up, then either driven to a different location and murdered there, possibly in the cab. Her assailant then drove to the M9, parked on the hard shoulder and took/rolled the body down the embankment, where he concealed it at the location where the police dog detected it. Alternatively, when the driver went down the M9 instead of continuing along the A904 or A905 to Stenhousemuir, Dawn realised she was being abducted. She tried to get out and was murdered, either in the vehicle, at the roadside, or dragged down the embankment and murdered at the deposition site.

The authors believe that Dawn was murdered using a ligature. This does not leave any obvious bruising and instantly cuts off the victim's air supply, rendering her incapable of resistance. The marks from a ligature would be under the neck tissue and not visible on the skin. It takes about two weeks for a bruise to fade out completely as the body breaks down and reabsorbs the blood. Given that the body had already been exposed to the elements for fifteen days, it is highly unlikely that bruising would still be visible. Particularly if the pathologists were not looking for bruising because they had already concluded the cause of death was a heart attack.

The victim was partially undressed, which indicates a murder with a sexual motive. It is not clear how Dawn had been undressed, if all her clothes were recovered, or where they were found. But fully or partially undressing the body is consistent with an attack by Sutcliffe. He usually lifted up the clothes of his victims. It is unclear where the body was stripped. If her clothes were not found, then this would indicate she was stripped at another location or in the vehicle. If Dawn was not murdered there, it is a secondary crime scene.

It took a police dog to find the body, indicating that it was not visible to the naked eye from the road and had been deliberately and skilfully concealed. Passing traffic would not have seen the attack if it took place at the deposition site, which was a secluded place. Sutcliffe sometimes masturbated over his victims. This fact was not released by the police at the time and it is such an unusual action that the pathologists would not have been looking for semen externally. The body had been in the open for fifteen days in September and October and was therefore subjected to rain and sun, which degrade forensic evidence. The autopsy report that it found no sign of sexual activity probably refers to an internal examination. If the assailant had masturbated onto the body, the effect of the weather would have removed the signs of this.

The murder occurred on a Friday, which would fit with Sutcliffe returning from a delivery in Peterhead to stay with Theresa for the weekend. Earls Road was in an industrial estate, so a lorry would not have looked out of place. Sutcliffe may have also delivered there and, if so, would be familiar with the area. Sutcliffe is known to have enticed hitchhikers into the cab of his lorry and into his cars.

When he was arrested, the cab of his lorry was searched and a rope which had been modified by the addition of a noose was discovered. It would have been perfect for use as a ligature in a confined space, such as the cab of a lorry. During his interrogation, Sutcliffe denied recognising the ligature from the lorry, although it was distinctive, so it is unlikely he would not remember it. Other similar ligatures with a noose were found in Sutcliffe's garage. His explanation was that he used them for lifting engines and the noose stopped the rope from slipping. It is completely implausible that he would be lifting the engine of a lorry, a procedure that would have been done at the Clarks' depot. So he had no innocent reason to be carrying this ligature in the cab. The only credible reason for it to be kept there was for an opportunistic attack on a hitchhiker or sex worker that he had lured into the cab. He denied knowledge of the noosed ligature because it could connect him to other crimes committed while he was driving his lorry.

The deposition site is on the M9 on the eastern route to Bradford and seventeen miles from the route to Theresa's house at Holytown.

In summary, the attack bears many of the classic indicators of an attack by Sutcliffe. It is inconceivable that there was another killer operating in the area with such a similar modus-operandi.

The retired police officer who was the initial suspect would have realised the risks he was taking in being recognised locally and that, as the last person to see Dawn alive, he would automatically become a suspect. It is inconceivable that he would commit such a brazen attack. Although he denied murdering Dawn, he had no alibi and he could not be cleared of involvement and remains the prime suspect. Because of this and because Sutcliffe was not until now suspected of murdering hitchhikers, the authors believe Sutcliffe has never been considered as a suspect for Dawn's murder.

Diagram 6 - Murder of Dawn Webster

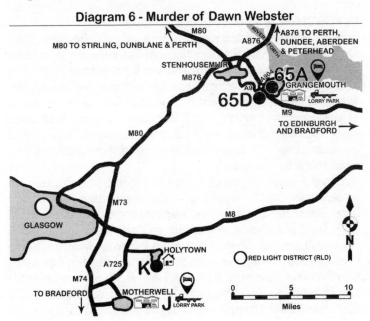

231

No	Name	Date	Cluster(s)	Route Package
J	Motherwell: Where Sutcliffe delivered to General Motors			
K	Holytown: Where Sutcliffe stayed with Theresa Douglas from April 1979 onwards			
65A	Abduction Point	14/09/79	North Western	7.1. Bradford to Peterhead Western Route, 7.2. Bradford to Peterhead Eastern Route
65D	Deposition Site			

Dawn's father was destroyed by the death of his daughter and died prematurely shortly afterwards. The authors would like to leave the last word on Dawn's murder to her family. Quoted in the *Daily Express*, her grandmother said: 'I know they could not find out what she died of, but she didn't end up on that motorway embankment on her own.'

INTERVIEW 6: 23 OCTOBER 1979
Sutcliffe was interviewed again at home to check his alibi for the murder of Barbara Leach, because he had been interviewed about the murders of Jean Jordan and Vera Millward and only eliminated by alibis provided by his wife and his mother. Neither interviewing detective knew of the Laptew Report. Sutcliffe stated that he had been at home with Sonia working on the house and Sonia confirmed this. A handwriting sample was obtained and used to eliminate him.

Chief Constable Gregory had resisted pressure to call in Scotland Yard, believing with some justification that local knowledge was more important and that the days of 'The Yard' being called in to take over large cases from the smaller city, county and borough forces were over. But following enormous pressure, in October 1979 he discussed the situation with MPS Commissioner Sir David McNee. Commander Jim Nevill, the head of the Anti-Terrorist Branch and arguably the MPS's most experienced detective, was sent to Leeds to do a full review.

Commander Nevill identified all the problems with the investigation. He made a series of recommendations – one of which was that suspects should not be eliminated on the basis of voice and handwriting alone – which were largely ignored (MPoF).

Commander Nevill also recommended the £5-note enquiry should be reopened. DCS Jack Ridgway of GMP agreed and took charge of a second £5-note investigation. The distribution of £5 notes from the Midland Bank at Shipley was reconstructed note by note until, in December 1979, GMP detectives had identified that the note found in Jean Jordan's handbag had been sent to eleven firms in West Yorkshire, which had 240 employees. One of them was T&WH Clark.

All 240 employees already had an index card because they had featured in the first £5-note investigation. Initial review of these employees' index cards did not arouse any suspicion about Sutcliffe, because his file had been mislaid or misfiled. Had it been in this review, the sightings in his Ford Corsair and Sunbeam Rapier would have been revealed and he would have been arrested (MPoF).

A separate '£5 Note Incident Room', run by GMP officers, was established at Idle Police Station, Bradford, to oversee the interviews, which were conducted by two detectives – one each from GMP and WYMP.

INTERVIEW 7: 13 JANUARY 1980
Sutcliffe was interviewed at home and said that when he was not at work, he spent his time with his wife working on the house. Sonia confirmed he rarely went out without her. The house, Rover and garage were searched, but nothing of interest was found. His footwear and tools in the house were checked, but the size-seven boots were in an upstairs cupboard and were not found. Sutcliffe told them he had been interviewed in connection with the sightings, which they were unaware of. The officers returned to the station

and found three separate index files concerning the first £5-note enquiry, the cross area sightings in the red Corsair and the triple area sightings in the Sunbeam Rapier, and DC Laptew's report. This should have led to Sutcliffe's immediate arrest, but only a follow-up interview was ordered (MPoF).

INTERVIEW 8: 30 JANUARY 1980

Sutcliffe was questioned about his use of sex workers, whether he had access to a tape recorder, his accent and his alibi for the Barbara Leach murder. Sutcliffe repeated that his work took him through the RLDs in Leeds and Bradford and his wife would confirm he was at home on the night of the Barbara Leach murder. The detectives had been ordered to search Sutcliffe's home, but did not do so because they had interviewed him at a work location. Instead, they searched the cab of his lorry. Had they interviewed him at his home and searched diligently, they would probably have found the size-seven boots, which would have linked him forensically to the Ripper murders and led to his arrest (MPoF). They noted that he had a Bradford accent and left.

The search of the cab found nothing, which is significant. Sutcliffe's tool bag was probably not in the cab, because if the detectives had found a ball pein hammer or a garrotte, he would have been arrested. It confirms the authors' view that Sutcliffe was forensically aware and kept the cab forensically sterile.

The GMP DI commanding the £5 Note Incident Room was still not satisfied and ordered two different detectives to interview Sutcliffe to find out when he had disposed of the two Ford Corsairs and to obtain a stronger alibi for the Barbara Leach murder.

INTERVIEW 9: 7 FEBRUARY 1980

Sutcliffe was interviewed at Clarks Transport. He stated that he had been to Leeds with Sonia on the night of Barbara's murder and had given a couple a lift home to the

Roundhay area, which was confirmed by Sonia. He said that the white Corsair had been scrapped, but there was no record of it at the scrapyard. They checked his logbook at Clarks and identified that on the night of the Josephine Whitaker murder, Sutcliffe had driven about 260 miles and had clocked off at 5.00pm. Sonia confirmed he was at home with her that night.

The officers reported that it was not possible to definitively eliminate Sutcliffe, but he should be interviewed again when the Ripper committed another attack. The DI commanding the incident room ignored their recommendation and signed off Sutcliffe as no further action (MPoF).

This was approved by DCS Ridgway on the basis that Sutcliffe was alibied by the housewarming party for the second visit to the Jean Jordan crime scene (MPoF). He did not know that after the party he had driven his parents back to Bingley and in fact did not have an alibi.

Like the first £5-note enquiry, the second had correctly identified Sutcliffe as a suspect and led detectives to him. However, failures in the WYMP Ripper Incident Room and the GMP £5 Note Incident Room, coupled with poor detective work, resulted in its failure.

66. Yvonne Mysliwiec
(Attributed to Sutcliffe by Detective Superintendent John Stainthorpe. Believed to be attributed to Sutcliffe by both ACC Hellawell and ACC Sampson.)

On Friday 11 October 1979, Yvonne Mysliwiec, a twenty-one-year-old reporter for the *Ilkley Gazette*, was attacked from behind with a ball pein hammer after crossing the footbridge at Ilkley railway station. Yvonne survived because the attack was interrupted by Bryan Copping, aged sixteen.

Bryan passed Yvonne going down the footbridge steps while he was going up. Sutcliffe was five yards behind Yvonne, following her, and briefly made eye contact with Bryan as they passed. Sutcliffe attacked Yvonne from behind, hitting her on the back of her head with a hammer at the bottom of the steps, hidden from view by high stone walls, trees and bushes. He was disturbed and fled back over the footbridge, passing Bryan, who had a good look at him. He described him as being in his thirties, dark, swarthy, with crinkly hair, who got into a flatbed lorry and drove off.

Bryan had previously seen Sutcliffe in Ilkley stalking a local park, which indicates that Sutcliffe was aware the RLDs were under surveillance and had stopped selecting his victims from them. Bryan reported this and it was ignored. It also suggests a detailed knowledge of Ilkley, which Sutcliffe probably acquired while doing his HGV driver training with the Apex School of Driving in 1975.

Given the identification of Sutcliffe, the fact that he was a lorry driver and that Yvonne was attacked from behind with a ball pein hammer, there seems no doubt that Sutcliffe was the perpetrator. Ilkley is thirteen miles from Clarks Transport. The late hour of the attack indicates that Sutcliffe was returning from a long-distance delivery on the Scotland West, Scotland East, Sunderland Docks, Scarborough or Darlington route.

Sutcliffe had made a serious mistake. Police now knew Yvonne's assailant was a lorry driver who drove a flatbed lorry. A search of HGV vehicles registered within West Yorkshire would have identified Clarks Transport. This, coupled with the fact it had been included in the £5-note enquiry, should have resulted in a request to interview the man driving Clarks' flatbed lorry at 9.00pm on 11 October 1979 and would have resulted in Sutcliffe's arrest (MPoF).

Detective Superintendent John Stainthorpe led the investigation and immediately realised it was a Ripper attack. But senior officers did not want the extra pressure caused by another Ripper attack and told him to keep quiet. He complied with this because he felt that WYMP needed to placate the public, not increase the criticism by admitting another attack. As a result, these lines of enquiry were ignored.

WYMP should have sent out a Special Notice to all forces asking them to notify it of any similar attacks where a lorry driver was involved, or suspected to be involved. This would have linked Sutcliffe to the murders of Barbara Mayo and Jackie Ansell-Lamb (MPoF). However, it appears that by this time WYMP was pursuing a policy of not classifying attacks as part of the series unless the evidence was overwhelming, to prevent further public alarm and dissatisfaction with WYMP. So this line of enquiry was ignored.

67. 'Margaret' AKA 'Bedgebury Forest Woman' and Harry Pennells (Acquitted)

On 23 October 1979, a woman riding on horseback through Bedgebury Forest, Kent, found the body of a woman. Despite multiple investigations, an arrest and a trial, she has never been identified and her killer never caught.

'Margaret' had been battered, mutilated and dumped, but little attempt had been made to conceal the body. She had suffered massive head injuries from a beating. A bloodstained wooden stake found near the victim's body was later concluded to have been the murder weapon. No handbag or means of identification were found.

The autopsy revealed that the victim had been killed up to five days prior to her discovery and had an ectopic pregnancy which had been present for four to six weeks and bleeding for two to three weeks. She would have been in severe pain.

The severity of the injuries prevented identification. She was white, aged between thirty and thirty-five, five-foot one-inch tall with a thin build. There was no evidence that 'Margaret' had ever visited a dentist. She had prominent, visibly decayed teeth. There was no nicotine staining, and her lungs were clear of carbon deposits, indicating that she probably lived in the countryside. She had straight shoulder-length dark brown hair.

'Margaret' was wearing black shoes, a black-and-white floral dress and a black polo neck jumper. The dress was homemade from furniture fabric and had been altered at the hem and at the chest area. An artist's impression of what she looked like was created.

The investigation failed to identify 'Margaret', but Kent Police believed she was possibly from the North of England, of no fixed address, and was a regular hitchhiker along the M1 and M6 motorways. She may have been a sex worker, operating from Spitalfields in London. The investigation focussed on the movements of lorry drivers.

In December 1984, the victim was featured on an episode of BBC TV's *Crimewatch* in which an appeal was made for the person who made the dress to come forward. This was successful and the case featured for a second time in the next programme in January 1985. It was revealed that the woman who made the black-and-white dress had made contact. She was from Stratford-upon-Avon and stated that she had given the dress to a charity shop in Evesham, Worcestershire. However, the police were unable to trace it back to 'Margaret'.

The case was reopened in October 1998, to take advantage of new forensic science techniques that allowed the generation of DNA profiles from much smaller samples than had been previously possible.

As a result of improved forensic techniques, more information was released, including an updated description. 'Margaret' was now believed to be aged between twenty-five and thirty-five, not between thirty and thirty-five; of medium build, not slight; and her eye colour was hazel, not brown. She had prominent decayed teeth. A more accurate image of 'Margaret' was also produced.

Lorry driver Harry Pennells had been questioned by police a few days after the discovery of the body and interviewed three times between 1979 and 1980. Specks of blood found in his lorry in 1979 were re-examined and linked to 'Margaret' through DNA. In January 1999 he was charged with 'Margaret's' murder.

The trial started on 4 May 2000 at Maidstone Crown Court. The prosecution case was that Harry Pennells had picked up the victim at Spitalfields Market on 19 October 1979 and taken her in his lorry to a delivery in Keighley, West Yorkshire, and returned to South London. Then on the morning of 20 October he had beaten her to death with the wooden stake.

Two witnesses from the Keighley lorry depot stated that they saw and spoke to a young woman who was with Harry Pennells. Staff at Henley Transport's Rochdale depot also stated that they saw Harry Pennells with a woman with a similar appearance to the artist's impression of the victim.

Samples of blood and flakes of hair found in a sleeping bag on the passenger seat of the lorry matched the DNA profile of the victim. Additionally, particles of foam from a mattress in the cab of the lorry were found on the victim's dress.

Harry Pennells pleaded not guilty; quoted in the *Birmingham Post*, his evidence was:

Mr Pennells told the court he had picked up a female hitchhiker at a service station on the M1, near Northampton, on October 19 and she had wanted to get to Liverpool. The woman, who said her name was Margaret or Marjory and lived in Stepney, East London, then changed her mind and decided to travel to London with him when he returned home the next day after making a delivery of fruit.

Mr Pennells said: 'Just before we got to London, she said there was no use going home as her landlady had gone to friends at the seaside. She asked if I drop her off as she was going to Dover to meet her mates to go to Scotland.'

Mr Pennells told the court he dropped the woman off at the Dutch House pub on the A20 in Eltham,

South London, and did not see her again. He claimed he had not picked up the hitchhiker for sex.

Mr Michael Hill QC, defending, told jury members that the prosecution case relied on circumstantial evidence and had several holes in it.

He said there was no evidence to link Mr Pennells with the scene of the murder or to prove that the murder victim had been in the cab on the date of the offence.

He was found not guilty in a unanimous decision. Neither author is surprised at the verdict. The presence of 'Margaret's' blood in the cab was not suspicious, because the victim had an ectopic pregnancy and had been bleeding for two to three weeks. Harry Pennells admitted he had given a woman resembling the victim a lift. This was entirely consistent with her hitching lifts up and down the M1 with lorry drivers in return for sex. This was a common practice at the time known as 'a ride for a ride'. So the presence of the foam on her dress just showed she had been in the cab, but that was all.

The prosecution was unable to refute Harry's evidence that he had dropped 'Margaret' off alive at the Dutch House pub. 'Margaret's' lifestyle meant that she could have been picked up by another man. Above all, two defence witnesses stated that they had seen a woman matching 'Margaret's' description in Bedgebury Forest on 21 October 1979, the day after the prosecution alleged Harry Pennells had murdered her.

The authors believe that Harry Pennells did pick up 'Margaret' and that he dropped her off at the Dutch House pub in Eltham unharmed. It is right next to the A20, and she probably asked to be dropped off there in the hope of getting another lift and a cab to stay the night of the twentieth in. Another lorry driver may have given 'Margaret' a lift to Central London so she could ply her trade at Spitalfields Meat Market, or to Kent. She ended up at Bedgebury Forest on the twenty-first, where she was seen by the two witnesses.

One of the areas that Sutcliffe regularly delivered to in London was the LEP Transport Depot just off the A2 at Charlton (now a business park with an Asda Superstore). Sutcliffe was familiar with this part of London, having stayed in Deptford when Sonia was at the Teacher Training College. This would put him in the area where Harry Pennells dropped 'Margaret' off. Sutcliffe also delivered to Dover and other parts of Kent, which could put him in the area where her body was found.

'Margaret' may have been a sex worker, which is consistent with Sutcliffe's victim preferences. She may have been working in Yorkshire or in truck stops. It is just possible that Sutcliffe may have known her from picking her up in Spitalfields Meat Market, a RLD in Yorkshire or truck stops on other occasions. She was beaten to death with blows to the head with a blunt instrument, which is consistent with Sutcliffe's modus-operandi. He was the only lorry driver known to be delivering in London and Kent that attacked victims in this way. Bedgebury Forest is two miles from the A21, which would have allowed a fast escape.

'Margaret' was buried in Hawkenbury Cemetery, Tunbridge Wells, with only police officers attending. Her identity is still unknown and her grave is unmarked.

68. Sally Shepherd

At about 1.00am on Saturday 1 December 1979, following an evening visit to friends, twenty-four-year-old restaurant manager Sally Shepherd caught the last bus to Peckham at New Cross.

She got off at the last stop and started walking home. Sally was struck on the back of the head with a blunt instrument. She was then dragged semi-conscious through a hole in a wire-mesh fence surrounding an unoccupied yard at the back of Peckham Police Station, to a secondary crime scene. There she was stripped of her boots and some of her clothes, which were strewn around. Her murderer then mutilated her private parts and caved in her chest by stamping up and down on her. Sally's body was discovered the next day.

The SIO said:

> It's the worst murder I have dealt with in twenty-six years. She suffered horrific injuries, including massive head wounds caused by a blunt instrument. This heinous crime defies normal logic. There was no need to inflict the terrible injuries she suffered. I believe we are hunting for a sex maniac who is extremely unbalanced.

At the time of her murder, four policemen were within earshot in the back yard of Peckham Police Station examining a stolen vehicle, but none of them heard anything. Whoever killed Sally attacked swiftly and silently, with a ruthless blow delivered expertly to the back of the head to immediately kill or render the victim unconscious. The implication is that he had probably done it before.

Sally's murder is a carbon copy of Sutcliffe's attack on Yvonne Pearson. He hit Yvonne on the head with a hammer, then undressed her and kicked her in the head and body. Then he jumped up and down on her chest with the weight of both feet, caving in her chest. A unique act not replicated by any other killer or murder.

Three hairs were recovered from the scene of Sally's murder, but science is not currently advanced enough to test them for DNA. The leader of the MPS Cold Cases Unit has been quoted as saying:

> The investigation team from Yorkshire visited the Met's homicide enquiry team at the time of the original investigation as it was known that the Yorkshire Ripper had a delivery run down through London at the time of Sally Shepherd's murder. There were no links found.

The hairs recovered at the scene were rootless and therefore, at this time are not viable for testing.

The location of this crime off the A202 Peckham High Street was only one mile from the junction with the A2 at New Cross Road, which Sutcliffe travelled through regularly to the LEP Depot at Charlton. The blunt instrument could have been a hammer. Given the late hour of the attack and the tachograph limitations on how many hours he could travel for, Sutcliffe could have been staying in a lorry park after a delivery to the LEP Depot six miles away. The Conquering Hero pub is six miles away from the crime scene. A bus conductress told police that she saw a white Ford Cortina (Sutcliffe's white Corsair?) with a dark patch of primer on one wing parked nearby and saw a man running from Staffordshire Street.

The attack bears all of Sutcliffe's hallmarks and the assertion that there were no links to him is untenable. Sutcliffe is in fact a very strong suspect. So why was he ruled out?

At the time of the WYMP visit to the Met, the SIO on the Ripper investigation was DCS Hobson. If he had confirmed that Sutcliffe had attacked a woman in South London, it would instantly have revealed that he was not just operating in a closely defined area of West Yorkshire, South Yorkshire and Manchester, but was operating all over the country. This would have opened up an even bigger controversy, resulting in even more criticism. Hence, as with Yvonne Mysliwiec, it was ignored as a Ripper attack (MPoF).

69. Diane Johnston
Diane Johnston's evidence is below:

> I remember the atmosphere of terror for women during this time. However, the belief was that the Yorkshire Ripper was only operating around the Leeds area, and attitudes to hitchhiking were very different at that time.

I was a twenty-two-year-old student nurse and was hitchhiking on my own to get home from Edinburgh to Essex, where I lived. It was February – April 1980. I was picked up by Sutcliffe in his flatbed lorry on the A1. It was daytime and he was the second or third lift I got that day. He stopped way after where I was hitching, started, then stopped again. The picture of him leaning over to open the passenger door is imprinted on my mind. What followed went quickly from normal to terrifying.

We started talking normally at first. He looked at me, but not in a lecherous or threatening way. He answered a few questions in a quiet spoken, high-pitched northern accent as we were driving along – I thought he was very shy – but he very quickly stopped talking, stared straight ahead and leant over the steering wheel and started fiddling with a bag of stuff on the floor to his right which obviously, I now know, contained a hammer. At that point I realised I was in serious danger and felt like screaming. I can't say at all how long I was in that cab, terrified. But I carried on talking and in my babbling I said I was a nurse. He then seemed to relax and said, 'Oh, you're one of the good ones,' which was the most terrifying part, the way he said it.

He pulled into the next services alongside a coach and asked where it was going and persuaded the driver to give me a lift. He agreed. I got on the coach in total shock. The following year his face was all over the papers and only then did I realise who he was and what a lucky escape I'd had. I presume he realised it was too dangerous in broad daylight to kill me but I do realise how very lucky I am and many women were not.

The A1 is on the direct route to Harwich from Bradford, which Sutcliffe used regularly. The authors believe Sutcliffe had attacked hitchhikers in daylight before and think the initial stop, start, stop when he picked up Diane was because he was initially hesitant about picking up a hitchhiker to murder so openly, but after some hesitation decided to proceed.

The tool bag contained the hammer and other tools he used as weapons. It would normally be stowed out of the way in the sleeping area behind the seats. Sutcliffe obviously kept it on his right side on the floor so that he could get to the weapons it contained easily, concealed by the steering column. He was fiddling with the tool bag to find the hammer shaft or the garrotte amongst the other tools.

Sutcliffe was forensically aware and would not have attacked a victim in the cab with a hammer, to avoid leaving bloodstains. The authors believe it was Sutcliffe's intention to stop the lorry in a secluded spot on the pretext of needing to urinate. Then he planned to walk around to the passenger door, pull Diane out (she wasn't wearing a seatbelt), smash the back of her skull in with the hammer, then strangle her with a ligature. The body would then be dragged to undergrowth to be undressed, mutilated and concealed. A carbon copy of the attacks on Jackie Ansell-Lamb and Barbara Mayo.

Diane was very lucky. Sutcliffe was devoted to Sonia, who had been a patient in a mental hospital. It is possible that Diane's revelation that she was a nurse may have influenced him to spare her.

70. Child C
Child C's evidence is below:

> I happened to be watching a documentary this evening on the Yorkshire Ripper. For what it's worth I wanted to let you know that I believe I had an encounter with Peter Sutcliffe in what I believe would have been 1980 on Checketts Road in Leicester. I vividly remember that day because he scared me to no end. His truck was parked on the opposite side to me and

he crossed over to my side of the road. I was on my way home from school and I remember the time to be around 3.40pm as he asked me what time it was. He then asked me if I was free which scared me so I said 'no' and started walking faster. I looked behind and he was following me. I started running and he also started running right up to my street. Luckily he didn't see me go into the house.

I peeked through the window and saw him walk all the way to the end of my street and back. I was terrified. I recognised him from the pic in the papers following his arrest a year later. I did not report this as I did not want to be associated with him. I'm not sure whether this disclosure matters at all but I had to let my story and him out of my system.

After watching the documentary last night, I Googled to check whether it was ever proven that he went past Leicester during his killing spree. Surprisingly I came across the *Leicester Mercury* article which I have just realised was from 2013. It had your email address and mobile number. I realised that your investigation or interest was linked to murders committed much earlier in Leicester but it seemed like a good idea to mention my encounter and lucky escape.

I had thought of reporting my encounter to the police numerous times but would not have known how best to go about it. He had parked the truck by the school on the opposite side of the road. He walked across the road clad in a denim shirt and trousers, very short and skinny. I remember not being scared at this point. I believe I had walked past Bernard's Rd but before Victoria Rd. My route that I took every day and on that day was Checketts Rd up to Loughborough Rd and crossing at the traffic lights and walking towards home.

I was lucky that when I approached the traffic lights, the road was clear but when he approached it, there was traffic, giving me time to get to my house in the middle of the street before he reached the corner. I would have been fifteen [at] the time but always looked a couple of years older and, yes, I was in my school uniform although it could have been mistaken for normal clothing: yellow shirt, blue skirt and cardigan. I know it was a warm day with blue skies. I don't remember wearing a jacket, just the shirt, cardigan and skirt.

I also remember that it was the beginning of holidays and we were let out early from school. So that would probably be the Easter break or half-term break after Easter. I don't think it would have been any term breaks after that as the temperatures would have been much higher. Also on the account that it was really quiet on Checketts Rd makes me think it was not a Friday as perhaps I would have expected more people around.

This verifies that Sutcliffe attacked schoolgirls and searched for victims in Leicester. It adds credibility to him as the murderer of Rosina Hilliard.

71. Patricia 'Patsy' Morris

Patsy Morris was a fourteen-year-old schoolgirl who it is believed 'bunked off' school for the afternoon of Monday 16 June 1980. A witness who knew Patsy saw her soon after noon near her home. Another witness saw a girl who might have been Patsy at a bus stop on the Hounslow Heath side of Staines Road between 12.20pm and 12.40pm that day.

On 18 June, Patsy's body was found by a police dog handler on Hounslow Heath, ten yards from a path. She was lying face down, hidden in a thicket, and had been strangled with her own tights. Her clothing had been pushed upwards, revealing her thighs. Her tights and knickers had been pulled down over her ankles – strongly suggesting a sexual motive for the killing. Unusually, there was no sign of sexual assault or evidence of rape. A second pair of tights, one leg missing from the gusset downwards, was tied around Patsy's leg and wound upwards until it was knotted four times around her neck. An identical pair of one-legged tights was wrapped three times around both wrists in front of her body and then over her breasts. No attempt had been made to conceal her body.

The 1980 Whit Bank Holiday Monday was on 26 May, and during that week Sutcliffe drove to Marianne's at Alperton with Sonia and her parents, where they stayed overnight. They then visited a relative in Middlesex before returning home.

During the early summer of 1980, Sutcliffe and his brother Mick were house-sitting at Alperton whilst Marianne and her family were abroad. While they were there they routinely picked up sex workers from Soho together in a car.

There was vehicle access to the crime scene via a concrete road that ran across the heath between the A314 and the A315, giving easy access for a quick exit. Scores of people were on the heath, but no one saw or heard anything. Previous sexual assaults and murders on or around the heath had invariably involved the penetrative rape of the victim. Whoever murdered Patsy Morris attacked efficiently and silently, found satisfaction without penetration and fled quickly. All classic Sutcliffe indicators.

Patsy was murdered twelve miles from Alperton and just over a mile from where Lynne Weedon was murdered. Like Eve Stratford, Patsy was found with her wrists tied behind her back with one of her stockings and with the other stocking tied around her ankle.

72. Woman A and Woman B

Chris was contacted with an account of an attack on two women having tea in a café in York at dusk in about May 1980. The only other customer was a man who frequently stared at them while writing in a notebook. They felt uneasy and left. He followed them and they started to run, with him running after them. They managed to hail a taxi and get away. They reported it to NYP.

After Sutcliffe's arrest, Woman A saw Sutcliffe's photograph and recognised him as the man in the café some nine months later. Sutcliffe was probably writing down his hours driving in the days before tachographs, probably parked up in a lorry park after a long journey, or having made a delivery in York.

Sutcliffe was familiar with York and this may not have been his first attack there. On 28 May 1977, Sutcliffe was drinking in a pub in York with two friends. At some point in the evening he followed a woman out of the pub, returning later. It is likely that he attacked this woman – he could have had no other reason to stalk her. Enquiries to ascertain if there was an attack reported that night were ignored by NYP.

INTERVIEW 10: 26 JUNE 1980
Sutcliffe had a heavy drinking session in the Royal Standard pub on Manningham Lane in Bradford. He was seen around 11.30pm by two uniformed police officers, who were manning a static observation point in an unmarked car as part of an operation to catch the Ripper while he was returning from an attack. Sutcliffe was driving his Rover erratically and was pursued home, breathalysed and found to be over the limit. He was arrested, then bailed until his trial, which was scheduled for January 1981. The officers passed his details to the Millgarth Incident Room, which confirmed he had been eliminated.

The authors believe that Sutcliffe committed four attacks in the period August to September 1980 and reverted to strangulation to ensure these murders were not attributed to him. Two murders were in Leeds and two in Sweden.

The murder of Marguerite Walls was the second of these attacks, but is considered first, so the Swedish murders can be considered together.

74. Second attack on Maureen Long, resulting in the murder of Marguerite Walls
(Convicted)

On the night of Wednesday 20 August 1980, Marguerite Walls, a forty-seven-year-old civil servant, had finished work at 10.30pm and started walking to her home in Farsley, Leeds. This was a very respectable area, so Marguerite would have felt quite safe. At about 11.00pm Sutcliffe attacked her. The bloodstains and drag marks showed that Marguerite was attacked at the entrance to Claremont House on New Street, Farsley. His initial blows from behind with the hammer did not subdue Marguerite. So Sutcliffe strangled her with a ligature, then dragged her from the entrance into the garden and completed strangling her there.

On the night of Marguerite's murder, a man was seen lurking in the bushes in Westroyd Park, less than fifty yards from where she was attacked. In his book *On the Trail of the Yorkshire Ripper*, Richard Charles Cobb concluded that this man was Sutcliffe and he was waiting there to kill Maureen Long. Sutcliffe took the *Daily Mail* and the *Argus* – which covered the Ripper story extensively – and used them to follow the investigation. On 11 July 1977 the *Argus* confirmed that WYMP had identified Maureen Long as a Ripper victim and that she could identify him. It published her address at 22 Donald Street, Farsley, which is a cul-de-sac exiting onto New Street. Sutcliffe stated that he subsequently saw Maureen while shopping. As the only surviving victim that could identify him, Sutcliffe must have realised that she was a major threat. Richard asserts that Sutcliffe intended to eliminate Maureen as a witness by killing her as she walked along New Street before turning into Donald Street and home, but mistook Marguerite for Maureen.

Maureen and Marguerite had similar facial features, were the same height and build, with short dark hair. Both were wearing dark clothing and carrying a large handbag. During the investigation, WPC Elizabeth Ross, who was the same height and build as Marguerite, participated in a reconstruction in which she walked the same route, wearing similar clothes and with the same hairstyle. WPC Ross looked more like Marguerite than Maureen. With a fleeting glimpse through the bushes, Marguerite would easily be mistaken for Maureen.

An attack on a woman that looks exactly like a key witness one hundred yards from that witness's home by the same man goes far beyond coincidence. The authors therefore concur with Richard's assessment that this was not an opportunistic attack, as Sutcliffe was to claim, but a carefully planned ambush.

The authors believe Sutcliffe was patiently lying in wait, observing New Street from Westroyd Park or Claremont House. Both locations gave good cover and observation of New Street so he could attack Maureen as she walked to the only entrance into Donald Street. When Marguerite walked past him, Sutcliffe mistook her for Maureen and either followed her from Westroyd Park to the entrance to Claremont House, or jumped out from Claremont House.

He dragged her into the overgrown gardens, which were secluded and concealed from view by thick vegetation and a fence. It was by far the best location on New Street for Sutcliffe to murder a victim and had obviously been pre-selected. There he knelt on her chest and strangled her. At this point, Sutcliffe took a major risk. Marguerite had served in the army and had screamed and fought like a banshee. Yet instead of fleeing, he lingered to rain blows on her body with his hammer, rip her clothes off and scatter them around the garden, before partially concealing it with a pile of grass clippings and leaves. The authors believe that when he was strangling Marguerite, he realised she was not Maureen and he had attacked the wrong woman. Overcome with rage, he had a need to vent his fury on her body as he had done with Jean Jordan. Hence the reason he delayed his departure so he could mutilate her body.

Sutcliffe had probably been observing New Street on other occasions. He was to use an observation point to select Upadhya Bandara and Jacqueline Hill as victims.

251

Although Marguerite had been beaten about the head with a hammer, WYMP eliminated her as a Ripper victim because she had been strangled, there was no use of a knife and Farsley was unlike any location the Ripper had attacked in before.

Maureen had recently moved away from Donald Street, so Marguerite's murder was not connected to her (MPoF).

When questioned about Marguerite's murder, Sutcliffe initially denied it, saying: 'No, that wasn't me. You have a mystery on your hands with that one. I've only used the rope once on that girl at Headingley.' (Upadhya Bandara.)

Then on 26 January 1981, he confessed to her murder. When asked why he had initially denied responsibility he stated:

Because when I was questioned initially I knew I was in such deep water through killing through the method I normally use, that this would possibly open completely new lines of enquiry into other murders which could have been committed [by himself] and which I knew I hadn't done.

Diagram 7 - The Murder of Marguerite Walls

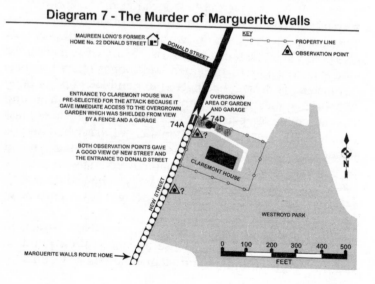

Initially, Sutcliffe had misrepresented the use of a ligature on Upadhya Bandara as an isolated incident to prevent it being connected to other murders committed using a ligature. The authors believe Sutcliffe had started using the ligature again but without using a knife, to avoid the attack being connected to other murders he had committed.

The Swedish Cluster. 73 Gertie Jensen and 75 Teresa Thörling

The Swedish Police Authority (*Polismyndigheten*) Investigations Unit (*Kriminalavdelningen*) has confirmed that it is satisfied that Gertie Jensen and Teresa Thörling were murdered by the same man and that both murders are consistent with Sutcliffe's modus-operandi.

GERTIE JENSEN

Gertie Jensen, aged thirty-one, was a prostitute in Gothenburg. At this time, sex work was legal in Sweden. Her naked body was found on a demolition site at 7.00am on Tuesday 12 August 1980. The back of her skull had been bashed in with a brick.

TERESA THÖRLING

Teresa Thörling was a twenty-six-year-old Malmö sex worker. She was seen soliciting in the early evening of Saturday 30 August 1980 in Malmö's RLD.

Two days later, Teresa's body was discovered in a derelict building, concealed beneath a piece of carpet. She had been hit on the back of the head with a blunt object, which was probably a brick. The cause of death was strangulation either with hands or a thin object (i.e. a ligature). Teresa had been murdered shortly after she was last seen. She was naked and was posed, lying on her front with a long wooden stick forced into her rectum. A substance was found on her back that could have been semen, indicating that she had been masturbated over.

By this time Sutcliffe was aware that the RLDs he usually used were under surveillance and was varying the areas he attacked in to evade it. This would explain why he would choose to attack in another country.

Both murders have features common to Sutcliffe's attacks. The victims were sex workers, lured into a vehicle, then hit over the back of the head with a brick. A brick was used in the stone in the sock attack, and to murder Mary Judge and Stephanie Spencer. Teresa had been strangled and masturbated over. Like Emily Jackson, she also had a stick forced into a body cavity. Both bodies were found in derelict buildings/wasteland, a type of location Sutcliffe favoured.

Sutcliffe hid the bodies of some of his UK victims and always fled quickly, so that he would be home before any police road blocks could be established. The E6 would meet Sutcliffe's need for a fast exit from the deposition site. Like Barbara Leach, Teresa's body was concealed under a carpet, delaying its discovery for two days and ensuring Sutcliffe was out of the country when the body was discovered.

Sutcliffe could have been travelling to the continent for Clarks Transport. However, the authors believe he was travelling privately in a car. He could have travelled on a freight ferry or a passenger ferry. Paying for the ticket in cash and changing cash into (Swedish) Krona would have ensured that there was no financial record of his presence on a ferry. He could have slept in a lorry park, in his car, or in the tent he used when Sonia was studying in Deptford, to avoid registering in a hotel.

Travelling by ferry would explain the use of a brick as the murder weapon. Sutcliffe would know his vehicle could be searched by customs, so he would have left his tool bag behind, depriving him of his usual variety of weapons and requiring him to use an improvised weapon picked up at the crime scene.

The interval between the Swedish attacks is consistent with Sutcliffe's intensity of offending at this time, as shown by the intervals between the attacks on Mo Lea, Theresa Sykes and Jacqueline Hill.

No	Name	Date	Interval between attacks without Swedish murders	Interval between attacks with Swedish murders
73	Gertie Jensen	12/08/80	N/A	
74	Marguerite Walls	20/08/80		8 days
75	Teresa Thörling	30/08/80	N/A	10 days
76	Upadhya Bandara	24/09/80	35 days	25 days
77	Mo Lea	25/10/80	31 days	31 days
78	Theresa Sykes	05/11/80	11 days	11 days
80	Jacqueline Hill	17/11/80	12 days	12 days

The authors' analysis of the route packages available to him show that Sweden was in easy striking distance for Sutcliffe. The E6 connects the ferry ports of Bergen, Stavanger, Oslo, Gothenburg, Varberg, Halmstad, Helsingborg, Limhamn and Rodyhavn. Thus putting Malmö and Gothenburg within convenient travelling distance of any of those ports, which in turn gave access to ferries direct to the UK and to Denmark. The road network would give access to ferry ports at Ebsjerg, Germany, the Netherlands, Belgium and France for the journeys to and from the UK.

This gave Sutcliffe a wide variety of routes to Gothenburg and Malmö:
- The direct route from the UK to Gothenburg would involve driving to Newcastle, Immingham or Harwich and on to Gothenburg by overnight ferry. If he also used this direct route package for the attack on Teresa, there would be an additional six-hour road journey from Gothenburg to Malmö.

- He could have travelled to Bergen or Stavanger in Norway from Newcastle, then driven along the E6 to Gothenburg and Malmö.
- He could have travelled to Ebsjerg in Denmark by overnight ferry from Newcastle, Immingham or Harwich. Then travelled to Gothenburg or Malmö by ferry from Denmark. If Sutcliffe travelled from Helsingor or Dragor, the delays on the ferry between Nyborg and Korsor would increase the journey time.
- He could have travelled from Newcastle, Immingham, Harwich or Dover to Dunkirk, Calais, Zeebrugge, Hook of Holland, Rotterdam, Amsterdam, Ijmuiden, Bremerhavn, Bremen, Cuxhavn or Hamburg and then driven to Denmark. Then:
- a) Travelled to Sweden by ferry and gone on to Gothenburg or Malmö by the E6. If Sutcliffe had used Helsingor or Dragor, the ferry journey between Nyborg and Korsor would have increased the journey time.

Or

- b) Travelled to Germany, ferry from Puttgarden to Rodbyhavn and road to Malmö.

The Route Package analysis below shows that all of these routes would allow Sutcliffe to travel to Sweden and murder Gertie in three to four days and Theresa in three to five days.

No	Name	Date	Possible Route	Days
73	Gertie Jensen	12/08/80	UK to Gothenburg	3
			UK to Norway, E6 to Gothenburg	4/5
			UK to Ebsjerg, ferry to Gothenburg	3/4
			UK to Ebsjerg, ferry Nyborg to Korsor, ferry from Helsingor or Dragor to Sweden, E6 to Gothenburg	4/5

No	Name	Date	Possible Route	Days
			UK to Channel/ North Sea port, road to Denmark, ferry to Sweden, E6 to Gothenburg	4/5
75	Teresa Thörling	30/08/80	UK to Gothenburg, E6 to Malmö	3/4
			UK to Norway, E6 to Malmö	5
			UK to Ebsjerg, ferry to Sweden, E6 to Malmö	3/4
			UK to Ebsjerg, ferry Nyborg to Korsor, ferry from Helsingor or Dragor to Sweden, E6 to Malmö	4/5
			UK to Channel/ North Sea port, road to Denmark, ferry to Sweden, E6 to Malmö	4/5
			UK to Channel/North Sea port, road to Denmark, ferry Nyborg to Korsor, ferry from Helsingor or Dragor to Sweden, E6 to Malmö	4/5
			UK to Channel/ North Sea port, road to Germany, ferry Puttgarden to Rodbyhavn E6 to Malmö	4/5

The above timings are approximate and only intended to give an indication of journey times

Sutcliffe enjoyed visiting RLDs and may have wanted to visit the large RLDs at Amsterdam, Hamburg or Copenhagen, which had an international reputation. He had the route-planning skills to organise journeys like this. The cities of North East France, Belgium, the Netherlands, North West Germany and Denmark all have RLDs. Like West Yorkshire, they are all connected by a fast road network, making them attractive areas for Sutcliffe to operate in.

Sonia was very home orientated, so other than their honeymoon in Paris and one family visit to Prague, the Sutcliffes did not go away on holiday. Sutcliffe routinely went on 'runs out' for four or five days. So disappearing for five or six days would not be out of the ordinary. It is highly likely that Sutcliffe would take his annual holiday in August. As a teacher, Sonia would be on her summer holiday break. So taking three or four days leave from the eleventh to the thirteenth of August would not have aroused any suspicion and would have allowed Sutcliffe to get to Sweden, murder Gertie, and return without arousing suspicion.

On 27 August, Sonia's grandmother arrived in the UK to visit Sonia's mother and Sonia. Sonia, her mother and grandmother stayed together in Morecambe in self-catering accommodation from 3 September. Sutcliffe visited them with his brother, nephews and nieces on Sunday 7 September.

Knowing that Sonia would want to be with her grandmother – whom she had not seen since 1975 – it is entirely credible that Sonia would agree he could go on a 'run out' from 27 August onwards. This means that Sutcliffe could have been away from home at various times between 27 August and 6 September (eleven days).

The visit of Sonia's grandmother was a unique event, giving Sutcliffe the opportunity for an extended 'run out', explaining how he could have been able to commit an attack in Malmö.

The calendar below shows that Sutcliffe could easily have travelled to Sweden and committed both murders and been able to return to the UK to murder Marguerite Walls.

Day and Date		Direct to Gothenburg by ferry from the UK	To Sweden via Denmark, Norway, France, Belgium, the Netherlands or Germany	Event
S	09/08/80			
S	10/08/80		Day 1	
M	11/08/80	Day 1	Day 2	
T	12/08/80	Day 2	Day 3	Murder of Gertie Jensen, Gothenburg
W	13/08/80	Day 3	Day 4	
T	14/08/80		Day 5	
F	15/08/80			
S	16/08/80			
S	17/08/80			
M	18/08/80			
T	19/08/80			
W	20/08/80			Murder of Marguerite Walls, Leeds
T	21/08/80			
F	22/08/80			
S	23/08/80			
S	24/08/80			
M	25/08/80			
T	26/08/80			

Day and Date		Direct to Gothenburg by ferry from the UK	To Sweden via Denmark, Norway, France, Belgium, the Netherlands or Germany	Event
W	27/08/80			Sonia's grandmother arrives in the UK to visit her daughter and granddaughter Sonia. Sonia preoccupied with her mother and grandmother, possibly leaving Sutcliffe free to travel until 6 September (11 Days). (Dark shading) 1
T	28/08/80		Day 1	2
F	29/08/80	Day 1	Day 2	3
S	30/08/80	Day 2	Day 3	Murder of Teresa Thörling, Malmö 4
S	31/08/80	Day 3	Day 4	5
M	1/09/80	Day 4	Day 5	6
T	2/09/80			7

Day and Date		Direct to Gothenburg by ferry from the UK	To Sweden via Denmark, Norway, France, Belgium, the Netherlands or Germany	Event
W	3/09/80			Sonia, her mother and grandmother leave Bradford and stay in self-catering accommodation in Morecambe 8
T	4/09/80			9
F	5/09/80			10
S	6/09/80			11
S	7/09/80			Sutcliffe visits Sonia and her family at Morecambe

Typically, Sutcliffe would return from an attack late at night. Sonia would normally be in bed and therefore would not see him in bloodstained clothes and shoes. He would check his clothing and shoes for bloodstains before going to bed. Heavily bloodstained clothes would be burnt in a garden incinerator shortly afterwards.

Sutcliffe's brother Carl has confirmed that in the 'late summer' of 1980, Sutcliffe turned up at his house unexpectedly in the 'late afternoon'. He took off the clean clothes he was wearing, then put on some dirty clothes and hid the clothes he had changed out of behind the boiler in the bathroom.

The visit to Carl was highly unusual and can only have been in order to conceal bloodstained clothing. Why did Sutcliffe deviate from his normal, forensically safe routine and risk involving Carl in the storage of incriminating clothing?

Sutcliffe had changed out of one set of clothing and into another set that to Carl's eye had obviously already been worn, possibly for a couple of days. This indicates that Sutcliffe was returning from a 'run out', having taken only one spare change of clothes with him, and that he had committed an attack, leaving his clothes bloodstained. The authors believe Sutcliffe stashed the bloodstained clothing at Carl's home to prevent Sonia from seeing it when he returned that afternoon.

The authors have not been able to identify any attack in the UK at this time. However, these circumstances are entirely consistent with returning home after an overnight voyage from Denmark or Sweden, following the murder of Gertie Jensen.

Sutcliffe retrieved the clothing from behind the boiler later, then presumably washed it at home or burnt it in his garden incinerator.

The murders were investigated separately by the Malmö and Gothenburg Investigations Units (*Kriminalavdelningar*) who cooperated closely. Sexual murders of this type occur perhaps once a year in Sweden. Two murders of this type within three weeks was unprecedented, and the *Kriminalavdelningar* detectives quickly identified that both murders had been committed by the same man. It was inconceivable that a Swedish man who was unknown to them had suddenly started murdering sex workers and then equally suddenly had stopped. They concluded that this was part of a wider series of offences committed by a foreign serial killer who had visited Sweden in August 1980, and then returned to his home jurisdiction.

In the forty-two years since these two murders, many serial killers have been convicted in European jurisdictions. None have been linked to these two murders.

Map 15A - The Swedish Cluster August 1980

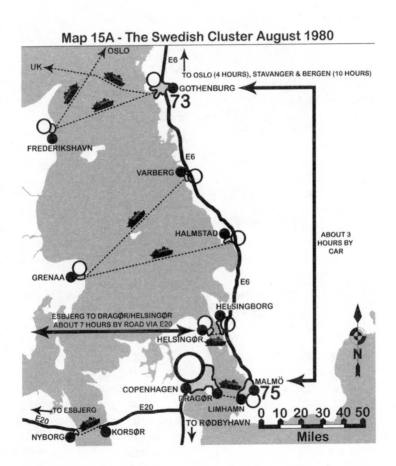

OSLO

UK

E6
TO OSLO (4 HOURS), STAVANGER & BERGEN (10 HOURS)

GOTHENBURG
73

FREDERIKSHAVN

E6

VARBERG

ABOUT 3
HOURS BY
CAR

HALMSTAD

GRENAA

E6

HELSINGBORG

ESBJERG TO DRAGØR/HELSINGØR
ABOUT 7 HOURS BY ROAD VIA E20

HELSINGØR

N

COPENHAGEN

MALMÖ
75

DRAGØR

LIMHAMN

TO ESBJERG

E20

E20

TO RØDBYHAVN

0 10 20 30 40 50

NYBORG

KORSØR

Miles

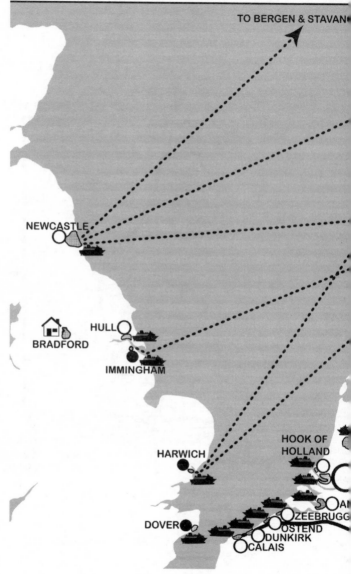

TO BERGEN & STAVAN

NEWCASTLE

BRADFORD

HULL

IMMINGHAM

HARWICH

HOOK OF HOLLAND

DOVER

ZEEBRUGG

OSTEND

DUNKIRK

CALAIS

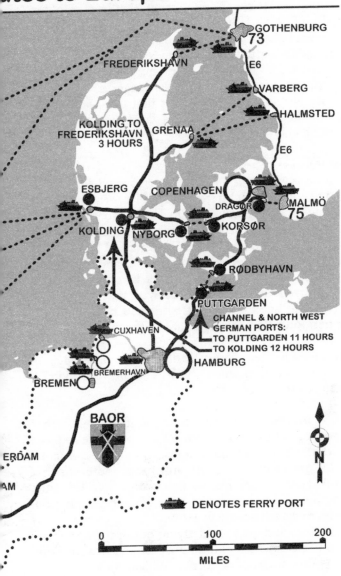

GOTHENBURG
73

FREDERIKSHAVN

E6

VARBERG

HALMSTED

KOLDING TO
FREDERIKSHAVN
3 HOURS

GRENAA

E6

ESBJERG

COPENHAGEN

MALMÖ
75

DRAGØR

KOLDING

NYBORG

KORSØR

RØDBYHAVN

PUTTGARDEN

CHANNEL & NORTH WEST
GERMAN PORTS:
TO PUTTGARDEN 11 HOURS
TO KOLDING 12 HOURS

CUXHAVEN

HAMBURG

BREMERHAVN

BREMEN

BAOR

ERDAM

AM

N

DENOTES FERRY PORT

0   100   200

MILES

Sutcliffe's Foreign Travel

Sutcliffe travelled abroad in 1974, when he and Sonia honeymooned in Paris. Then during the late summer of 1975, Sutcliffe and Sonia visited Prague with Sonia's parents to visit relatives, also stopping in Rome. Because of the considerable latitude Sonia allowed Sutcliffe, it would have been easy for Sutcliffe to slip away one evening in Paris, Prague or Rome and commit an attack.

Assuming Sutcliffe applied for his first passport for his honeymoon, he would have had a valid passport from 1974 until he was arrested.

54. Carol Reeves

According to a *Newcastle Journal* report from 8 July 1978, Carol and her husband John travelled to Hyeres in the South of France for a diving holiday. On Friday 16 June 1978, John went diving at a beach four miles from Hyeres while Carol sunbathed on a jetty. When he returned he was told that Carol had been involved in an accident and was dead.

The French Police started a murder investigation after two post-mortem examinations showed that Carol had been hit on the head and an attempt had been made to strangle her. John Reeves was quoted as saying:

> I went to see her and could hardly make out her face. I was informed that when she was found her bikini had slipped round her neck.

At the UK inquest, a Home Office pathologist said that all of Carol's injuries resulted from blunt violence or force and could be placed in three groups:

- Areas of grazes on her trunk and limbs indicated that she rolled over from her stomach onto her left side, striking her body against a rough surface before her fall onto the rocks where she was found.
- Cuts, bruises and grazes chiefly on her upper and lower limbs and head which could have resulted from striking against blunt surfaces or corners of slab rock.

Map 16 - Foreign Travel 1974 to 1980

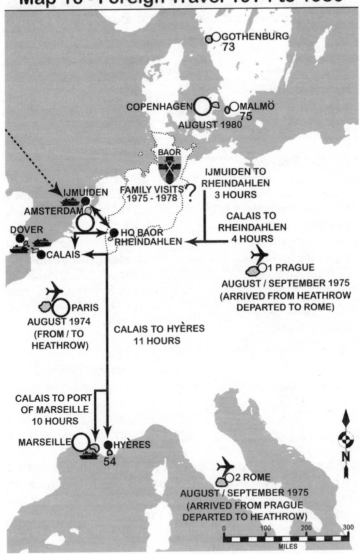

GOTHENBURG 73

COPENHAGEN

MALMÖ 75

AUGUST 1980

BAOR

IJMUIDEN

FAMILY VISITS 1975 - 1978

AMSTERDAM

DOVER

CALAIS

HQ BAOR RHEINDAHLEN

IJMUIDEN TO RHEINDAHLEN 3 HOURS

CALAIS TO RHEINDAHLEN 4 HOURS

1 PRAGUE

AUGUST / SEPTEMBER 1975 (ARRIVED FROM HEATHROW DEPARTED TO ROME)

PARIS

AUGUST 1974 (FROM / TO HEATHROW)

CALAIS TO HYÈRES 11 HOURS

CALAIS TO PORT OF MARSEILLE 10 HOURS

MARSEILLE

HYÈRES 54

2 ROME

AUGUST / SEPTEMBER 1975 (ARRIVED FROM PRAGUE DEPARTED TO HEATHROW)

N

0   100   200   300

MILES

- Multiple fractures of both jaw bones on her right side, her right cheek and right eye socket and nose, with flattening of the right side of her face, possibly resulting in it making contact with a hard surface such as a slab of rock after a fall from height.

No	Name	Cluster	Dates
Honeymoon in Paris			**12/08/74 – 24/08/74?**
?	?	French?	12/08/74 – 24/08/74?
Holiday in Prague			**September 1975**
?	?	Czech?	September 1975
Stopover in Italy			**September 1975**
?	?	Italian?	September 1975
Delivery to Marseille for Clarks Transport			**15/06/78 – 17/06/78**
54	Carol Reeves	French	16/06/78
Short visit to Sweden by ferry			**11/08/80 – 13/08/80**
73	Gertie Jensen	Swedish	12/08/80
Annual leave touring in Europe via the channel ports while Sonia was visiting her family			**27/08/80 to 11/09/80**
75	Teresa Thörling	Swedish	30/08/80
?	?	French, Belgian, Dutch, German, Danish?	27 August 1980 to 11 September 1980

He opined that these injuries indicated an accidental fall of ten feet onto rocks. The cause of death was multiple fractures to the skull and bones of Carol's face.

The French authorities rejected the findings of the UK inquest and confirmed they would continue to treat Carol's death as murder.

The authors have examined the facts of the case and have identified the following inconsistencies in the Home Office pathologist's analysis:

- If Carol had rolled over from her stomach onto her left side – an entirely normal act in sunbathing – it would not have left graze marks on her trunk and limbs.
- 'Striking her body against a rough surface before her fall onto the rocks' is completely inconsistent with a fall off a jetty onto rocks. But it is entirely consistent with a struggle on the jetty before the fall. There is no explanation of what rough surface this was, the reason for the fall, or why she fell on the rocks.
- The French post-mortem was performed shortly after Carol's death, so the signs of bruising from strangulation would still be fresh and visible. It takes about two weeks for a bruise to fade out completely. The UK post-mortem was performed some considerable time after death, when the bruising would have faded. Yet the UK pathologist has provided no explanation for the French pathologist's identification of signs of strangulation and appears to have completely ignored this possibility.
- The cause of death was multiple fractures to Carol's skull and the bones of her face. There is no mention of any other broken bones, e.g. ribs, arms or legs, that you would expect from a fall onto rocks. This indicates several blows targeted to the head, not one impact from falling off a jetty onto rocks.
- In 1986, Chris investigated a suspicious death when a body was found lying on the rocks at the foot of cliffs near King's Lynn, Norfolk. The cause of death was head injuries following a forty-five-foot fall. Two men were subsequently convicted of manslaughter. The description of Carol's injuries indicates that they were more severe, even though she only fell ten feet.
- A fall could not have caused Carol's bikini top to be lifted up to expose her breasts. The UK pathologist provided no explanation for this clear indication of a sexual assault.

The authors have concluded that:
- The UK pathologist's report is unreliable.
- The UK pathologist did not have access to the crime scene or information on the state of Carol's clothing. So he would not have been able to assess how Carol fell, if there had been a struggle on the jetty, or if Carol's clothing had been interfered with. He may also not have had access to the French police and pathologists' reports or the crime scene photographs. So the French pathologist's report is much more credible because all this evidence was available to the French pathologist, who conducted the autopsy shortly after death, before the bruising had dissipated.
- Carol's injuries are too severe to be consistent with a fall ten feet onto rocks.

The authors therefore concur with the opinions of David Yallop, the French pathologist, the French Police and the investigating magistrate that Carol was murdered.

Considering Sutcliffe as a suspect:
- Sutcliffe could have travelled to Hyeres and returned to Bradford in three or four days.
- The murder took place on a Friday, which fits with a 'run out' by Sutcliffe to visit Marseille's RLD while on a 'run out' over an extended weekend in the summer, using his holiday allowance.
- Hyeres is about an hour-and-a-half's drive from Marseille, the biggest port in France. Clarks Transport regularly delivered to UK ports. If it had an export cargo for North Africa or the Far East, delivering it to Marseille would ensure faster onward delivery. Sutcliffe was Clarks' top driver and had a reputation for being able to navigate complicated routes, so would have automatically been selected for this delivery.
- Carol's injuries are entirely consistent with her having been beaten with a weapon to the head and strangled, then being thrown or rolled off the jetty to conceal the body.

- Carol's bikini top was lifted up to expose her breasts, which is consistent with her murderer obtaining necrophilic pleasure.
- The murder weapon was not found.
- There were no witnesses and no one heard any screams, indicating that the attack was swiftly and ferociously executed.
- There is a fast exit from the coast at Hyeres on the A570.
- The attack took place in daylight, which is inconsistent with Sutcliffe's modus-operandi. However, the controls on lorry drivers' working hours in France were very strict and entry to ports was controlled, so if Sutcliffe had delivered to the port of Marseille that day, there would be a record of it. He may have attacked in the hours of daylight immediately after leaving Marseille because he had to be back at a ferry port at a specified time for the return journey. He would also want to get away as quickly as possible from the crime scene to establish an alibi of being on route to the ferry, after being logged entering the port.
- Attacking a woman in daylight on a jetty, presumably in full view of anyone passing, was a very risky and brazen attack. Sutcliffe may have been disturbed, or was pressed for time, or the risk of being observed deterred him from mutilating the body and masturbating over it.

So Carol's murder is consistent with Sutcliffe's modus-operandi and he is a credible suspect.

The UK inquest verdict will have ensured that Sutcliffe was not considered as a suspect in any of the UK Police antecedent investigations and may have precluded the UK Police cooperating with the French investigation. It therefore appears that Sutcliffe has not been considered as a suspect in this investigation, or eliminated as a suspect.

In summary, Sutcliffe is known to have visited three European cities and the authors believe he had three other visits that can be linked to crimes there, summarised below.

Sutcliffe could have gone on an extended 'run out' for up to eleven days from 27 August to 6 September, while Sonia was visiting her family. This would have allowed him to murder Teresa Thörling in Malmö and commit other attacks across Northern Europe.

Other European attacks?

There are no attacks attributed to Sutcliffe in the UK in:
- August 1977.
- June, July and August 1978.
- July 1979.

Serial killers do sometimes have extended periods between attacks. However, given the short interval between some of Sutcliffe's attacks, these gaps could indicate that there were other visits to Europe and victims there or elsewhere that have not been linked to him.

Chris travelled by hovercraft and channel ferry to France regularly in the 1980s. The service was fast and reliable. He explains that: 'The cross-Channel car ferry crossing from Dover to Calais took one hour and thirty minutes, with probably half an hour loading time extra and the same time disembarkation.'

The ferry from Newcastle to Ijmuiden in the Netherlands – about an hour's drive from Amsterdam – would probably have been the most convenient choice for Sutcliffe. This would have put many cities in North-West Europe within easy range during a three-day 'run out', allowing the opportunity to attack women in RLDs and hitchhikers.

From September 1975 to April 1976, then from October 1976, Sutcliffe was in employment with an annual holiday entitlement. This allowed him to take leave in the summer months without arousing suspicion. Clarks Transport may also have allowed him time off in lieu if he had been on several long deliveries – a common practice in the road haulage industry at the time. This would allow him to have time off, which would not have appeared on his holiday record. This would have given him the opportunity to go on 'runs out' to the continent using the multiple route packages provided by the ferries.

Robin Holland was posted to Germany with BAOR from 1975 to 1978. The authors have not been able to identify where he was stationed. All the garrison towns in Germany – where prostitution was legal – had RLDs. Sutcliffe was devoted to his sister and her children. It is possible that he visited Robin and Maureen at their married quarters. If so, he could have slipped away one evening and attacked a woman locally.

If indeed Sutcliffe is responsible for the Swedish attacks, the question arises: why did he choose such a faraway foreign jurisdiction? The answer could be that he had already committed attacks in France, Belgium, the Netherlands and/or Germany, and was changing his area of operation to prevent them from being linked.

This would explain the above gaps in the attacks.

76. Upadhya Bandara
(Convicted)

On Wednesday 24 September 1980, a thirty-four-year-old doctor, Dr Upadhya Bandara from Singapore, who was attending a course at the Leeds Nuffield Centre, was walking home after visiting friends at about 10.30pm. As she walked along Otley Road, she noticed Sutcliffe staring at her from the Kentucky Fried Chicken (KFC) restaurant, but thought nothing more of it. Sutcliffe had been keeping observation on the street from the KFC restaurant and other places for about an hour and a half until he identified a suitable victim walking alone.

He unobtrusively left the KFC restaurant and followed closely behind her without being detected for about half a mile, before attacking her in Chapel Lane, which was a suitable, secluded, dimly lit and deserted location. Upadhya heard footsteps from behind her and thought it was someone walking faster than her, so she moved aside to let him pass. Sutcliffe hit her head with a hammer at least twice, rendering her semi-conscious. He then expertly looped the ligature he had used to murder Marguerite Walls around her neck and dragged her down the lane to the bin area at the back of some houses. Hearing her shoes making a dragging noise, he removed them and threw them and her handbag over a wall. Upadhya was able to release the pressure from the ligature and breathe. Sutcliffe kicked her in the head and then she passed out.

At this point, a resident heard the noise and came out to see what was happening and a police car passed at the bottom of the lane, so Sutcliffe fled.

Upadhya was examined by Professor Mike Green, who identified that she had been strangled with a plaited cord that had been thrown over her neck and looped behind. She confirmed that her attacker was the same man she had seen in the KFC restaurant and described him as aged mid-thirties, five-foot six-inches in height, with black hair and a full beard and moustache.

Despite this excellent description, which was consistent with the descriptions of other victims and the use of a hammer, this incident was eliminated from the Ripper series because a ligature was used and there were no knife wounds (MPoF). Instead, WYMP linked the attack to the murder of Marguerite Walls and concluded that there was a second serial killer in West Yorkshire who was attacking women with a hammer.

Sutcliffe must have been pleased that varying his weapon of choice and location had ensured that the attacks on Gertie Jensen, Marguerite Walls, Teresa Thörling and Upadhya Bandara were not linked to him. This would no doubt have increased his confidence and belief in his invincibility. This may explain why he stopped using a ligature and reverted to his old modus-operandi and geographical area of operations.

77. Maureen 'Mo' Lea
(Attributed to Sutcliffe by Chief Constable Byford. WYP later confirmed that it had enough evidence to charge Sutcliffe with this offence, but he was never prosecuted.)

On Saturday 25 October 1980 at 10.50pm, art student Mo Lea, aged twenty, was walking along Hillary Place in the grounds of Leeds University. Sutcliffe followed her and said: 'Hey you, don't I know you?'

Thinking it was a friend, Mo stopped. When Sutcliffe came closer, she realised he was a stranger, became fearful and started to run. He chased after her, caught up with her, and hit her on the back of the head multiple times with a hammer, rendering her unconscious. Sutcliffe continued hitting Mo's head, then pushed two sharpened screwdrivers into her spine, nearly severing it. Sutcliffe was disturbed by a passer-by and fled.

Mo was a lone female walking at night attacked with a hammer from behind. However, the attack – which was the fourth in the Leeds University Sub-Cluster – was not connected to the Ripper series (MPoF). It occurred within two miles of the attack on Upadhya Bandara, but was not connected to that attack or the attack on Ann Rooney (MPoF). WYMP consequently failed to identify that Sutcliffe had changed his geographical area of operation to the area of Leeds University (MPoF).

Despite this horrific experience and being stigmatised as a prostitute, Mo was determined not to let Sutcliffe ruin her life. After years of therapy she overcame long-term post-traumatic stress disorder and went on to be a university lecturer and teacher in the UK, America, Malaysia and the South Pacific. She also developed her artistic skills and has exhibited her work in London and the United States. She wrote a book about her experience, *Facing the Yorkshire Ripper – The Art of Survival*, and raised funds for victim support. Mo is obviously a courageous and determined character who was able to overcome the psychological and physical injuries she suffered. Many victims were not so fortunate.

The process of overcoming her terrible experience continued until Sutcliffe's thirty-year sentence was coming to an end in 2011. WYP then revealed that if Sutcliffe was released, he would immediately be re-arrested for attempting to murder Mo.

Mo subsequently obtained the withheld Page 55 of the Byford Report, which confirmed that Sir Lawrence Byford had identified her as a Sutcliffe victim. Despicably, WYP had maintained the fiction that Sutcliffe was not her attacker, thereby denying her closure and the satisfaction of knowing her attacker had been detected, in order to evade admitting that it had bungled the investigation. For all of that time, Mo lived in fear that her attacker was free and could still come after her.

78. Theresa Sykes
(Convicted)

On Guy Fawkes Night, Wednesday 5 November 1980, sixteen-year-old Theresa Sykes was returning to the flat she shared with her boyfriend, Jim Furey, and their baby son in Willwood Avenue, Huddersfield, at around 7.30pm.

Sutcliffe had been using a telephone box as an observation point to look for victims. He stalked Theresa for about 700 yards from New Hey Road while she walked beside a playing field. Unusually, he was detected. Theresa saw his shadow, turned and saw him about ten feet away. She remembered his eyes were dark and he had a long, thin face and neatly trimmed beard. He turned and disappeared, going down a passageway between two of the buildings that backed onto the playing fields.

Reassured, she pressed on, but Sutcliffe had moved parallel with Theresa in another street and then moved back onto the pathway. He appeared behind Theresa and rained blows onto her head. Jim heard her screams, rushed out and chased Sutcliffe, but lost him when he hid behind a hedge.

Theresa survived her injuries but was left with a half-moon shaped scar on her forehead from one of the hammer blows. She was so badly affected by the attack that she never recovered from the psychological harm it did to her. Sutcliffe had ruined the lives of both Theresa and Jim.

Again, the police failed to link the attack as one of the Ripper series, because Theresa described Sutcliffe as having a ginger beard. This was because the orangey-coloured light emitted by street lamps distorts colours. Accordingly, the different colour of hair and beard should not have been given significance (MPoF).

79. 'Anita' Unknown victim
See Antecedent Investigations DI Megan Winterburn.

WYMP was perplexed that there had been no more attacks since Barbara Leach in September 1979. There was the usual speculation that he was dead, in jail, in a mental hospital or had settled down with a woman. Again, no one considered that the Ripper had committed other attacks they had not been linked to the series (MPoF).

80. Jacqueline Hill
(Convicted)
On Monday 17 November 1980, Sutcliffe clocked off at Clarks at about 7.00pm. He phoned Sonia and told her he was in Gloucester and would finish work very late. He then drove to Headingley, and by 9.30pm he was sitting in his Rover eating a takeaway from the same KFC restaurant he had targeted Upadhya Bandara from, observing Otley Road.

Sutcliffe saw twenty-year-old student Jacqueline Hill get off the bus at the Arndale Centre and walk on alone to her hall of residence. He followed her unobtrusively in the Rover. When she entered the dimly lit Alma Road, Sutcliffe stopped and waited for her to walk past. He then got out of the car and followed her on foot before delivering a blow to her head with a hammer. Seconds later, another woman appeared, so Sutcliffe dragged Jacqueline approximately thirty yards to a secluded area behind the Arndale Centre.

There, he stripped Jacqueline and repeatedly stabbed her with a screwdriver in the chest and once in the eye. When he had finished he returned to his car and drove home. Unusually, he drew attention to himself by driving down Alma Road – a one-way street – the wrong way.

Shortly afterwards, a student found Jacqueline's handbag and took it home to show his flatmates, one of whom was a retired police officer. He became alarmed when he saw that nothing had been taken from the bag and that it was bloodstained. He called the police at 11.30pm.

It was some time before two policemen arrived at the flat, and at the student's insistence they reluctantly made a cursory search by torchlight of the area where the handbag was found. They missed Jacqueline, who was still alive, less than thirty yards away. They then left to attend another call and handed the handbag into lost property at the end of their shift. No one knows if Jacqueline would have survived if the initial search had found her.

Jacqueline's body was discovered the following morning. The first policeman to attend was PC Keith Tordoff. He stayed with the body in situ then took her father to identify her.

The week prior to Jacqueline Hill's murder, eighteen-year-old Julie Bindel was followed by a man fitting Sutcliffe's description while she was returning home to her hall of residence in Headingley at night. She reported this to WYMP, but was dismissed. This was about half a mile from where Jacqueline was murdered. Again, WYMP had failed to identify that Sutcliffe was targeting the Leeds University area (MPoF).

WYMP initially confirmed that Jacqueline's murder was not a Ripper attack (MPoF), demonstrating WYMP's determination to evade criticism by minimising the number of Ripper attacks. The next day, Professor Gee confirmed his autopsy finding that it was indeed a Ripper attack.

This demonstrated publicly how incompetent the investigation was and was a turning point. Prime Minister Margaret Thatcher and Home Secretary William Whitelaw intervened. They ordered a review of the investigation by Chief Constable Sir Lawrence Byford of HM Inspectorate of Constabulary (HMIC).

The Byford Review

Chief Constable Byford identified immediately that the senior officers were not capable of running the investigation. On 25 November 1989 there was a change in the management of the investigation. ACC Oldfield was removed and replaced by DCS Hobson. Chief Constable Byford also brought in a new team of experts to lead the enquiry. It was called a 'Consultative Committee' to placate the chief constable.

For two weeks the Consultative Committee went through all the papers, including DI Zackrisson's report, interviewed detectives, and visited the incident room and the crime scenes.

One of the members of the Consultative Committee was Home Office forensic scientist Stuart Kind. He had been a navigator in the RAF during the war and used this experience to narrow down the area where the Ripper lived. He assumed that the Ripper started and finished from his home. He deduced that the earlier in the day an attack took place, the further away it was from home, and the later at night, the closer it was because it required less time to get home. Using graphical analysis he deduced that the Ripper lived in Bradford. This was the first time that what we now call Forensic Geographical Profiling was used in the UK. The Consultative Committee issued its report on 20 December 1980, which stated a series of deductions (inaccurately described as hypotheses). Illustration 12 shows the report.

Hypotheses 2 (Selects target towns that are different to the previous incident locations) and 4 (The next incident is unlikely to be in Leeds and is likely to be in Manchester, Huddersfield or Bradford) were wrong, because not all of the attacks had been linked and they could not therefore identify that Sutcliffe was operating on a wider geographic basis.

Hypothesis 3 (If unsuccessful obtaining a victim in the target town, he would look for another victim on the way home) was shown to be wrong, based on the information that became available on the pattern of Sutcliffe's offending when he was arrested.

The report identified that the Ripper had a local accent and exposed the letters and tape as a hoax, and the approximate location of Sutcliffe's home in Bradford was identified.

The authors believe the new team would have led WYMP to Sutcliffe's arrest early in the new year. However, events in Sheffield were to pre-empt this and in a final humiliation, WYMP was to be cheated of Sutcliffe's arrest.

Phase 9. January 1981: Arrest and confession

Following the murder of Jacqueline Hill, the reward for information leading to the conviction of the Ripper was increased to £50,000. The police were inundated with information from the public, including receiving 8,000 letters, 7,000 of them anonymous. One of these was from Trevor Birdsall, which was received on 25 November 1980. He had been suspicious of Sutcliffe since the attack on Olive Smelt. But his suspicions were allayed because the police had interviewed Sutcliffe on many occasions and he did not have a Geordie accent. In the letter he named Peter Sutcliffe as the Yorkshire Ripper, giving his address and place of work. The next day he repeated his allegations to the constable manning the front desk at Bradford Police Station, who took a report.

This information should have been entered onto Sutcliffe's nominal index card, collated with the vast amount of intelligence already held on Sutcliffe and assessed. This should have resulted in Sutcliffe's immediate arrest. But overwhelmed by the enormous volume of information arriving in the incident room, the information was still waiting processing when Sutcliffe was arrested (MPoF). When Trevor Birdsall heard nothing more, he assumed his information had been investigated and his concerns were groundless.

Sonia had suffered multiple miscarriages, and at this time the Sutcliffes successfully applied to Bradford City Council for permission to adopt a child. This demonstrates how Sutcliffe had successfully projected an image of a respectable married man in stable employment.

The attacks on Carol Wilkinson, Marguerite Walls, Upadhya Bandara, Mo Lea, Theresa Sykes and Jacqueline Hill demonstrate that Sutcliffe pre-selected some victims and had surveillance and stalking skills.

Sutcliffe will have realised that following Jacqueline's identification as one of his victims, the area around Leeds University would be put under surveillance. So he again changed his area of operations to Preston and Sheffield.

Reconnaissance in Preston

A witness who saw Sutcliffe in Preston about the first or second week of September 1980 contacted Chris. She recognised him from his photograph published after his arrest and gives this account:

> I was an art student in Preston. As I exited the building I looked across the road to see a man staring at me who looked like a cross between a young Rolf Harris and the singer Cat Stevens. He wore all denim and black polished leather shoes. I thought he matched the photofits so I stopped two policemen that night. Both laughed. The next day I chatted with another student who also saw the man. We reported it to a policeman at lunchtime but he just laughed as well.

Preston is about an hour-and-a-half's drive from Bradford and has a RLD near the docks. Humble had alleged in his first letter that Sutcliffe had committed the murder of Joan Harrison in Preston in 1975. If there was a Ripper murder in Preston, it would increase the credibility of the Humble hoax letters and keep the police looking for a Geordie. Sutcliffe was obviously looking for a victim in Preston to decoy the investigation by reinforcing the credibility of the hoax tapes.

Reconnaissance in Sheffield

A witness has confirmed to Chris that Sutcliffe had started operating in Sheffield in November 1980:

> I had a conversation with a guy who I am convinced was Peter Sutcliffe on the night of 26th November 1980, which I remember being a Wednesday night. I just wondered if you still have access to Peter Sutcliffe's log book from his job as a lorry driver as I would be interested to know where he had been delivering to that day. **I guess he would have clocked off work around 5pm that night and driven to Sheffield in his car that night as if you think about it, Leeds Bradford and Huddersfield would have been too hot for him as his last murder was the week before** [murder of Jacqueline Hill, 17 November 1980] **and 3 weeks to the night in question he attacked a girl in Huddersfield** [attempted murder of Theresa Sykes, 5 November 1980] **so I think he would have been sizing Sheffield up as his next hit,** the conversation took place in a north Sheffield pub not too far from the M1 motorway and just south of a district in Sheffield called Chapeltown which ironically he could have been targeting this as his next place.
>
> Chapeltown is right next to the M1 and is signposted which he would have seen driving up and down the M1 in his lorry; I think he would have on the night had a look around there but didn't find it too busy so came a little further into Sheffield. I remember getting into the pub at 9.35 that night. My girlfriend at the time was working behind the bar; she was only 16 at that time and Peter had had his eye on her. Peter asked me who that 'lass was'. I replied that she was my girlfriend. He said she seems a nice girl but she can't count. I asked why and he said that

he gave her a £5 note for a pint of bitter and she had given him change for a £1 note instead.

During the conversation he had mentioned to me that he was a lorry driver from the North East. I had read that the Ripper may be a lorry driver and with him saying he was from North East, but he was talking in a Yorkshire accent more north of Sheffield, as he reminded me of how a friend of mine from York spoke. I said to him that with you being a lorry driver and from the North East that it's a wonder you not been quizzed by police about being the Ripper. I remember the startled look on his face and he replied that he had **but his wife just confirms who I am and they leave me alone**.

He then said to me whilst it was my turn to be startled, he said the Ripper hasn't struck in Sheffield has he? I said no. He asked is that because Sheffield hasn't a RLD? **I said it had and gave him a rough direction as to where it was.** We were about 5 miles from the RLD (not that I frequented it). I remember telling him after he asked me that it was near to Bramall Lane football ground just up from it on the main road. It was at this point my girlfriend was collecting the empties then after saying my girlfriend couldn't count I quizzed him about it been a wonder police hadn't quizzed him about being the Ripper. I remember walking my girlfriend home and she asked me who that man was I was talking to. I said I don't know but I am very suspicious about him. I asked her if she could remember serving him and she said yes. I told her what he said about her not been able to count and I remember her telling me that he gave her a £1 note as **she noticed oil stains on his hands.**

When pics of him in the paper appeared they were all from him from his wedding which threw me off a little, but shortly after my girlfriend phoned me up asking me if I seen an interview with a girl who worked at his place, think she was a wages clerk, she described the clothes he wore at work and my girlfriend said she describes the same clothes the man I was talking to was wearing which were **a lumber type jacket or shirt** and with brown corduroy trousers.

I have been in touch with Carl Sutcliffe and asked him if he can remember Peter wearing a lumber jacket and he said that he did and that it was probably Peter I was talking to. I am not looking to make money on what I said and described, am not one for making a fuss about all this, I just wonder that if I had not gone to the pub that night I am certain Sutcliffe would have followed her home that night and she could well have been the next victim.

[Authors' emphasis in bold]

Enquiries with SYP have confirmed that there were no attacks on women in Sheffield on 26 November 1980. The authors nevertheless remain concerned that there could have been other attacks in Sheffield in November and December 1980 that may not have been reported to the police or identified as part of the Ripper series.

81. Olivia Reivers
(Sutcliffe had not harmed Olivia and she got into his car willingly, so he could not be charged with any offence)
On Friday 2 January 1981, Sutcliffe told Sonia that he was going to collect the key of his sister's red Mini, which had broken down, and left home just after 4.00pm. He then drove to a scrapyard near Dewsbury and picked up two number plates from a scrapped Skoda, which he fixed onto his Rover. Then he went to Sheffield's Havelock Square RLD, which was five minutes' drive from the Bramall Lane football ground as indicated to him in the pub in November.

Sutcliffe propositioned Olivia Reivers, who was aged twenty-four. They agreed a price and he drove her to Melbourne Avenue and reversed his car into a space in the driveway of the Light Trades House. This was so he would be able to drive straight off after he had murdered Olivia, without having to back out first and then turn, thus saving precious seconds in making his getaway.

Sutcliffe turned the lights off, took off his coat and placed it on the back seat, and asked Olivia to get in the back. Olivia declined this and removed her panties in the front passenger seat but Sutcliffe could not get an erection, so they talked.

At about 10.30pm, Sergeant Robert Ring and Probationary Constable Robert Hydes of SYP in a panda car saw the Rover. They immediately suspected that it contained a punter with a sex worker. They parked in front of the Rover and questioned Sutcliffe.

INTERVIEW 11

Sutcliffe told PC Hydes that Olivia was his girlfriend, that his name was Peter Williams and gave a false address. Simultaneously, Sergeant Ring returned to the panda car to check the index plates with the PNC, which confirmed that the number plates belonged to a Skoda.

Sergeant Ring and PC Hydes arrested Sutcliffe for car theft. Although the intervention of these officers had saved Olivia's life, the arrest and follow-up were bungled and Sutcliffe nearly escaped.

Arrest

Both officers told Sutcliffe that the number plates were not for his car, removed the ignition keys from the steering column and arrested Sutcliffe and Olivia for car theft. PC Hydes noticed that the false plates were only held on by tape, and the two officers escorted Olivia to their car.

Sutcliffe immediately realised the situation was serious, but stayed calm. He surreptitiously grabbed the ball pein hammer and knife he had concealed under the driver's seat without either officer noticing (MPoF). Then he walked off, saying he was 'bursting for a pee'. Instead of going with him, Sergeant Ring and PC Hydes let him out of their sight to urinate (MPoF).

Sutcliffe dropped the knife and hammer by an oil tank. They made a slight noise when they hit the ground. Sergeant Ring said he heard a clatter but did not investigate it (MPoF). Sutcliffe retained the knife and garrotte he had in his jacket.

Leaving the Rover at the scene, the officers took both Sutcliffe and Olivia to Hammerton Road Police Station. Neither Sutcliffe nor Olivia were searched or handcuffed (MPoF). Chris comments:

> This was a very unsatisfactory arrest. Both suspects were transported in the same car and without being searched. Sutcliffe was allowed to ditch crucial evidence and was armed with a knife while being transported in the back of the car, which put the lives of both officers and Olivia at risk. Unbelievable.
>
> That's not what I would have done. I'd have got him out, searched him and placed him cuffed in the police car and then searched the suspect car, in the meantime organising a separate unit to take Olivia.
>
> It then took them twenty-four hours to investigate what had made that noise!
>
> Additionally, neither officer, upon realising that they had a man with a gap in his teeth that fitted the description of the Yorkshire Ripper with a sex worker in a car, considered the possibility that it could be the Ripper.

When they got to the police station, Sutcliffe again asked to use the toilet and was again allowed to go without being searched or supervised (MPoF). When he was there, he took the other knife out of his jacket and dropped it in the cistern, but for some reason retained the garotte.

INTERVIEW 12

Sutcliffe was interviewed and admitted stealing the plates and to being Peter Sutcliffe of 6 Garden Lane, Heaton, Bradford, the registered owner of the Rover. He said he had stolen the plates because he was due in court on drink-driving charges and, as he was about to lose his licence, it wasn't worth renewing his insurance which had expired.

(Sutcliffe's workmates later confirmed he had arrived at work on a number of occasions with false plates on the Rover. This was obviously to thwart the PNC checks made on him in the various red-light areas he frequented.)

Sutcliffe obviously intended to deceive the investigation by murdering a sex worker in Sheffield with a garrotte. So the new location and use of a garrotte would ensure that, as with the murders of Marguerite Walls and Upadhya Bandara, Olivia's death would not be attributed to him. Sutcliffe knew he should be bailed to report to Dewsbury Police Station over the theft of the plates.

He intended to get a cab back to Light Trades House, collect the knife and hammer and then return to Bradford in the Rover. However, WYMP had issued a directive to all neighbouring forces that if a man was arrested in the company of a prostitute, the Millgarth Incident Room was to be notified. This triggered a chain of events which led to Sutcliffe being exposed as the Yorkshire Ripper.

Sergeant Ring telephoned Millgarth and asked the duty DS if Sutcliffe was of interest in the Ripper enquiry, who said he would check and ring back. Being a diligent officer, he reviewed Sutcliffe's index card and gathered all the other papers on him. He read that Sutcliffe was a lorry driver, which was a suspect occupation; he had been interviewed in connection with the £5-note enquiry; and his cars had been sighted in RLDs. Sutcliffe had the same shoe size, a gap in the centre of his upper teeth, and had previously been eliminated from the enquiry solely on handwriting or generalised alibis from his wife. Some of the detectives who had interviewed Sutcliffe were not satisfied with his explanations. Now he had been arrested with a sex worker, having previously denied using them.

Because of the pressure on the investigation and the failure to consolidate all of the information available on

Sutcliffe onto one index card, this may have been the first time when all of the papers relating to Sutcliffe had been gathered together and assessed by a senior detective (MPoF). He rang SYP back and ordered that Sutcliffe be held overnight then taken to Dewsbury Police Station. He arrived just before 9.00am on Saturday 3 January. The Rover was also driven there and Sonia was notified of his arrest for theft.

INTERVIEW 13

Sutcliffe was interviewed by DS Desmond O'Boyle, who was familiar with Sutcliffe's nominal index file information and the notes on the interviews he had had. DS O'Boyle had interviewed and cleared many suspects who had a weight of circumstantial evidence against them, and found Sutcliffe to be cooperative. He was initially reluctant to provide a blood sample, but did so, which confirmed he was B Negative, the same as the Ripper. DS O'Boyle concluded that Sutcliffe was innocent and recommended his release (MPoF).

Chief Superintendent John Clark, who commanded Dewsbury Police Station, still considered that Sutcliffe was a credible suspect. At 6.00pm he contacted DI John Boyle, the duty officer in the incident room, who concurred. He ordered DS O'Boyle to continue the interrogation.

Meanwhile in Sheffield, Sergeant Ring came back on duty and updated himself on developments with Sutcliffe's arrest. He remembered that Sutcliffe had gone out of sight to urinate and decided to return and check the area, where he found the hammer and knife. SYP immediately informed DI Boyle, who realised that Sutcliffe was the Ripper. He went straight to the location and had the weapons photographed before removal and re-interviewed Olivia Reivers.

DI Boyle briefed Detective Superintendent Holland on the developments, who organised an initial search of 6 Garden Lane, including the garage. They removed a number of tools, including ball pein hammers, a hacksaw and a screwdriver. They also recovered lengths of rope, women's underwear and a leather apron (these articles were never shown as exhibits or made public). They then left, taking Sonia with them for questioning at Bradford Police Station. Other tools were recovered from Sutcliffe's Rover and three screwdrivers were recovered from the glove compartment of the Sunbeam Rapier.

The weapons displayed at his trial were seven ball pein hammers, one claw hammer, one hacksaw, three carving knives (one with a serrated edge), one long, thin-pointed kitchen knife, one wooden-handled cobbler's knife, a chisel, eight screwdrivers, and one length of rope.

Sonia was questioned extensively, building up a personal profile of her husband, their life together and his movements on specific dates during the last two months. By the end of her interrogation, WYMP were satisfied that she had not known that Sutcliffe was the Yorkshire Ripper.

Confession

Sutcliffe was interviewed by DI John Boyle and DS Peter Smith at lunchtime on Sunday 4 January 1981. DS Smith was probably the longest-serving member of the Ripper squad and had a detailed knowledge of all the attacks.

INTERVIEW 14

Initially, DI Boyle and DS Smith asked general questions, trying to systematically close later possible avenues of escape for Sutcliffe when it came to specific facts. He appeared to them to be friendly, articulate, very calm and cooperative, and not once asking for bail or a solicitor.

Then they questioned Sutcliffe about his whereabouts on the dates of the attacks. Sutcliffe stated that on 5 November 1980, when Theresa Sykes was attacked at 8.00pm in Huddersfield, he was home no later than 8.00pm, which gave him an alibi. However, Sonia had already confirmed that she distinctly remembered him returning home at 10.00pm.

They then questioned him over his arrest and went over the circumstances of the night of his arrest on Friday 2 January 1981 and built up to the point when he went to urinate. At this point Sutcliffe realised that they had found the hammer and knife and that the game was up. He said, 'I think you have been leading up to it,' and DI Boyle replied, 'Leading up to what?' Sutcliffe replied, 'The Yorkshire Ripper.' DI Boyle asked, 'What about the Yorkshire Ripper?' and Sutcliffe replied, 'Well, it's me.'

Sutcliffe went on to make a partial confession, admitting to murdering twelve women. He only confessed to those murders and attempted murders he knew were undeniable. Sutcliffe did not confess to the murders of Marguerite Walls and Debbie Schlesinger, or to the attempted murders of Tracy Browne, Ann Rooney and Mo Lea, even though there is no doubt that he committed them. His account was unemotional, giving an accurate description, taking care to include information that only the killer would know. He also revealed where he had discarded some of the weapons. He denied any knowledge of Joan Harrison's murder or the letters and tapes.

At this point, Chief Constable Gregory was informed. He organised a press conference where he, DCS Hobson and ACC Oldfield appeared jubilant at the arrest of the Yorkshire Ripper and pandered to media interest. This was severely criticised at the time, because Sutcliffe's case was sub-judice and the chief constable's comments prejudiced Sutcliffe's right to a fair trial (MPoF).

A press conference by SYP also ignored the way an announcement of this type should normally be made (MPoF). This set the standard for the subsequent media coverage.

After the press conference, Chief Constable Gregory and ACC Oldfield visited the cells and interrupted the interrogation to gawp at Sutcliffe. Both DI Boyle and DS Smith were still taking down his confession and were exhausted. Chief Constable Gregory ordered them to get Sutcliffe into court that day and so the interrogation that had proven so successful was cut short (MPoF). The confession was still not complete and there was still a lot more information to extract from Sutcliffe before he was charged. Under normal circumstances he would not have been charged until the interrogation had finished. Nevertheless, the interrogation was terminated prematurely (MPoF).

Sutcliffe was then strip-searched for the first time (MPoF). His underpants and a piece of blue-and-red plaited nylon rope were found in his jacket pocket. The rope was about three feet long, knotted with two knots at each end and two knots a few inches apart in the middle. He was found to be wearing an under garment consisting of two sleeves of a jumper made of a silky material crudely sewn together, which left a gap that exposed his penis. The arms of the jumper were padded to protect his knees. It was obviously designed to allow him to kneel on the ground and give speedy access to his penis to masturbate over his victims.

Sutcliffe was then charged. His house, garage and car were searched with Sutcliffe and Sonia present. His arrest photograph is shown as Illustration 11. Further pieces of rope were seized, including one that was about four feet long found in their bedside cabinet. The boots that he was wearing when he left their imprints at the murders of Emily Jackson and Patricia Atkinson were recovered. Later searches recovered the discarded weapons, including the Phillips head screwdriver, from locations Sutcliffe described.

Phase 10. January to May 1981: Remand, trial and sentencing

Sutcliffe was taken to Dewsbury Magistrates Court on 5 January 1981 and remanded in custody at HMP Armley, Leeds.

Sutcliffe was brought to trial at the Old Bailey very quickly due to the public interest in the case. This did not allow enough time for a full antecedent investigation to be conducted to identify the full range of his victims (MPoF).

Whilst on remand, Sutcliffe had said he had been hearing voices from God which told him to murder prostitutes since he had been working at Bingley Cemetery. Psychiatrists diagnosed him as a paranoid schizophrenic. The prosecution accepted this diagnosis and both defence and prosecution agreed that at trial, Sutcliffe would be found not guilty of thirteen charges of murder but guilty of manslaughter on the grounds of diminished responsibility and guilty of seven charges of attempted murder.

The judge, Mr Justice Boreham, determined that Sutcliffe's guilt or innocence should be decided by a jury, not predetermined by the defence and prosecution, and directed that there should be a full trial. It started on 5 May 1981. The key issue was Sutcliffe's sanity. The prosecution established that the psychiatrists had made their diagnoses purely on what Sutcliffe had told them. He was known to be a plausible liar and he had been overheard in prison telling his wife that he might be able to only get ten years if he could convince everyone that he was mad.

It took the jury six hours to determine that Sutcliffe was sane and guilty of all the charges by a majority of ten to two on Friday 22 May 1981. He was sentenced to life with a minimum term of thirty years.

Phase 11. May 1981 to March 1984: HMP Parkhurst

In May 1982 the Court of Appeal rejected Sutcliffe's appeal that the murder convictions be reduced to manslaughter on the grounds of diminished responsibility.

In December 1982, Home Secretary William Whitelaw overruled prison psychiatrists who recommended that

Sutcliffe be transferred to a secure mental hospital and ordered that Sutcliffe should stay in Parkhurst. The following month, Sutcliffe was seriously assaulted by another prisoner.

In March 1984 a new Home Secretary agreed that Sutcliffe should be transferred from HMP Parkhurst to Broadmoor Secure Psychiatric Hospital.

Aftermath: January 1981 to present

Sutcliffe's arrest revealed the way the investigation had been mismanaged. There was a furore of criticism, with calls for heads to roll and the formation of a national police force, or a national CID. The newspaper headline (Illustration 13) gives a flavour of public outrage.

The failure of the Yorkshire Ripper investigation followed the catastrophic failure of the Donald Neilson 'Black Panther' investigation. Neilson was a prolific and highly skilled burglar who graduated to armed robberies. Coincidentally, Chris investigated two of his burglaries in King's Lynn. In 1974, Neilson murdered postmasters in Harrogate (NYP), Baxenden (Lancashire Police) and Langley (West Midlands Police). In 1975 he kidnapped heiress Lesley Whittle in Shropshire (West Mercia Police), shot a security guard in Dudley (West Midlands Police), then murdered Lesley Whittle at Kidsgrove (Staffordshire Police). The police operation to free her failed because these forces failed to cooperate, resulting in Lesley's murder. Like Sutcliffe, Neilson was only arrested because of a routine stop by two PCs. This demonstrated that the police were not capable of conducting large, complex investigations across force boundaries. Following public concern over the conduct of this investigation, assurances were given to the House of Commons that:

The case had been discussed by chief officers of police collectively and that she [the minister] was quite sure that they were fully aware of the need to learn any lessons which may be learned from such an investigation.

Home Secretary William Whitelaw appointed Chief Constable Byford to conduct an official enquiry into the Yorkshire Ripper investigation. Chief Constable Byford commented:

Regretfully, some of these lessons were previously identified at the conclusion of the 'Black Panther' case in 1975 but, in the light of the Ripper case, quite clearly the Police Service has not learned from them, particularly those relating to the management and control of a multi-force murder investigation.

Home Secretary William Whitelaw made the following statement to Parliament:

I have now received and considered Mr Byford's report, and I am extremely grateful to him for it. I should like to let the House know of its main conclusions and recommendations. A more detailed summary has been placed in the Library.

It is apparent from the report that there were major errors of judgment by the police and some inefficiencies in the conduct of the operation at various levels. In particular, excessive credence was given to the letters and tape from a man claiming responsibility for the series of murders and signing himself 'Jack the Ripper'. Another serious handicap to the investigation was the ineffectiveness of the major incident room which became overloaded with unprocessed information. With hindsight, it is now clear that if these errors and inefficiencies had not occurred Sutcliffe would have been identified as a prime suspect sooner than he was. Mr Byford's report concludes that there is little doubt that he should have been arrested earlier, on the facts associated with his various police interviews.

I remind the House that the Ripper case gave rise to the largest criminal investigation ever conducted in this country, imposing a great strain on all concerned. It would have been surprising if in this unprecedented situation there were no mistakes. What we now have to do is to respond constructively to the considerable experience gained in the course of it in order to ensure that future investigations of crimes such as this are carried out as effectively and quickly as possible.

I turn, therefore, to the lessons for the future and to the recommendations made by Mr Byford. As will be seen from the statement in the Library, they deal comprehensively with the management requirements of the investigation of a series of major crimes, the training of senior detectives and personnel working in major incident rooms, the command of investigations involving a number of crimes which cross force boundaries, the harnessing for such investigations of the best detective and forensic science skills in the country, and the use of computer technology.

The following extracts from some of the questions asked by Members of Parliament give an indication of public outrage over the failings of the investigation:

Mr Edward Lyons (Bradford, West):
'Will the Home Secretary agree that the Byford recommendations make it clear that scarcely a police force in the country is adequately trained or equipped to deal with an inquiry on the scale of that required as a result of the activities of my constituent, Mr. Sutcliffe?'

Mr Jack Ashley (Stoke-on-Trent, South):
'Although I welcome the constructive proposals and hope that they will be accepted by the police, what will the Home Secretary do if any police force is not

prepared to give the constructive commitment for which he is asking?'

Mr Whitelaw:
'I believe that the commitment will be given, and it is most important that it should be. Under the Police Act 1964, there is a safeguard. The Home Secretary has a right, through the inspectors of constabulary, to make proposals to various police forces if they do not carry out their duties to the standards expected of them.'

Mr Geoffrey Lofthouse (Pontefract and Castleford):
'Will the Home Secretary now confirm to the House that he has already taken action in putting a ban on the promotion chances of senior officers of the West Yorkshire police force?'

Mr Whitelaw:
'I have represented to the West Yorkshire police authority that there are certain officers in the force whom I would not be prepared to agree should go forward for promotion to assistant chief constable.'

Mr Martin Flannery (Sheffield, Hillsborough):
'Does the Home Secretary agree with me that, no matter what computer facilities existed or did not exist, the number of leads to this man, who was interviewed about nine times, was so massive that there must have been culpable negligence in not following them up and arresting him much earlier?

'Would he finally accept it from me that if some major heads in West Yorkshire do not roll as a result of this, and if that police force is left undisturbed at the top level as a result of this inquiry, there will be grave disquiet throughout the whole of West and South Yorkshire?'

In summary, the Byford Report revealed that the investigation had been incompetent, many senior officers had been inadequate and these failures were endemic to all forces, not just WYMP. Uniquely, chief officers had been exposed for their failings and held to account. The Home Secretary had intervened to impose a promotion ban on those officers that were assessed as ineffective. He made it clear that there had to be change across all forces and that he would remove chief constables that did not embrace change.

This was the worst criticism the police service had ever had, causing lack of public confidence in the police and concern throughout the higher ranks of the police service. Hence the reason why only a summary was made available to MPs and why the Byford Report has never been released in full. It was partially released by the Home Office on 2 June 2006 and instantly caused controversy over the unacknowledged murders.

One casualty of the aftermath was DC Andy Laptew, who had wanted to arrest Sutcliffe but was overruled by Detective Superintendent Holland. He was a Uniform Branch sergeant when Sutcliffe was arrested and was tracked down and interviewed by a journalist. Andy was inexperienced in dealings with the press and made comments which were justifiably critical of the investigation, but which were published. WYMP officers of all ranks never forgave him for this. He should have gone on to other promotions to senior rank, but, perceived as being disloyal, he was ostracized and his career finished. Andy was very badly affected by the failure to arrest Sutcliffe and the treatment he received from some of his colleagues in WYMP.

Chris knew Andy and corresponded with him. Some of their correspondence is reproduced below:

Hi Andy,

I know that it is some while since we have spoken but I just wanted you to know that the public hold you in high esteem. As we both know, serving in the police force doesn't necessarily mean that the cream rises to the top (Keith Hellawell an exception, John Stalker another). When I look around during the era of particularly the 1970s there were numerous bad decisions made by inept guvnors around the UK.

In your case you have nothing to reproach yourself about in not nicking Peter Sutcliffe as both your hands were tied behind your back. The guilt was and should remain with Oldfield, Holland and Hobson, who all lacked direction and purpose. I also feel that the Home Secretary should have ordered in the Super Squad, including Stuart Kind, at a much earlier stage to review the cases.

You can hold your head up high along with Keith Hellawell for being an honest guy doing the job to the best of your ability. I am proud of you for the way you dealt with all the shit which came your way in the aftermath. Well done, Andy.

Chris.

Andy's response is below:

Hello Chris,

Many thanks for your kind and encouraging words. It means a lot to me when my own peer group make the effort to support me.

Kind regards

Andy L

He was a good copper and did not deserve the treatment he received. He died in 2019.

Phase 12. March 1984 to August 2017: Broadmoor Secure Psychiatric Hospital

Sutcliffe received an enormous amount of romantic correspondence from women, some of them attracted by his notoriety, some by a desire to reform him. He corresponded with multiple women at any one time, writing to them and sending them Christmas cards, poems, drawings and paintings. He enjoyed causing them emotional upset by toying with their emotions, and in some cases encouraged competition between them, building them up, then dropping them.

There were attempts made to murder Sutcliffe by Broadmoor patients in 1996, 1997 and 2007. The 1997 attack left him without the sight of one eye and with reduced vision in the other.

In 2005, WYMP reopened the investigation into the hoax letters and tape sent to ACC Oldfield. One of the envelopes was tested where it had been licked to seal it, which produced a DNA profile. A search of the DNA database identified forty-nine-year-old alcoholic John Humble from Ford, near Sunderland, as the man who had licked the envelope. He was sentenced to eight years' imprisonment, of which he served four.

Sutcliffe's sentence of a minimum term of thirty years' imprisonment was increased by the Home Secretary to a full life tariff in 2010. His appeal against this failed.

In August 2016, Sutcliffe was deemed fit to return to the prison system and transferred to HMP Frankland, Durham, in August 2017.

Phase 13. August 2017 to November 2020: HMP Frankland

Sutcliffe died on 13 November 2020. Forensically aware to the end, his body was cremated, thereby preventing it being used for future forensic analysis.

The antecedent investigations:
January 1981 to present

Sir Lawrence Byford's investigation was explicit that Sutcliffe started his attacks in 1969 and committed more than he was convicted of:

> Between 1969 and the start of the known Ripper crimes in 1975, there is a curious and unexplained lull in Sutcliffe's criminal activities and there is the possibility that he carried out other attacks on prostitutes and unaccompanied women during this period.
>
> ...we feel it is highly improbable that the crimes in respect of which Sutcliffe has been charged and convicted are the only ones attributable to him. This feeling is reinforced by examining the details of a number of assaults on women since 1969, which in some way, clearly fall into the established pattern of Sutcliffe's overall modus-operandi.

The authors have identified fifteen occasions when antecedent investigations were conducted into – or retired police officers identified – attacks by Sutcliffe that were never attributed to him.

However, no chief constable wanted to admit that his force had failed to detect a Ripper attack, thereby associating his force with this failed and controversial investigation. Nor did they want to expend resources on investigating the crimes of a man that was primarily seen as a WYMP problem who was in prison for life. Had the full number of attacks and the circumstances of them been released in 1981, there would have been uproar and chief officers' heads would have rolled. It was in this atmosphere that the various investigations (AI) to identify the full number of Sutcliffe's victims took place. A *Daily Express* article showing the continuing controversy over the Byford investigation is shown as Illustration 14.

WYMP Taken in Consideration form 1981

DC Alan Foster was the Exhibits Officer at the Old Bailey. He revealed that after Sutcliffe's arrest, the investigation team were aware that Sutcliffe had committed more attacks than he had been charged with. They wanted to identify all of these attacks and bring some element of justice for the victims and their families. A list of forty-seven attacks Sutcliffe was believed to have committed was compiled on a Taken in Consideration form, which is standard procedure. The form was supressed and DC Foster was ordered to destroy all the exhibits (MPoF).

In 2005 the *Yorkshire Evening Post* reported that DC Foster had retained the leggings and some of the other exhibits so they could be used for DNA analysis and returned them to WYP after his retirement. The article reported that the murder of Fred Craven, the attack on John Tomey and the undated murder of an unidentified prostitute in Hemel Hempstead, Hertfordshire (probably the attempted murder of Marie Burke), were on this list.

Kriminalavdelningar 1981

In January 1981, investigative journalist David Yallop wrote that the murders of Gertie Jensen and Teresa Thörling in Sweden were committed by Sutcliffe. When Sutcliffe was arrested in 1981, Malmö *Kriminalavdelningar* detectives became aware of media comment that he appeared on the passenger lists of ferries between Dragor and Limhamn on the days before and after Teresa's murder. This media comment was subsequently found to be erroneous.

The obvious similarities between the attacks and the original assessment that both murders were committed by a foreign serial killer visiting Sweden caused the Kriminalavdelningar detectives to telex (a teleprinter-based forerunner of fax machines) WYMP on 12 January 1981, asking for confirmation of these media reports.

WYMP responded twelve days later that Sutcliffe had not been to Sweden. It is possible that WYMP had alibied Sutcliffe by checking the records at Clarks Transport and confirmed he was at work on the days preceding or following the Swedish murders. However, to draw the conclusion that Sutcliffe had not been to Sweden, WYMP would have had to confirm through the ferry companies that Sutcliffe had not travelled to Sweden, Denmark, Norway or any of the Channel and North West Europe ports from the UK. The records were probably not computerised, so this would have been a major task and does not seem to have occurred (MPoF).

WYMP may have concluded this because there were no stamps for immigration into Sweden in Sutcliffe's passport. However, Nigel Ward has confirmed to the authors that:

> I travelled back and forth to Sweden by ferry from Germany via Denmark in the 1970s, on more than one occasion. Border controls between the Scandinavian countries were very lax/non-existent. I cannot once remember my passport being checked and it was certainly never stamped with an immigration stamp from those countries.

So Sutcliffe's passport would not have shown any evidence of him visiting Sweden or Denmark.

The Interpol enquiry arrived at the height of the furore over WYMP's failed investigation. The authors suspect that some time prior to the murder of Yvonne Mysliwiec, WYMP had started pursuing a policy of not classifying attacks as part of the series unless the evidence was overwhelming, to prevent further public alarm and criticism. The knowledge that Sutcliffe had committed another two murders would have added to this unprecedented outburst of criticism of WYMP. Hence perhaps the reason that WYMP quickly responded that he had not been to Sweden, without conducting an adequate investigation.

Whilst passport controls were lax, it would have been impossible to bring a foreign-registered car into Sweden without an official record of it entering the country being made. Unfortunately, the Swedish Police accepted the assurances of WYMP that Sutcliffe had not entered Sweden and understandably did not search the passenger lists for Sutcliffe or the cars he owned and had access to.

WYMP DS Desmond O'Boyle 1981

Immediately after Sutcliffe's arrest, Fred Craven's son rang ACC Oldfield to ask whether Sutcliffe could have killed his father. ACC Oldfield responded that he was too busy handling Sutcliffe's confession to speak with him. He promised to call back but never did, thereby preventing a full investigation of Fred Craven's murder.

DS O'Boyle spotted the similarity in modi-operandi between the Fred Craven and John Tomey cases and Sutcliffe's attacks. He also noted that the detailed description John had given matched Sutcliffe. He showed him a double spread of photographs of men with beards and without hesitation he picked out Sutcliffe's mugshot taken two years after the attack when he was arrested in September 1969.

DS O'Boyle correctly linked the attacks on Fred Craven and John Tomey and recommended that Sutcliffe should be interviewed about both attacks. He was ordered not to pursue this line of enquiry by DCS Hobson, on the grounds that Sutcliffe only attacked women (MPoF).

Chief Constable Byford said in his 1981 antecedent investigation into Sutcliffe:

I should perhaps say here that I have given considerable thought to the extent of my responsibility in this review of the Ripper Case having regard to the opportunity it has given to interview Sutcliffe and his associates and in particular, Birdsall. I came to the conclusion that consideration of any other crimes **which might have been committed by Sutcliffe and any of his associates** was a matter for the West Yorkshire Metropolitan Police and the other police forces where such crimes have been committed. [Authors' highlighting in bold]

Chief Constable Byford suspected that Sutcliffe had committed some attacks with an accomplice or accomplices. He clearly expected DCS Hobson to investigate this and any other unsolved crimes that Sutcliffe and his associates could be responsible for and this did not happen (MPoF).

DCS Hobson was a very senior and experienced detective. It is inconceivable that he overlooked the similarities in the attacks. The authors suspect the reason DCS Hobson rejected DS O'Boyle's recommendation is because he did not want to admit that ACC Oldfield had bungled the investigation into the murder of Fred Craven in 1966 by arresting Sutcliffe's brother. Thereby allowing Sutcliffe to go on to continue murdering. Had this emerged, it would have led to an outcry and ACC Oldfield's sacking.

Chris and Fred Craven's elder daughter, Irene Vidler, campaigned to have WYP reopen the case. Irene confirmed to Chris:

In early 2000, officers went to see my mum, who has since died, and they told her they were 99 per cent sure Peter Sutcliffe killed her husband. But they admitted even if he confessed, they could not do anything about it as they'd lost the evidence when the police station moved from Keighley. All I want is for Sutcliffe to say 'yes, I've done it' and I'd get closure. It's always there in the back of my mind. It never goes away.

In 2018, Chris sent a FOI to WYP asking for a copy of the pathologist report. Their response was:

West Yorkshire Police can confirm that they hold a copy of a crime file for the murder of Fred Craven. The Pathologist report contained within this file is exempt by virtue of Section 30(1) – Investigations and proceedings conducted by a public authority.

So in fact, WYP did have a crime file which may hold fingerprint evidence, but will not release any information on the case or reopen it to consider if Sutcliffe was one of the murderers.

Sadly, Irene died without ever getting justice for her father's murder.

There are too many coincidences with the Craven, Tomey and Ellis cases to ignore them. All three attacks happened in or close to Sutcliffe's hometown of Bingley, where he grew up. He knew two of the people that died, and John Tomey positively identified Sutcliffe as his attacker. It appears the victims and relatives have been fobbed off with an excuse.

Quite apart from the fact that this denies victims and their families justice and closure, it also effectively closed down any investigation into Sutcliffe's accomplice(s), who was/were almost certainly still alive at the time and still represented a danger to the public (MPoF).

Strathclyde Police 1981
After his arrest, Strathclyde Police discussed the possibility that Sutcliffe may have been responsible for crimes in Glasgow with WYMP. DCS Hobson examined the files on four murders and ruled out any connection to Sutcliffe.

HMIC Sir Lawrence Byford 1981
Sir Lawrence Byford identified thirteen attacks committed by Sutcliffe which he was not charged with.

WYMP ACC Colin Sampson 1981
Chief Constable Gregory directed there should be an internal WYMP review of the Ripper investigation conducted by ACC Colin Sampson. The *Yorkshire Evening*

Post ran articles on 26 May 1982 (Illustration 15) and 15 October 1987 (Illustration 16) stating that Sampson suspected Sutcliffe was guilty of other crimes.

The authors have not been able to identify which cases ACC Sampson was referring to. However, the two articles, which are obviously based on briefings from WYP, specifically mention the attacks on Tracy Browne, Yvonne Mysliwiec, Barbara Mayo, two murders in Glasgow (later attributed to Angus Sinclair), Anne Marie Harold (husband later convicted) and Barbara Young.

WYMP Chief Constable Keith Hellawell 1982–1992

In 1982, Chief Superintendent Keith Hellawell was ordered by the newly promoted WYMP Chief Constable Sampson to review unsolved attacks to see if they could be attributed to Sutcliffe.

An officer from this investigation has confirmed to the authors that it investigated the possibility of Sutcliffe commuting to commit the two Swedish murders and could find no evidence to prove he ever visited that country. The investigation checked all the records and concluded that he was not in Sweden on the relevant dates. This would indicate that the original enquiry following the telex from the Malmö and Gothenburg *Kriminalavdelningar* on 12 January 1981 was unsatisfactory, requiring this line of enquiry to be reopened and pursued by Hellawell's team. (Swedish AI 2.)

It appears from the form of words used that the investigation was unable to establish an alibi for Sutcliffe and had to try and identify if Sutcliffe had travelled from the UK to Sweden. Given the laxity of passport controls into Sweden in August 1980 and that Sutcliffe could have travelled into Sweden directly from the UK, or via Denmark, the Netherlands, Germany, Belgium or France, from Dover, Immingham, Harwich or Newcastle, this would have been a massive investigation. Unless the investigation was able to alibi Sutcliffe for both days from his records at Clarks Transport, or a witness, the authors do not believe it would be possible to come to this conclusion with 100 per cent certainty.

In 1983, Chief Superintendent Hellawell was promoted to ACC and transferred to Humberside Police. He transferred to be chief constable of Cleveland Police in 1990 and in 1993 transferred to be chief constable of WYP, but nevertheless kept contact with Sutcliffe and interviewed him throughout this period.

In November 1992, Sutcliffe finally admitted responsibility for the attacks on Tracy Browne and Ann Rooney. This was a brilliant piece of detective work. Unfortunately, Chief Constable Hellawell was severely criticised in the media for sending Sutcliffe a Christmas card, as part of the process of developing a rapport with him, which led to this remarkable breakthrough.

In 1996, Chief Constable Hellawell took part in the ground-breaking documentary *Silent Victims – The Untold Story of the Yorkshire Ripper*. He revealed that he had examined sixty unsolved attacks from 1966 onwards across England, Wales and Scotland which WYP or other forces suspected Sutcliffe could have committed. His review identified that Sutcliffe varied his modus-operandi, but nevertheless, he was able to sift them down to twenty unsolved crimes which fitted Sutcliffe's pattern of offending.

Chief Constable Hellawell retired in 1999 and asked for his notes of interviews with Sutcliffe, to assist in writing his memoirs. His request was denied, which was unprecedented. The authors are of the opinion that this was to prevent any more information being released into the public domain that, even then, could be embarrassing to WYP and to all the retired officers who participated in the investigation.

Chief Constable Hellawell included six Scottish cases in the original unsolved cases he considered at the start of his antecedent investigation. The authors believe he eliminated all of them except Dawn Webster.

Essex Police 1983 – 1984
Essex Police requested permission to interview Sutcliffe in connection with the murder of Alison Morris in 1983. The request was denied because Sutcliffe was a patient

at Broadmoor, and it was not followed up when he was transferred to HMP Frankland in 2017.

WYMP Detective Superintendent John Stainthorpe 1996
Detective Superintendent Stainthorpe led the investigation into the attempted murder of Yvonne Mysliwiec in October 1979 at Ilkley. He stated in the programme *Silent Victims – The Untold Story of the Yorkshire Ripper* that he believed that the attack on Yvonne had been committed by the Ripper and that he was ordered by Chief Constable Gregory not to attribute it to him, because it would result in further criticism of the police.

WYP 2002
In 2002, the Law Lords found against the Home Secretary being able to increase the minimum life sentencing tariff recommended by the judiciary. The implication being that Sutcliffe, having served more than thirty years, would be released. In response, WYP initiated an antecedent investigation and announced that should he be released, he would be re-arrested and charged with the murder of Debra Schlesinger and the attempted murder of Mo Lea.

Until that time, the official WYP line was that there was not enough evidence to bring charges in any other cases. This shows that WYP had enough evidence to charge Sutcliffe for many years but had not revealed it until forced to by the prospect of his release. In the event, the full life term was reinstated and neither case went to trial.

WYP Carol Wilkinson 2005
In October 2005, Kay Lintern was interviewed by journalists investigating Carol's murder. She was told that a WYP DI would contact her, but no one ever called (MPoF).

WYP Carol Wilkinson 2008
In 2008 the WYP Major Investigation Review Team started interviewing witnesses to the Carol Wilkinson murder.

This appears to have been a review of a cold case, not an antecedent investigation into Sutcliffe. Predictably, it did not criticise the original investigation (MPoF).

WYMP DI Megan Winterburn

Retired WYMP DI Megan Winterburn, who ran the Millgarth Incident Room, revealed that she had interviewed a woman who had been the victim of a brutal attack. DI Winterburn was certain that this was an attack by the Ripper but was ordered by Chief Constable Gregory not to record it as one (MPoF).

Accordingly, this woman was ignored and denied justice. The authors have allocated her the name 'Anita' and she is recorded as attack 79.

The authors have no doubt that there were other attacks that Chief Constable Gregory ordered should be ignored, to prevent any more criticism of him or his force.

After Sutcliffe's death, DI Winterburn told ITV News she suspected there were many more victims, saying, 'I'm sure he has taken secrets to the grave.'

WYP Operation Painthall and the *Polismyndigheten* 2016 – 2017

According to media reports, in August 2016, detectives from WYP's Operation Painthall contacted the Swedish *Polismyndigheten* concerning a telex received by WYMP from Interpol in the 1980s. The telex indicated that Sutcliffe had travelled on a car ferry between Dragor and Limhamn before and after Teresa Thörling's murder. (Swedish AI 3.)

WYP subsequently confirmed its original finding that Sutcliffe had not been to Sweden. Although it appears to be based on a superficial investigation.

In 2018, WYP confirmed that there was 'no evidence at all to suggest that Peter Sutcliffe offended abroad'. This is different to the 'Sutcliffe had not been to Sweden' position that they adopted in 2017, which is definite and explicit, and rules Sutcliffe out of any offending in Sweden. The new form of words indicates they have found no evidence that he went to Sweden, Denmark, France, Belgium, the Netherlands or Germany but does not definitively rule this out.

WYP Operation Painthall 2016 – 2018
According to media reports, detectives from Operation Painthall interviewed Sutcliffe at HMP Frankland in connection with attacks going back to 1964.

On 21 December 2017, Chris issued the following FOI request to WYP:

> With regards to Operation Painthall. It was announced earlier this year (2017) that West Yorkshire Police were re-interviewing Peter Sutcliffe over other unsolved cases. Has this Operation been completed? What is the outcome?

WYP responded:

> West Yorkshire Police can neither confirm nor deny that Operation Painthall exists.

WYP subsequently confirmed that Operation Painthall was tasked with reviewing thirteen unsolved cases, as featured in the Byford Report. In February 2018, Detective Superintendent Jim Dunkerley of WYP was widely quoted in the media as saying:

> West Yorkshire Police continues to review and where possible re-investigate all unresolved homicides and serious sexual assaults to bring offenders to justice and to bring much needed closure to the victims and their families.
>
> At this moment in time, West Yorkshire Police **have no intention to seek a CPS decision to charge Peter Sutcliffe with any further matters.**
> [Authors' highlighting in bold]

Sutcliffe had already confessed to ACC Hellawell that he was the man who attacked Tracy Browne and Ann Rooney, and WYP had stated in 2002 that there was enough evidence to charge Sutcliffe with the attacks on Debra Schlesinger and Mo Lea. The authors are of the opinion that there was at the time enough evidence to successfully charge Sutcliffe with the attacks on Yvonne Mysliwiec, Gloria Wood, Maureen Hogan, Rosemary Stead, Bernadette Cassidy and Carole Montgomery.

Having 'no intention to seek a CPS decision to charge Peter Sutcliffe with any further matter' does not mean that there is not sufficient evidence to charge Sutcliffe with some of the attacks. It just means that WYP does not intend to charge him. It appears to the authors from the above form of words that WYP would prefer not to reopen the controversy and bring more discredit on the history of the force by reopening the cases and admitting just how many women he attacked.

In summary, once Sutcliffe was convicted, senior officers ordered all of the evidence – which could have progressed the unsolved cases – to be destroyed. To this day, no official estimate of the number of Sutcliffe's victims has been issued and none of the antecedent investigations have ever been released to the public in full.

Why did the investigation fail?

Based on Sir Lawrence Byford's conclusions and the authors' observations, there are a number of reasons for the total failure of the investigation.

Sutcliffe
Sutcliffe was a very capable criminal:
- He kept fit, was able to outrun pursuers and was physically very strong. This enabled him to strike with great force and move bodies out of sight quickly.
- He changed cars, used other people's cars and false number plates to defeat surveillance.
- He varied his modus-operandi by using different weapons and locations to prevent the police linking his crimes.
- He used weapons like hammers and screwdrivers that appeared innocent if he was caught with them.
- He had modified his coat pocket to hide the garrotte and the hammer, so they were unobtrusive.
- He regularly discarded weapons.
- He concealed bodies and planted post-dated items to obscure the date of death and make it difficult for police to break his alibi.
- He was forensically aware and usually did not leave a weapon, fingerprint or possession at a crime scene.
- He checked his face, clothing and shoes for bloodstains after an attack and cleaned them carefully. He burnt bloodstained clothing in a garden incinerator. He did not take trophies from his victims. He made a major

mistake by not discarding his boots. But because he kept them upstairs in the bedroom, they were not discovered when the house was searched.

- He varied his appearance, sometimes having long thick hair, sometimes short, variously having a full beard, moustache and beard, or sideburns. He had swarthy skin and afro hair, so at night he was sometimes described as black. This led to a plethora of photofits and descriptions the police were unable to link.

- He attacked at locations where there was a fast exit to a motorway or an A road, so he could quickly leave the crime scene.

- He parked his car facing in his direction of escape, so he could just drive off quickly, not reverse out and manoeuvre around.

- He attacked in different force areas, thereby making the coordination of the investigation more difficult.

- He led a quiet life, appearing to be a hard-working, married man in stable employment and did not draw attention to himself.

- Sutcliffe and Sonia did not go out much, so when questioned, Sonia would always say that they stayed in most nights, so he was probably at home. Not a strong alibi, but strong enough.

- He did not confide in anyone, so no one could inform on him.

- He was quiet spoken, neat and tidy, which put people at their ease and made it easy for him to pick up victims.

- He monitored the progress of the investigation by listening to the news and reading both a local and a national paper.

- He realised that the hoax letters and tapes were of great assistance to him, so he tailored his attacks to manipulate the investigation into believing they were genuine. Thereby distracting it and preventing it from effectively investigating him.

- When arrested or interviewed, he always remained calm and controlled, and did not break under the strain. He appeared cooperative and reasonable and this put the detectives at ease in most of these interviews. Only in Interviews 5 and 7 were the detectives suspicious, and they were overruled when they wanted to make further enquiries.

• He had surveillance and stalking skills

Failures endemic to all forces

FAILURE TO STANDARDISE POLICE PROCEDURES

In the 1960s, there were about 500 police forces in England and Wales and these were systematically amalgamated into the large forces we know today. Prior to the amalgamations, all major enquiries were run by Scotland Yard, which would send a detective superintendent to lead the investigation and a detective sergeant to run the incident room, so all investigation procedures were standardised by Scotland Yard. The mergers created larger forces with large teams of detectives that did not need Scotland Yard. So inevitably, they abandoned the nationally standardised Scotland Yard method and adopted their own procedures. Consequently, multi-force investigations were hampered because officers from different forces used different processes which could not interoperate.

FAILURE TO ESTABLISH A CENTRALISED INTELLIGENCE SYSTEM

When a criminal was convicted, the arresting force would raise two card indexes. One would be retained by that force, the other would be held centrally in Scotland Yard. The card for Sutcliffe sent to Scotland Yard in 1969 recorded his arrest for possession of a hammer in the RLD in Bradford and conviction for going equipped to steal. The card created by the BCP did not mention the hammer. So when the WYMP detectives looked at it, it did not arouse their suspicions. The Scotland Yard card with the reference to the hammer was not available to them, nor were the cards held by GMP in its system.

INABILITY TO PROCESS THE VAST AMOUNT OF DATA THE INVESTIGATION CREATED

The Ripper investigation generated thousands of statements, suspects, house visits and vehicle sightings, which all had to be transcribed onto more than 250,000 index cards. Other than Scotland Yard, no county force had the experience or specialised trained personnel to process, store and access that amount of card-indexed data. WYMP used untrained police cadets and constables. Consequently, index cards were duplicated, triplicated and misfiled, and the information amassed on Sutcliffe was not held on one card.

RELIANCE ON INDIVIDUAL FORCE INCIDENT ROOMS

No central incident room was established. All four forces ran their own separate incident rooms.

FAILURE TO APPOINT AN OVERALL SIO

There was no single SIO for the investigation with authority over officers from all four forces.

Issues specific to WYMP

Most forces faced with an investigation of this magnitude would have failed. There were, however, specific factors relating to WYMP and the investigation team.

DIVISIONS WITHIN WYMP

WYMP was a force joined at the top, but not integrated. The individual divisions did not talk to each other and still acted as if they were individual independent forces. It did not have a centralised intelligence system; the intelligence was held in individual city divisions, which resisted centralised recording and sharing of information. Each murder had a separate card index system which was not cross-referenced to the others. The reality was that WYMP could not conduct an investigation into linked offences committed in multiple locations.

There were also intense rivalries between officers from WYMP's former constituent forces. Particularly because the senior officers leading the WYMP were 'county' officers from the former WRC. They were referred to contemptuously as 'Donkey Wallopers' or 'Gurkhas', (allegedly because they never took any prisoners). As a consequence of this, there was personal division within the Ripper Squad. This came to a head when Sutcliffe was arrested. Detective Superintendent Holland ignored DCS Hobson – who was the SIO but from the LCP – and immediately informed his old WRC colleague, ACC Oldfield, who was on sick leave recovering from a heart attack. ACC Oldfield then drove to Dewsbury Police Station and seized control of the investigation.

FAILURE OF FORCE LEADERSHIP

Chief Constable Gregory was not capable of managing an investigation of this size and complexity. He did not have a CID background and failed to bring in new leadership when it became obvious the investigation was failing. Eventually, Sir Lawrence Byford sidelined him and the senior WYMP leadership.

Commander Nevill of Scotland Yard visited the Ripper Investigation and made a series of recommendations that would have improved the investigation. Chief Constable Gregory did not ensure they were actioned by CID and consequently they were all ignored (MPoF).

FAILURE OF CID LEADERSHIP

On 4 February 1974 the Provisional IRA bombed a bus on the M62, killing nine soldiers and three civilians and injuring thirty-eight others. Detective Superintendent Oldfield was the SIO and his investigation resulted in the conviction of an innocent former soldier for the bombing, who was exonerated on appeal in 1992.

At the time this was widely seen as a successful investigation into a complex mass murder and secured both Oldfield's promotion to ACC in May 1976 and his reputation as one of the UK's best detectives. This ensured his promotion to ACC and that he would lead the investigation into Sutcliffe, although the M62 investigation was bungled and the IRA gang was never arrested. He was appointed because of his seniority, not his capability as a detective (MPoF). His health was failing; the brutality of the murders had deeply affected him and he had become personally involved to the point where his judgment had become unsound. He should have been relieved much earlier (MPoF).

Detective Superintendent Holland was ACC Oldfield's number 2 on the M62 coach investigation and played a major role in the notorious conviction of Stefan Kiszko for a murder he did not commit. He was appointed because he was ACC Oldfield's protégé, not because of his ability as a detective (MPoF).

Both ACC Oldfield and Detective Superintendent Holland had dominant personalities, which resulted in valid lines of enquiry suggested by junior officers being ignored. When Detective Constable Laptew suggested that Sutcliffe should be arrested, Holland prohibited it because Sutcliffe did not have a Geordie accent and threatened to put DC Laptew back on the beat. Consequently, although many of the detectives believed that the letters and tape were a hoax, no CID Officer dared confront ACC Oldfield over this (MPoF).

Major policy decisions were taken without being formally recorded or properly disseminated (MPoF). This led to Detective Superintendent Stainthorpe eliminating Sutcliffe on the basis of handwriting, even though the elimination criteria had been changed to prohibit this.

The tyre-tracking and cross-area-sighting enquiries did not have clear objectives or adequate resources and a single officer was not appointed to individually lead them (MPoF).

FAILURE OF INCIDENT ROOM MANAGEMENT
To quote Sir Lawrence Byford:

The ineffectiveness of the major incident room was a serious handicap to the Ripper investigation. While it should have been the effective nerve centre of the whole police operation, the backlog of unprocessed information resulted in the failure to connect vital pieces of related information.

A card index system is supposed to ensure that every piece of information is collated with all the other information and assessed. Because there was a backlog of sometimes up to nine months of filing to update the index cards, the interviewing detectives were not aware of key information about Sutcliffe (MPoF).

Of all the thousands of letters, telephone calls, and visits to police stations that occurred during the investigation, the best two leads were when Trevor Birdsall wrote to the police then visited Bradford Police Station and denounced Sutcliffe as the Ripper. The letter and assessment of it were waiting filing and the report of Birdsall's allegations was lost. Despite all of this information, the incident room was not able to coordinate it into one place and alert CID to arrest Sutcliffe (MPoF).

When Sutcliffe was first interviewed on 2 November 1977, the incident room had several photofits of Sutcliffe, his wellington boot imprints, a partial handprint, imprints of his vehicle tyres, plus details of his vehicles seen multiple times in several different RLDs. They had clear imprints of the weapons he used, and knew he was a lorry driver with a local Bradford accent. Had a simple CRO name search been made with New Scotland Yard, this would have revealed his previous conviction for 'going equipped' with a hammer. This would have given the officers at the first police interview more than enough reasonable suspicion that Sutcliffe was the Ripper and he would have been arrested at that point in time. The interviewing detectives could have checked the tyre treads on his car for a match, had his palm prints compared and recovered the tools from his car and garage for comparison.

The Ripper Squad was exhausted and had low morale. No attempt was made to address this or rotate detectives and incident room staff to other duties. This is probably why so much information was misfiled (MPoF).

The incident room did not have an intelligence unit. One was set up after the recommendations of Commander Nevill and did useful work but was then disbanded. Had one been in place, it could have identified that the information in the hoax letters was in the public domain and that there had been other attacks that the Ripper was responsible for (MPoF).

Investigative failures within the enquiry

ABANDONING THE TYRE IMPRESSIONS LINE OF ENQUIRY

The tyre impressions Sutcliffe left at the Irene Richardson, Marilyn Moore and Vera Millward crime scenes could have identified Sutcliffe. However, this line of enquiry was abandoned more than halfway through due to lack of resources.

PREMATURE FOCUS ON SEX WORKERS AS VICTIMS

Because Wilma McCann and Emily Jackson were sex workers, the investigation rigidly followed the belief that Sutcliffe only attacked sex workers to the exclusion of all other victims. Prior to Wilma McCann's murder in October 1975, WYMP knew there had been three attacks in as many months on unaccompanied females where a hammer was used. Had they connected them to Wilma McCann's murder they would have had Sutcliffe's photofit, his description, the fact that he spoke with a high-pitched Bradford accent, had a gap in his front teeth which would match a later bite mark, suffered with hay fever and that he drove a light-coloured Ford car. They also had at this stage a sample of his semen left on the clothing of Wilma McCann, of the rare Blood Group B Non-secretor, which only 6 per cent of the male population have.

FAILURE TO CONSIDER ALL THE PHOTOFITS

Early photofit impressions of the murderer were not linked. Had the ninety photofit impressions from the surviving victims of all known hammer attacks or assaults involving serious head injuries on unaccompanied women been assembled, it would have revealed that the same man was involved in all the attacks.

UNQUESTIONING ACCEPTANCE OF THE HOAX LETTERS AND TAPE

The investigation team fell for a hoax involving three letters and a tape sent by John Humble. This was despite multiple victims saying the Ripper had a local accent. The confirmation from Northumbria Police that all of the information in the letters was in the public domain and that the hoaxer had rung Sunderland Police Station to confess it was a hoax was ignored (MPoF).

MISOGYNISTIC ATTITUDES AMONGST WYMP

The police were disdainful of sex workers and only started to investigate the attacks seriously when 'innocent' women were murdered. Victims who described a man with a local accent had their accounts dismissed by the police. When Tracy Browne went to Keighley Police Station with vital information that would have assisted the investigation, she was ridiculed.

FAILURE OF MEDIA OPERATIONS

Project R and the appeals for information were initiated without regard to the capacity of the incident room. This overwhelmed the incident room with an enormous amount of spurious information which it could not process (MPoF).

Senior officers were not experienced in media operations. Although a senior officer was appointed as press officer, he was ignored by chief officers, who allowed journalists to come to them directly (MPoF).

Information was routinely leaked to the press by police officers, one of whom was prosecuted for it (MPoF).

RELIANCE ON OVERLY RESTRICTIVE ELIMINATION CRITERIA

All forces were circularised and asked to consider if they had any crimes that had been committed by the Yorkshire Ripper. Criteria were drawn up to identify Ripper attacks. However, Sir Lawrence Byford assessed they were 'very restrictive'. This resulted in attacks which had been perpetrated by Sutcliffe being eliminated (MPoF).

POLICY OF SUPRESSING REPORTS OF RIPPER ATTACKS

Such was the criticism and pressure on WYMP that Chief Constable Gregory directed that attacks which were obviously perpetrated by the Yorkshire Ripper should not be acknowledged as such (MPoF).

Forensic failures

FAILURE TO RECORD AND DISSEMINATE SCIENTIFIC INFORMATION

The scientist that examined the boot prints at the Josephine Whitaker crime scene stated verbally that they could be used to identify the individual boot, but did not express this in writing, so this evidence was not given the weight it deserved (MPoF). Consequently, when Sutcliffe was interviewed while wearing those boots, he was not arrested.

MEDICAL MISDIAGNOSES

In the case of the Harrogate schoolgirl attacked in 1979, x-rays showed three semi-circular injuries to the head which were not consistent with an accidental fall, but the case was nevertheless recorded as one (MPoF).

The wider concern is that other murders and attempted murders were also wrongly classified as accidental, preventing them from being investigated.

Sutcliffe's impact on policing today

Following the 'Black Panther' fiasco, it took the public criticism arising from another catastrophic investigative failure to force reform.

Sir Lawrence Byford's report recognised that most of the police forces in England and Wales could not manage an investigation the size of the Ripper enquiry. It made wide-ranging recommendations for improvements in the investigation of multi-force series crimes. In summary, these were:

- The police service should introduce standardised computer systems.
- Standardised incident room procedures should be implemented across all police forces.
- Major incident rooms had to be staffed appropriately relative to the number of enquiries they were likely to receive, and the staff had to have specialist training.
- A continuous audit of index cards should be maintained in future large enquiries to prevent misfiling and duplication of index cards.
- Incident room staff should be rotated to prevent them from becoming stale.
- Senior detectives should receive enhanced training in the management of investigations into serial crimes.
- Detectives should receive improved training in interview techniques.
- For large multi-force enquiries, an overall SIO of ACC rank should be appointed to command the

investigation with the mutual consent of each chief constable.
- A specialist senior scientific officer should be appointed as advisor to an investigation.
- Large investigations should have a senior officer appointed to handle media comment.

This led to the introduction of a standardised cross-referenced index card system across all forces in 1983 and the Association of Chief Police Officers (ACPO) standard manual procedures in 1984. In 1986 the Home Office Large Major Enquiry System (HOLMES) was implemented. This revolutionised policing and prevented the information overload that destroyed the Yorkshire Ripper enquiry.

However, analysis of subsequent cases shows that the same failings present in the Sutcliffe investigation still exist and it is still not able to efficiently conduct investigations into serial killers and serial sexual offenders.

Failure to use HOLMES or to link crimes in a series

ROBERT BLACK

In 1983, Deputy Chief Constable (DCC) Hector Clark became the first chief officer since the Byford Report to command a multi-force investigation into a serial killer, following the murders of Susan Maxwell in 1982 and Caroline Hogg in 1983 by Black.

This was the first major cross-force investigation into a serial killer since the arrest of Sutcliffe and it failed. Like Sutcliffe and Neilson, Black was only arrested in July 1990 when caught abducting a six-year-old girl by Uniform Branch officers, because an alert witness called the police.

Some of the same failings were present in this investigation:
- In March 1986, Black murdered Sarah Harper from Leeds. The SIO was Detective Superintendent John Stainthorpe, who wrongly rejected any link between

Sarah's murder and those of Susan and Caroline. DCC Clark failed to overrule Detective Superintendent Stainthorpe, the very reason that a DCC was appointed to lead this type of investigation, and WYP was allowed to follow a separate investigation. It was only because a WYP sergeant studied the case and wrote a report, which he took over the head of Detective Superintendent Stainthorpe to the Home Office, that it was included in the investigation. Consequently, it took two years before all three investigations were linked and considered together.

- In April 1988, Black attempted to abduct Teresa Thornhill from Nottingham and this was not linked to Black in any way.
- The antecedent investigation after Black's arrest linked him to twenty-one other murders, disappearances and attempted abductions in England, Scotland, Northern Ireland, the Republic of Ireland, France, Germany and the Netherlands, none of which had been identified or linked prior to his arrest.

In 1987, all of the information on the murders of Susan Maxwell and Caroline Hogg was entered into HOLMES. Had all twenty-four cases been identified and entered into HOLMES, it is possible the correlation of all the available information could have detected Black earlier and saved lives.

Black was later convicted of four murders and one attempted murder. As with Sutcliffe, the true toll was probably very much higher and no official estimate of his crimes has ever been published.

JOHN CANNAN

In July 1986, Suzy Lamplugh disappeared in Fulham, South London, after going to an appointment with a 'Mr Kipper'. No trace of her was ever found. This was a major investigation which received massive media publicity, which in turn generated an enormous number of contacts from members of the public. All of which had to be recorded on index cards. Chris was one of the first collators to be trained on HOLMES. He recalls:

> HOLMES only became available in some forces in 1986 and then only with basic functionality. It was systematically enhanced over time. As it was rolled out across the police service, there was a period of training and familiarisation. It was only fully operational by about 1988.

The MPS was not therefore able to use HOLMES to manage the investigation, so as with the Yorkshire Ripper investigation, the MIRIAM card-based incident room was overwhelmed. This was a major factor in the failure of the investigation.

In October 1987, Shirley Banks was murdered in Bristol. A&SP ran the investigation on HOLMES, and after a very skilful investigation, John Cannan, a serial rapist and killer, was convicted of Shirley's murder and of attempting to abduct Julia Holman. Media comment – not police intelligence analysis – suggested Cannan as a suspect for Suzy's murder. The MPS liaised with A&SP and concluded there was 'no evidence' connecting Cannan to Suzy's murder.

In May 2000, the MPS put a new team onto the Lamplugh investigation, which entered all the index cards onto HOLMES. The HOLMES information coordination function revealed that 'Mr Kipper' had visited several estate agents in Fulham on the pretext of visiting properties but actually to select victims. In 2002 the MPS requested permission to charge Cannan with Suzy's murder, but the Crown Prosecution Service (CPS) decided there was insufficient evidence to obtain a conviction.

The original failure to use HOLMES demonstrated that the police service had still not grasped the importance of using computer technology, linking in investigations and sharing information. Had the index cards been entered onto HOLMES in 1987, the incident room would not have been overwhelmed and this would have revealed critical information, which could have led to Cannan's conviction.

DELROY EASTON GRANT

Grant was a serial burglar and gerontophile (sexually attracted to the elderly) rapist, who raped hundreds of elderly women in South-east London and Surrey from about 1990 onwards. The investigation into Grant was codenamed Operation Minstead and ran from 1998, when a series was first identified, until his arrest in 2009. The investigation generated an enormous amount of documents, photographs, CCTV etc. Instead of being stored individually in HOLMES, they were stored in summary files, which prevented them from being individually searched. Essentially preventing the location and recall or identification of any individual piece of evidence and negating the advantage of using HOLMES for a large, complex investigation.

Separately, Delroy Easton Grant was confused with another man named plain Delroy Grant. Delroy Grant's DNA did not match the DNA profile obtained from the crime scenes. So Delroy Easton Grant was marked up in HOLMES as eliminated as a suspect on the basis of a DNA sample taken from Delroy Grant.

Failure to openly assess the number of victims of a serial offender

HAROLD SHIPMAN

On 31 January 2000, Dr Harold Shipman was convicted of murdering fifteen of his patients in Manchester. The initial investigation by GMP had cleared him of any wrongdoing. It was only when he tried to defraud the estate of one of his victims using a forged will that he was arrested for fraud, leading to the full extent of his crimes being revealed. To allay public concern, the Home Office initiated an investigation by Her Honour Dame Janet Smith, who identified that Shipman probably killed about 250 of his patients.

This is the only time the findings of an independent investigation into a serial offender to identify the full number of his victims, based on the balance of probability – not the legal definition of beyond reasonable doubt – has been issued to the public.

Misclassification of murders as RTAs, suspicious deaths or missing persons

'HOPE'
'Hope's' case is listed as a suspicious death, not a murder. NYP has resolutely refused to comment on the possibility that 'Hope' was murdered by Sutcliffe.

HELEN SAGE
The normal indicator for the police of a 'no body murder', where a murder is committed and the body is concealed, is 'no proof of life'. That is when there is no contact with relatives, activity on social media, mobile phones, credit cards or bank accounts. Manchester sex worker Helen Sage, aged twenty-two disappeared in August 1997. Helen was a devoted mother and it is highly unusual for a mother to disappear and abandon her children. This is also accepted as the key indicator of a 'no body murder' of a woman. However, although there is 'no proof of life' and most forces would accept that Helen has been murdered and her body concealed, GMP has ignored this and categorised Helen as missing.

The National Crime Agency has confirmed there is no proof of life for Helen since 1997. Categorising her as a missing person allows GMP to evade expending any effort on investigating a 'prostitute murder' and exclude it from GMP's crime figures.

Analysis of crime patterns can only be as good as the linking of offences. Misclassifying murders prevents series of offences being linked, which thwarts the intelligence analysis that is essential to identify a serial offender.

Misogynistic policing 1997 to present

ANN SMITH

Such is the lack of interest in resolving Ann's murder that a request by the authors in 2022 to consider Sutcliffe as a suspect on the basis of fresh evidence was ignored. The MPS would only issue this very general statement to the authors:

> The case of Ann Smith, like all unsolved murders, remains open and is subject to periodic review. As part of the investigation into her murder, connections to other cases were explored and discounted.

When pressed to confirm when Ann's case was reviewed, if Sutcliffe had ever been considered as a suspect, and if so, how he had been eliminated, the MPS declined to respond. Essentially preferring to assume that Sutcliffe had been eliminated in the past.

So in fact, it is unclear if Sutcliffe was ever considered as a suspect for any murder or assault in the MPD and if so, how he was eliminated.

'HOPE'

In 2019 Tim's investigation into the murder of 'Hope' revealed a new witness who recognised 'Hope' as an alcoholic sex worker from Scarborough. For three years NYP refused to interview this witness, although this could have led to 'Hope's' identification and her family being informed of her fate.

BECKY GODDEN-EDWARDS

The Independent Office for Police Conduct (IOPC) found that WP did not pursue the investigation of the murder of Swindon sex worker Becky Godden-Edwards by serial killer Christopher Halliwell, although lines of enquiry were still available to it. It also did not share information with the CPS that should have resulted in Halliwell being convicted.

If Ann, Helen, 'Hope' or Becky had been a teacher, civil servant, housewife or related to a police officer, there would have been a huge manhunt that would have been maintained to this day.

It appears the police still see sex workers as choosing to accept male violence as a result of a lifestyle choice and therefore do not want to expend any effort on investigating 'fish and chip prostitute murders'. Exactly the same misogynistic attitude that infected WYMP in the 1970s.

Refusal to abandon elimination criteria and lines of enquiry that have obviously become erroneous

JACKIE ANSELL-LAMB: CARPET FIBRES
In 1991 a joint appeal for information on both murders by Cheshire and Derbyshire Constabularies was broadcasted on BBC TV *Crimewatch*.

A detective announced that fragments of carpet found on Jackie's body had been identified as coming from a sample or roll of carpet. He said there had been a carpet exhibition that weekend at Earl's Court; he believed her killer was connected to the carpet industry and that the smartly dressed man she was reported to have been seen with at the Poplar transport café near Warrington on the day she was killed may have been a carpet salesman.

This deduction is completely spurious. Jackie had attended a party at Earl's Court, then stayed the weekend with David Sykes, who worked as a colour consultant in the textile industry. David then drove her to Hendon in his car. It is probable that there was an innocent transfer of carpet fibres at the party, at David's flat, or in his car. Jackie could then have had multiple lifts along the M1 and it is possible that the carpet fibres could have come from one of them.

Yet Derbyshire Constabulary is still maintaining that the murderer works in the carpet industry (MPoF).

BARBARA MAYO: DNA

In 1997, ACC Don Dovaston announced that a sample of human material recovered from an article of Barbara's clothing had given them a DNA 'fingerprint'. He maintained that: 'I am satisfied the DNA sample will lead us to the identity of the person responsible for this murder.'

It is unclear if Sutcliffe had his DNA taken when compulsory DNA testing for prisoners started in 1995, because he was a patient in Broadmoor. However, the Home Office have confirmed that his DNA has been taken at some point.

This DNA finding was used to eliminate Sutcliffe and other suspects as Barbara's murderer. According to unfounded media comment, this also eliminated Sutcliffe as Jackie Ansell-Lamb's killer, because both murders were linked. In fact, the police have never linked the two murders.

The authors identified that in 1970, WPC Lindsay Wallace retraced Barbara's journey dressed in the clothing Barbara wore when she was murdered for a television reconstruction (the first colour reconstruction). WPC Wallace participated in another reconstruction in January 1971 showing her being picked up by a Morris 1000 Traveller in Kimberley, again dressed in Barbara's clothes.

Barbara's clothes would have been stained with blood and mud. Yet the clothes in both reconstructions are clean. A retired Derbyshire Constabulary officer confirmed to Chris that 'the clothing had been dry cleaned so a Policewoman could wear it for the reconstruction'.

Crime scene and evidence storage procedures in the 1970s were poor. The fingerprint could have been innocently transferred to the clothing either prior to Barbara acquiring it, from undressing the body, bagging the clothes, the dry cleaning, the policewoman getting dressed and undressed for the reconstruction, or in storage.

The DNA has never been matched. This indicates that neither the killer nor any member of his family has ever come into custody for anything from 1970 to the present day. This is highly unlikely for a serial killer operating from 1970 onwards. It supports the authors' view that the DNA does not belong to the murderer and has been innocently transferred from contamination of the clothing in the period 1970–1997, probably from WPC Wallace or an evidence technician. The DNA cannot therefore be used to eliminate Sutcliffe, or indeed anyone else. Nor can it be used to rule out a link from Barbara's murder to the other murders where DNA has been obtained. A classic example of what the Americans call 'junk forensic science'.

In January 2023, Chris submitted a FOI request to Derbyshire Constabulary, pointing out there was a reconstruction using Barbara Mayo's actual clothing in 1970, that the clothing had clearly been cleaned and handled by a number of people at that time, and asking how a fingerprint/DNA crime stain from the clothing could be used for elimination purposes. Derbyshire Constabulary refused to acknowledge that its elimination criteria were flawed by claiming that it had 'No Information Held'.

Chris then submitted a request for an internal review of this finding under Part 1 of the Freedom of Information Act 2000, which elicited the admission in March 2023 that:

> The position taken in terms of 'No Information Held' was not an accurate reflection of the actual position as there had been no enquiries to establish if there was any 'information' held that addressed your request.

In short, when Derbyshire Constabulary was confronted with evidence that it had been using completely unsound elimination criteria to eliminate suspects in a murder enquiry since 1997, it ignored the Freedom of Information Act and responded by issuing a blanket denial that it held any information. Thereby evading its duty to acknowledge this inexcusable mistake.

The review went on to confirm that Derbyshire Constabulary did hold information on the contamination of the DNA evidence, saying that: '...searches were conducted within Derbyshire Constabulary to locate any relevant information. The searches located some information relevant to your request.'

But then they justified not responding to Chris's enquiry – which would admit that the DNA evidence was contaminated and therefore unreliable – on the grounds that: 'On this occasion I am unable to provide you with the information you requested under the Freedom of Information Act 2000 as I have applied Section 12 of the Act – "Excess Fees".'

So Derbyshire Constabulary evaded admitting that the Barbara Mayo investigation had been fundamentally flawed since 1997 and had used a contaminated and unreliable DNA profile to eliminate suspects (MPoF). This also evaded the need to reinstate every suspect that was wrongly eliminated on the basis of the DNA sample, including Sutcliffe (MPoF).

This shows the dangers of unquestioning reliance on DNA evidence, which is not the silver bullet it is held out to be. It also shows how determined and unscrupulous the police can be when trying to conceal investigative failures and evade legitimate criticism.

DELROY EASTON GRANT: ELIMINATION CRITERIA

Grant's attacks were first linked through DNA found on two of his victims in October 1992 and September 1998. However, thirty-two other rapes committed between these dates were not linked to the series because the exclusion criteria were too restrictive.

Two of Grant's crimes were excluded because the victims were men and the detectives assumed – wrongly – that he only attacked women.

Failure to liaise and share information

TONY SNOW

Snow was a serial rapist who also committed an attempted murder in the Hertfordshire Constabulary and Bedfordshire Police force areas in 1991. It was only when the Hertfordshire rape featured in a BBC TV *Crimewatch UK* reconstruction that Bedfordshire Police realised it was looking for the same man. It transpired that liaison procedures between police forces were so inadequate that, as with the Yorkshire Ripper investigation in the 1970s, there was no process to identify a series of offences across multiple force areas. Detectives were watching *Crimewatch UK* to identify linked offences.

TREVALINE EVANS

In March 2020 the media reported that serial killer Christopher Halliwell was a suspect in the 1994 murder of Liverpool sex worker Julie Finley and he had been working in North Wales. Tim wrote to North Wales Police (NWP), bringing this to their attention. Initially, NWP refused to comment, then it responded that it was liaising with Merseyside Police (MP). Indicating that MP had not passed on information to NWP that a serial killer had been operating in its force area, and NWP was unaware of this until the authors contacted them.

CHRISTOPHER HALLIWELL

WP are refusing to release details of sixty items of women's clothing found at a trophy store Halliwell used at Ramsbury, Wiltshire, or images of twelve sketches he did, thought to show deposition sites for his victims. Even though the release of the images could progress other investigations by other forces.

DELROY EASTON GRANT

In May 1999, Grant committed a burglary in Bromley, South-east London, which was notified to Operation

Minstead detectives. The burglary was incorrectly assessed as not being an attack in the series because the elimination criteria were too rigid, and it was therefore eliminated from the investigation.

Bromley CID did not then proceed with the investigation into the burglary, because it had notified it to Operation Minstead. A witness had provided the registration of the vehicle used in the burglary, so if Operation Minstead or Bromley CID had investigated the burglary, Grant would certainly have been traced and arrested for the burglary. A DNA sample would have instantly revealed him as the serial rapist sought by Operation Minstead.

Inability to analyse patterns of activity and proactively identify the existence of a serial offender

CHRISTOPHER HALLIWELL
The NCA Serious Crime Analysis Section (SCAS) was established in 1998 to provide:

> ...a national service for investigators of serious sexual offences. Its main objective is to use data collected from police forces to identify the potential emergence of serial killers and serial rapists.
> [The quotation above is taken from Kent Police Crime and Intelligence – Serious crime analysis section policy (SO4) document.]

In 2011 serial killer Christopher Halliwell was arrested by WP for the murders of Becky Godden-Edwards in 2003 and Sian O'Callaghan in 2011. Both the detective superintendents who were SIOs on the case have stated they have no doubt he committed other murders. In 2019, Chris and co-author Bethan Trueman identified twenty-eight murders Halliwell was a viable suspect for in their book *The New Millennium Serial Killer*. He could have been murdering women from about 1982 onwards.

However, SCAS completely failed to identify Halliwell's offending. He was only detected by chance, because his car was recorded on CCTV when he abducted Sian O'Callaghan and by coincidence, a police car with ANPR passed him shortly afterwards. This revealed his number plate, which in turn identified him as a prime suspect. Following a very skilful investigation by Detective Superintendent Stephen Fulcher, Halliwell was arrested and eventually convicted for both murders.

The authors believe SCAS is ineffective in identifying serial offenders because a local SIO has to call on SCAS for assistance in an investigation before it can commence analysing patterns of crime. Consequently, SCAS is not able to independently review all intelligence material from all sources across all forces to identify patterns of activity that would reveal the existence of a serial offender 'at the earliest stage of their offending'. Hence perhaps the reason that Halliwell evaded detection from 1982 until 2011. It is also prevented from analysing all murders because some murder victims are misclassified as missing persons or suspicious deaths, and some, such as Becky Godden-Edwards, have not been reported missing.

STEPHEN PORT

Port murdered four men in east London between June 2014 and September 2015 with the date rape drug gamma-hydroxybutyrate (GHB). In 2021 an inquest ruled that investigative failures by the MPS meant the deaths were only identified as murders after the fourth victim.

In 2023, His Majesty's Inspectorate of Constabulary and Fire & Rescue Services (HMICFRS) identified key failings in the way the MPS investigated unexplained deaths and found failures in training, supervision, record-keeping, policies and intelligence procedures.

HMICFRS Inspector Matt Parr was quoted by the BBC as saying:

Among the deaths the Met Police did not classify as homicides, there were some that were. The risk of a homicide being missed is way higher than it should be.

We've seen poor supervision, poor training and poor record-keeping. The Met hasn't learnt any lessons from what happened eight years ago. The chance of this happening again is too large.

The Met have no system for analysing patterns. If there was a link between murders, they would only spot them if they are lucky.

Several officers told us that linking deaths at a local level relied frankly on luck, there was no formal process to spot the similarities, to link deaths, and it relied on officers talking to each other about the deaths that they've dealt with.

Lack of review by independent specialist officers

TREVALINE EVANS

In 2023, Tim participated in a documentary broadcasted on Channel 4 on the 1990 disappearance and murder of Mrs Trevaline Evans in Llangollen, North Wales. NWP arrested Trevaline's husband in 2001 but released him without charge. A witness came forward to the programme who had reported seeing a man resembling Christopher Halliwell outside Trevaline's shop the day before her disappearance.

When Tim wrote to NWP's chief constable asking her to request an impartial independent review of the case by another force in the normal way, she responded by refusing to either designate Halliwell as a suspect, follow up on the new evidence, or request an independent review.

NWP does not have a separate Cold Case Unit. All cold case investigations in NWP are performed by its Force Major Incident Team (FMIT). This was the same team that arrested Trevaline's husband. The investigation has never been reviewed by anyone except the FMIT, so Halliwell has been ignored as a suspect since 2001 because the

FMIT does not want to admit that it had wrongly focussed on the husband to the exclusion of all other suspects.

Premature focus on one suspect or line of enquiry

CLAUDIA LAWRENCE

In 2023, Tim forwarded enhanced CCTV images to NYP which appeared to show Halliwell at the rear of Claudia Lawrence's home in York on the day of her disappearance. NYP did not follow up with the NYE reader who produced the images. NYP has already arrested five men who were released without charge. If it now designates Halliwell as a suspect, it will have to admit that it pursued the wrong line of enquiry from 2009 onwards and wrongfully arrested innocent men.

Ignoring contrary evidence to obsessively pursue a single line of enquiry is exactly the same mistake WYMP made when it fixated on the belief that the Ripper only attacked sex workers.

Concealing or denying failings, for the sake of the public image of the force

TREVALINE EVANS

NWP's chief constable refused to order an independent review of the Trevaline Evans investigation, protecting NWP's reputation by avoiding admitting that the investigation had been bungled.

DANIEL MORGAN

Daniel Morgan was murdered in Sydenham, South London, in 1987. There were six failed investigations into his murder. It was alleged that police corruption had played a part in both his murder and the failure to produce a conviction.

To address public concern, the Home Secretary established the Daniel Morgan Independent Panel. Its 2021 report found that the MPS had focussed not on bringing the perpetrators to justice, but on protecting its own reputation by concealing evidence of corruption and a bungled investigation:

> Concealing or denying failings, for the sake of the organisation's public image, is dishonesty on the part of the organisation for reputational benefit and constitutes a form of institutional corruption.

JIMMY SAVILE AND PETER JACONELLI

In 2007, Surrey Police investigated Savile and asked for intelligence on him from all forces. NYP responded that it had none.

In 2011 the Jimmy Savile scandal broke. NYP issued a statement that:

> When the allegations surrounding Jimmy Savile were publicised, we carried out extensive searches of force records which did not reveal a local connection.

When the NYE published that Savile lived in Scarborough and had been abusing children there with Peter Jaconelli and had been protected by NYP because Jaconelli was the Mayor of Scarborough, DCC Sue Cross conducted an investigation in which she failed to consider the victims traced by the NYE and stated that there was no intelligence held on Savile and Jaconelli, and no evidence of any offending. In fact, multiple complaints had been made about both men to Scarborough CID and Jaconelli had been charged with raping a man in 1972. According to media reports, both men were suspects in a major 2003 paedophile investigation by NYP, which was put onto HOLMES.

In February 2014, Tim and NYE journalist, Nigel Ward, participated in an investigation by the BBC into Savile and Jaconelli, which interviewed the victims and set out the evidence to support their allegations. The next day NYP referred itself to the Independent Police Complaints Commission. Subsequently, thirty-five victims came forward with allegations against Jaconelli and Savile of indecent assault, inciting a child to engage in sexual activity, gross indecency, sexual assault and rape. Two people were victims of both men. An NYP spokesman said:

> ...there would have been sufficient evidence from thirty-five individual victims for the Crown Prosecution Service to consider criminal charges against Peter Jaconelli and Jimmy Savile, had they been alive today. The available information indicates that, historically, the police missed opportunities to look into allegations against these men whilst they were still alive.

The 2007 Surrey Police investigation was the closest the police ever came to arresting Savile. Had NYP shared the intelligence it undoubtedly had on him, he would have been arrested and convicted. It is irrefutable that NYP had known all about Savile and Jaconelli and done nothing about them. This was the worst case of police failure in the history of policing in North Yorkshire. When faced with the possibility of having this revealed in public, DCC Cross chose to protect the reputation of the force by supressing victims' evidence.

The MPS, NWP and NYP followed exactly the same policy as WYMP did in 1981.

Failure of media policy
In a democratic society with an open and accountable police service, the media are tasked with holding the police to account. The police service has a duty to cooperate with the media and respond openly to media criticism.

In the Yorkshire Ripper enquiry, WYMP senior officers initially confirmed that Jacqueline Hill was not a victim of the Ripper. The next day they had to concede that she was. So understandably, the media severely criticised them for mishandling the investigation into Jacqueline's murder. They then punished the media for criticising them by stopping media briefings. This retaliation undermined police–media relations and further damaged the investigation. The authors have found exactly the same approach exists in 2023.

Here are a few examples:

- In the case of Ann Smith, the MPS would not give any media comment on the possibility of Sutcliffe being responsible for her murder. It also refused to confirm if Sutcliffe had been considered as a suspect in any attacks in the MPD, on grounds of cost.
- When Chris pointed out that the DNA sample that Derbyshire Constabulary was using to eliminate suspects in the Barbara Mayo investigation was flawed, it claimed it could 'not locate information relevant to your [FOI] request'. It was subsequently forced to admit this information existed, but still refused to release it.
- When challenged over the refusal of NWP to designate Christopher Halliwell as a suspect and interview him in prison for the murder of Trevaline Evans, NWP refused to give any explanation for this decision and refused to comment on the case.
- When challenged over the failure of NYP to follow up on the images of Christopher Halliwell outside Claudia Lawrence's home, or to interview a witness who recognised 'Hope', NYP just refused to respond.

This policy of evading criticism by not responding to media enquiries prevents journalists from holding the police to account for failures in police investigations. This was exactly the same response adopted by WYMP when it was justifiably criticised for bungling the Jacqueline Hill investigation in 1980.

WYMP's policy of describing victims as prostitutes or 'good time girls' alienated public sympathy from the victims, which discouraged the public from coming forward with information. In the Claudia Lawrence investigation, NYP stated that Claudia had a 'complex and mysterious love life'. Predictably, this released a barrage of salacious headlines that alienated public sympathy, caused distress to Claudia's family, and discouraged witnesses from coming forward.

Failure to appoint an effective overall SIO

TREVALINE EVANS AND CLAUDIA LAWRENCE
One of the reforms introduced in multi-force investigations into serial offenders after the failure of the Yorkshire Ripper investigation was that a chief police officer should be the overall SIO. Tim wrote to Chief Constable Kier Pritchard of WP informing him that both NWP and NYP were ignoring lines of enquiry on the murders of Trevaline Evans and Claudia Lawrence. He asked him in his capacity as chief constable on the lead force for this investigation to order both chief constables to pursue these lines of enquiry, and received no response.

The continued failure to appoint an overall SIO for multi-force investigations into serial offenders ensures they are not properly coordinated. It also allow individual chief constables to continue to protect the reputations of their forces by supressing evidence and not pursuing all lines of enquiry, as Chief Constable Gregory did in the Yorkshire Ripper investigation.

Refusal to effectively pursue antecedent investigations
Quoted in the *Bradford Telegraph and Argus*, Detective Superintendent Holland said:

> I am against any further trials or further inquiries; it would be a waste of time and public money. I do not think he will ever be released.

In the authors' view, this reflects the current position held by most chief constables, that antecedent investigations into criminals like Sutcliffe, Cannan and Halliwell who are serving a full-life term should not be pursued.

Whilst this allows them to use resources on investigating current crimes, it ignores the victims' right to justice and the need for closure for their relatives and friends. It also conveniently prevents any previous errors in the investigation from being revealed and evades the need to apologise to those, like Stephen Downing, who were wrongfully convicted.

Even now, these factors prevent the open investigation of the full number of attacks by serial offenders.

In 2022 the IOPC reviewed the WP investigation into Becky Godden-Edwards's murder by Halliwell. It found that WP was not capable of running an incident room using HOLMES:

> Between 2011–14 the murder inquiry was poorly progressed and supervised, reasonable lines of enquiry were not pursued, and key evidence was not forensically examined.

* During the Yorkshire Ripper investigation, the independent review by Scotland Yard made very helpful recommendations, which were ignored. The IOPC found that WP 'did commission two independent reviews, but one was subsequently cancelled. The other review was completed but at the time of the managed investigation the recommendations were still to be actioned'. In other words, it was also ignored. The report goes on to state: 'The evidence suggests that a more robust system of review may have identified areas for improvement and led to a more expeditious outcome for the murder investigation.'

* Senior officer meetings (now called 'Gold Groups'):

> ...did not have clear objectives or terms of reference covering the oversight of investigations, roles and responsibilities, and wider organisational objectives. Their meetings had no clear objectives and/or were not held. The absence of a Gold Group with clear

objectives overseeing this murder investigation meant that there was no clear accountability for ensuring that the investigation was progressed and supervised in an appropriate manner.

- Senior officers took key decisions, but did not document or disseminate them properly.

  Decisions and policy issues were not consistently recorded and were not centrally logged. In one instance, a Gold Commander did document their decisions and policy issues but this was done within Gold Group minutes only, which were not centrally logged. It appears the lack of a policy log in this case led to WP missing significant opportunities to bring the perpetrator to justice sooner.

- The incident room was not properly resourced and organised.

  The IOPC recommends that WP ensures all force policies concerning the resourcing and administration of major incident rooms adhere to the Major Incident Room Standard Administrative Procedures (MIRSAP).

- The incident room was not staffed with appropriately trained and experienced specialist staff.

  ...a HOLMES review which identified the absence of key roles such as a Document Reader, which was not in line with the guidance provided for staffing a major incident room. The relevant guidance recommends that for a Category A murder, the full support of HOLMES is utilised, properly supported by a fully staffed HOLMES major incident room team, in order to properly record and review actions, read documents and raise and allocate new actions, to maintain momentum in the investigation. In this case, the full support of HOLMES was not utilised. The investigation found that a number of statements and reports had been moved prior to being read and assessed, meaning that reasonable lines of enquiry could not be identified and pursued. It appears the lack of adherence to MIRSAP in this case led to WP missing significant opportunities to bring the perpetrator to justice sooner.

- Despite being equipped with HOLMES, the incident room was overwhelmed by information. Documents were filed marked as read, when in fact they had not been read and assessed.

The IOPC recommends that WP reviews how it handles and categorises documents in HOLMES that have not been read by a Document Reader. We made this recommendation as the investigation found that within HOLMES a number of statements and reports had been moved to Reading Complete and Indexing Complete folders. This course of action would have been problematic to the investigation as it implied that all documentation had gone through the reading process. With this in mind, a senior officer or review team would have considered that all of the documents had been read, when in fact this process had not been completed. This was potentially misleading because the documentation had not been reviewed with a view to identifying investigative opportunities for further action. Additionally, conversations with HOLMES staff suggested that the issue was wider than just this investigation.

- Documents were lost. The IOPC was 'unable to definitively establish several facts owing to relevant documentation, including Gold Group minutes, not being found and corresponding information not being logged on HOLMES'.

- Standard incident room procedures were ignored.

The IOPC recommends that WP ensures SIOs are aware that, when MIRSAP is not to be complied with, this should follow a policy decision by the SIO that is documented with their rationale and saved centrally. We made this recommendation as the investigation found that the SIO did not properly document their decisions about deviation from MIRSAP. It appears the lack of such a policy decision in this case led to documentation not being reviewed with a view to identifying investigative opportunities for further action.

- Staff were inadequately trained or experienced to work in the incident room.

The IOPC recommends that WP ensures that its guidance and training for SIOs includes the information that should be recorded in HOLMES about reviews of investigations, to include: decisions that a review will take place or not, the reasons for any changes (including cancellation) to previously agreed reviews and decisions about what action to take (including no action) in response to review recommendations. WP should also ensure that the Brunel collaboration (a joint Wiltshire, Avon and Somerset and Gloucestershire Police investigation team) has a process in place to regularly review the HOLMES knowledge and skills of SIOs and to take appropriate action where a need for additional training or support is identified. We made this recommendation as the investigation found that reviews were not carried out in line with national guidance and also that 'natural' opportunities for reviews were missed. In policing terms, a review is a formal and independent examination which is undertaken to ensure that an investigation is thorough, conforms to national standards, has been conducted with integrity and that no investigative opportunities have been overlooked.

The key statement here is that 'Additionally, conversations with HOLMES staff suggested that the issue was wider than just this investigation'. The investigation was jointly run with A&SP, indicating that these issues are endemic not just to WP, but also to A&SP and other forces. In response to the IOPC report, the chief constable of WP stated:

> I acknowledge that there was confusion at the time concerning the oversight of the investigation into Becky's murder, as highlighted within the IOPC investigation. This arose, in part, **due to major crime collaboration being in its infancy**.
> [Authors' emphasis in bold]

This was exactly the same line the police took after the 1974 investigation into Donald Neilson. In fact, the police had been running multi-force investigations for many years.

Conclusion
The conclusion is inescapable that the British Police Service still does not have the intelligence capability to identify the emergence of serial offenders at the earliest stage of their offending, or the capability to perform multi-force investigations into serial offenders and operate incident rooms in large complex investigations.

Lessons still to be learned

The way the police investigate serial offenders needs to be reformed. Going forward:
- The NCA SCAS should be mandated to proactively search for linked offences across all forces, not wait to be called in by a local force. It should also be empowered to order chief constables to investigate clusters of incidents and specific suspects implicated by its analysis.
- The NCA should be given authority over all missing persons cases with power to overrule individual forces if it appears the victim has been murdered.
- The NCA should conduct a full review of all missing persons on a 'proof of life' basis to identify which of them are in fact murder victims and then correct their status.
- The NCA should appoint a chief officer to conduct cross-force serial offender investigations, and who is empowered to overrule individual chief constables.
- Following the conviction of a serial offender, there should be an antecedent investigation led by a judge supported by a specialist squad from the NCA so the investigation is conducted impartially without concern for the reputations of individual forces and officers. It should state on the balance of probabilities which crimes the perpetrator committed, as occurred with the Harold Shipman investigation.
- All forces should have a specialist Cold Case Unit and investigations should be reviewed by an officer from another force.

- The NCA Missing Persons Unit should extend its database to cover European cases.

Until this occurs, serial offenders like Sutcliffe, Halliwell, Black and Cannan, who could all have been arrested earlier, will continue to commit multiple rapes, femicide and infanticide with a high degree of impunity.